INDONESIAN HERITAGE

The Human Environment

This encyclopedia project was initiated and guided by the

Yayasan Dana Bakti

It was also made possible thanks to the generous and enlightened support of the following companies

Sinar Mas Group
Bakrie Group
Bank Artha Graha
Satelindo
Telekomindo
Telekomunikasi Indonesia
Indobuildco
Indosat
Inti
Pasifik Satelit Nusantara
Plaza Indonesia Realty
Siemens Indonesia
WES Intratama Consortium
Wahana Tigamas Buana/AT&T
Shangri-la Hotel, Jakarta
Japanese Telecommunications Association (NTT, Sumitomo, Fujitsu, Itochu, Kanematsu, KDD, Marubeni, Mitsui, Nisshoiwai, Tomen, Denki Kogyo, Fujikura, Furukawa, IKI, Infotama, JRC, Nesic, Bukaka, NEC, NNC, NTC, Sarana Ekacitra Indonesia, Tamura Denki, Voksel)
Konsorsium Promindo Ikat
Artha Telekomindo
Amalgam Indocorpora
Elektrindo Nusantara
Jatimas Fadjar Satryo Group
Komselindo
Citra Permata Sakti,
Adcor Utama

Published by Archipelago Press,
an imprint of Editions Didier Millet Pte Ltd,
593, Havelock Road, #02–01/02
Isetan Office Building, Singapore 169641

Jakarta Office:
Buku Antar Bangsa
Graha Unilever, lt. 10
Jl. Gatot Subroto 15
Jakarta, Indonesia 12930

Printed by Tien Wah Press Pte Ltd. Singapore
ISBN 981–3018–27–5

INDONESIAN HERITAGE

The Human Environment

VOLUME EDITOR

Dr. Jonathan Rigg
Department of Geography, University of Durham

AUTHORS

Sian Jay - *Centre for Southeast Asian Studies, University of Hull*
I Made Sandy - *Faculty of Mathematics and Natural Sciences, University of Indonesia*
Neville Nichols - *Bureau of Meteorology Research Centre, Melbourne*
Lily Kong - *Department of Geography, National University of Singapore*
Lewis Hill - *Centre for Southeast Asian Studies, University of Hull*
Pinna Indorf - *Department of Architecture, National University of Singapore*
Roxana Waterson - *Department of Sociology, National University of Singapore*
Mike Parnwell - *Centre for Southeast Asian Studies, University of Hull*
Joan Hardjono - *Faculty of Arts, Padjadjaran University, Bandung*
Lesley Potter - *Research School of Pacific Studies, Australian National University*
Victor King - *Centre for Southeast Asian Studies, University of Hull*
John Janes - *Indonesia Australia Eastern Universities Project*
Alan Wilson - *Indonesia Australia Eastern Universities Project*
Colin Barlow - *Research School of Pacific Studies, Australian National University*
Adrian Horridge - *Division of Neuroscience, Australian National University*
Dean Forbes - *Department of Geography, Flinders University*
Lea Jellinek - *Institute of Technology, Melbourne University*
Joep Bijlmer - *Ministry of Foreign Affairs, The Netherlands*
Anne Booth - *Department of Economics, School of Oriental and African Studies*
Graeme Hugo - *Department of Geography, University of Adelaide*
Meiwita Iskandar - *Centre for Health Research, University of Indonesia*
Terry Hull - *Centre for Health Research, University of Indonesia*
Clem Tisdell - *Department of Economics, University of Queensland*
Tony Whitten - *World Bank*

ARCHIPELAGO PRESS

Contents

THE INDONESIAN WORLD

SENSE OF PLACE - THE ARCHIPELAGO

THE HUMAN CONTEXT

PADI AND SAWAH: RICE IN INDONESIA

FIELD AND FOREST

LITTORAL LIVELIHOODS

CITY AND TOWN LIFE

DEVELOPMENT AND CHANGE

LEGEND

- Capital
- Towns
- Mountains
- Provincial Capital
- Regency Capital
- Villages
- International Boundary
- Provincial Boundary

Note: This legend applies to all the maps in this volume

Indonesia is the world's largest archipelago, stretching some 5,120 kilometres from west to east, and comprising approximately 13,677 islands. A general map, such as that below, showing the various provinces and the main islands, belies the complexity that is the Indonesian world. It does not reveal the heterogeneity of the different regions, or the survival strategies adopted by the Indonesian people to adapt to terrains that are very different as one travels from one end of the country to the other.

Detailed satellite photographs can reveal more, as the three examples at the bottom of the page illustrate. The first (left) reveals the network of lakes on the Mahakam River in Kalimantan, the Manado Peninsula in North Sulawesi and the third (right), the area around Jambi, Sumatra.

These images provide very different clues as to how people live in their own worlds. The inhabitants of the Mahakam River basin see the world in terms of the river on which they live. Their relationships with the interior and the outside world are mediated by the people living upstream and downstream from them.

For people living on the coast, the world is far bigger as their view encompasses other Indonesian islands as well as the rest of Southeast Asia, and

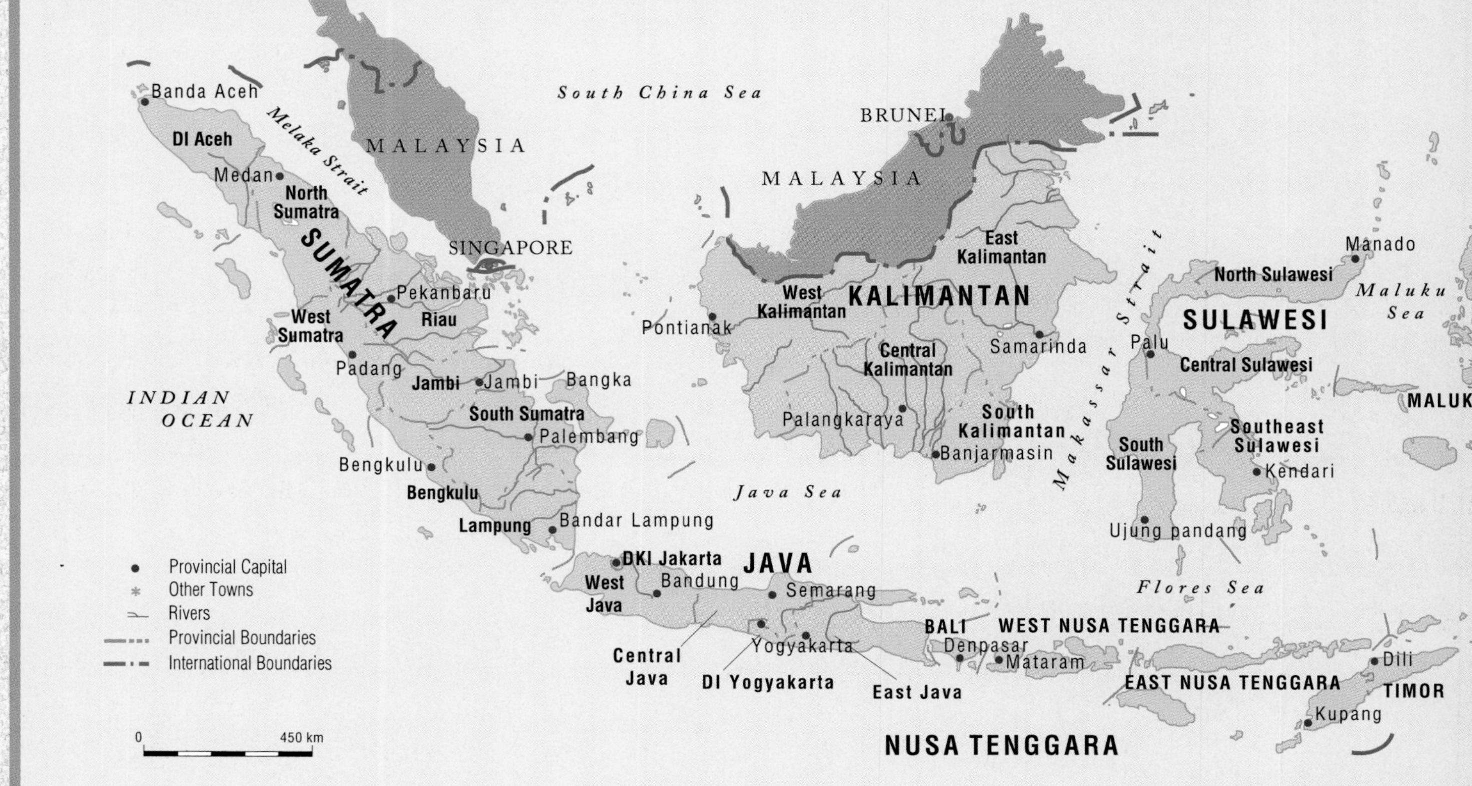

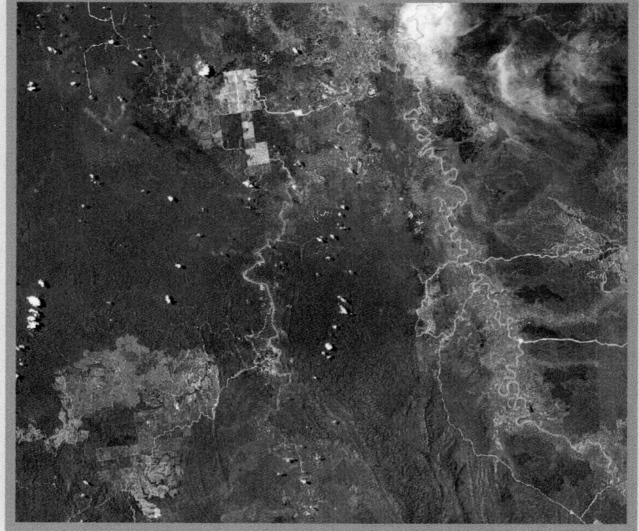

The Mahakam River system, Kalimantan

Peninsula of Manado, North Sulawesi

indeed the world. Whereas the interior living Dayak of Kalimantan were generally inward looking, the coastal and maritime peoples of Indonesia traded with the inland dwellers and with those outside of the islands. Their world is far wider.

Batang Hari River, Jambi area, Sumatra

THE INDONESIAN WORLD

Indonesia is a complex place of varied human and environmental patterns. This variety and diversity is now seen as the key defining characteristic of the country–the very essence of the personality of Indonesia. In this way many scholars have made sense of the country by stressing the extent to which it resists neat definition. This chapter presents the image of Indonesian diversity, encompassing both the human and physical environments. The emphasis is not on nature and culture as two distinct and separate elements within the Indonesian world, but on the interactions and interrelationships between them. The environment provides a canvas for culture to work and re-work. In some cases, there have been phases of evolution as areas have been developed, abandoned and then re-settled. Recently, archaeologists have unearthed evidence of intense agriculture in areas of Irian Jaya that are now sparsely settled, while formerly degraded places have been revitalised through innovations in agriculture.

The chapter also examines the various ways in which groups have tried to order, and therefore to understand, Indonesia through the development of maps and other conceptions of Indonesian order. These spatial frameworks of understanding are informed by different sets of priorities, and therefore result in differing frameworks. Places are mapped and recorded through the eyes of the people who are either charged with that task, or who have the power to decide the image that is to be presented. Local villages, district officials, national planning agencies, men and women, the elderly and the young have mental maps that are 'drawn' by the unique set of variables that each brings to the task of understanding. There are many, overlapping Indonesian worlds, each highly personalised. But the world that most people see 'mapped' is a singular place, one created by consensus and officialdom, informed by the methods of the cartographer.

So, what is one to make of Indonesia? There is the individualised Indonesia, each Indonesian's own personal country that is moulded and informed by their own unique set of circumstances, and which is in a constant state of flux as their circumstances change and they proceed through the cycle of life. At the same time, there is also the Indonesia of the text book and the official. Segmented, static and ordered by defined criteria, it brings understanding in a bureaucratic and academic sense, but not always in terms of human activities, perceptions and aspirations.

Living on the Edge: Tectonics of Life in Indonesia

The surface of the Earth, despite its apparent stasis, is unstable–in places highly so. It consists of a mosaic of continental (sima), and oceanic (sial) plates made up of crust and upper mantle which, together, comprise the lithosphere. Oceanic plates may be 60 kilometres thick; continental plates, 100 kilometres. These plates are in continuous movement over the partially molten hot layer beneath, called the asthenosphere.

People living in the shadow of Mount Merapi in central Java face the threat of eruptions that destroy villages, agricultural land and human lives.

Plate Tectonics

The motion of the earth's surface is called plate tectonics. The boundaries between the plates do not coincide with the boundaries of the continents and oceans, although the great landmasses ride upon these moving plates. The plates can move away from each other (divergent plate boundaries), towards each other (convergent plate boundaries), or side by side (lateral plate boundaries).

The Formation of Indonesia

Plate movements help explain the physical development of the Indonesian Archipelago, and the distribution of earthquakes, volcanoes, and other tectonic features. Running south-eastwards from Myanmar, along the west coasts of Sumatra and Java, and through the islands of Nusa Tenggara are a series of deep sea trenches. Some geologists would also extend the boundary northwards through Maluku and possibly into Sulawesi—although this is one of the most geologically complex areas in the world. These trenches mark the subduction zones where the Indo-Australian, Pacific and Philippine plates are forced beneath the Eurasian plate. Two arc basins run parallel to this trench along Sumatra, Java and Nusa Tenggara. The inner arc, particularly, is a zone of intense, and often violent volcanic activity.

The Human Factor

Communities in Indonesia living close to these zones have faced the prospect of destruction from volcanic eruptions, earthquakes, and tidal waves. Some of the most densely populated areas of Java and Bali, for example, exist in the shadow of active volcanoes. Extreme climatic events have also raised the spectre of calamity. On 12th December 1992 an earthquake struck eastern Flores in Nusa Tenggara, killing 1,500 people, and causing extensive damage in the districts of Sikka, Ende and East Flores. Low-lying islands off the north coast were swamped by the ensuing tidal wave, with only 300 of Pulau Babi's population of 1,000, for example, surviving the event.

The most violent eruption in Indonesia during the historic period, exceeding in violence even that of better-known Krakatau, was that of Mount Tambora (2,800 metres) between 5th July and 15th July 1815. The eruption directly killed 12,000 people, and a further 44,000 died in the ensuing famine. The quantity of ejecta was such that the volcanic eruption significantly altered the climate of the northern hemisphere. The following year became renowned as the 'year without summer'; there were summer frosts in New England, while Europe recorded its latest wine harvest on record. Similar periodic, but devastating, natural events threaten lives and livelihoods in many areas of Indonesia.

THE FORMATION OF SULAWESI

Eastern Indonesia is one of the most geologically complex zones in the world. This geological complexity is, in turn, based on great tectonic intricacy: Eastern Indonesia is the only region where three major tectonic plates converge. As a result, even today geologists are far from decided on the area's geological evolution, although it is widely accepted that a series of 'riftings' have occured as parts of the supercontinent Gondwanaland have broken off and drifted northwards over a period of some 200 million years. Of the islands of the area, it is Sulawesi which holds the key to an understanding of the sequence of tectonic events. Even within the context of Eastern Indonesia, its geology is remarkably complex, indicating diverse origins and large-scale crustal movements.

1. It has been suggested that western Sulawesi broke away from Gondwanaland about 200 million years ago. Eastern Sulawesi detached itself from Australian Gondwanaland (present day New Guinea) rather later, about 90 million years ago. The two then collided and fused about 15 million years ago.

2. The collision caused the southwest peninsula to rotate counter-clockwise. The Gulf of Bone was created between South and Southeast Sulawesi. The impact also caused the northern peninsula to rotate clockwise 90 degrees.

3. There have also been suggestions that western Sulawesi collided with eastern Borneo about three million years ago, closing the Makassar Strait. Evidence for this collision is sketchy so far, although the submarine contours of eastern Borneo fit closely into western Sulawesi.

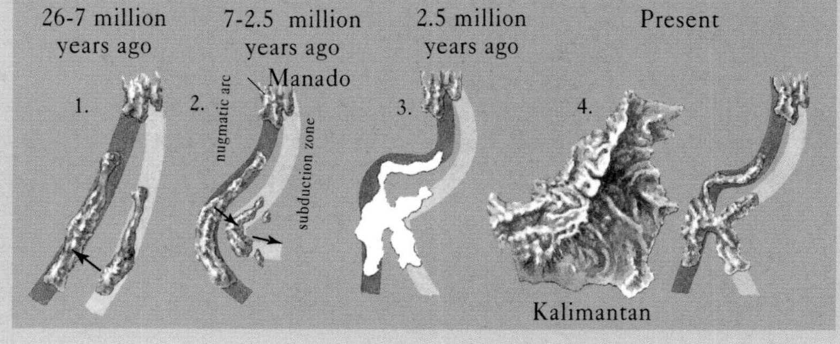

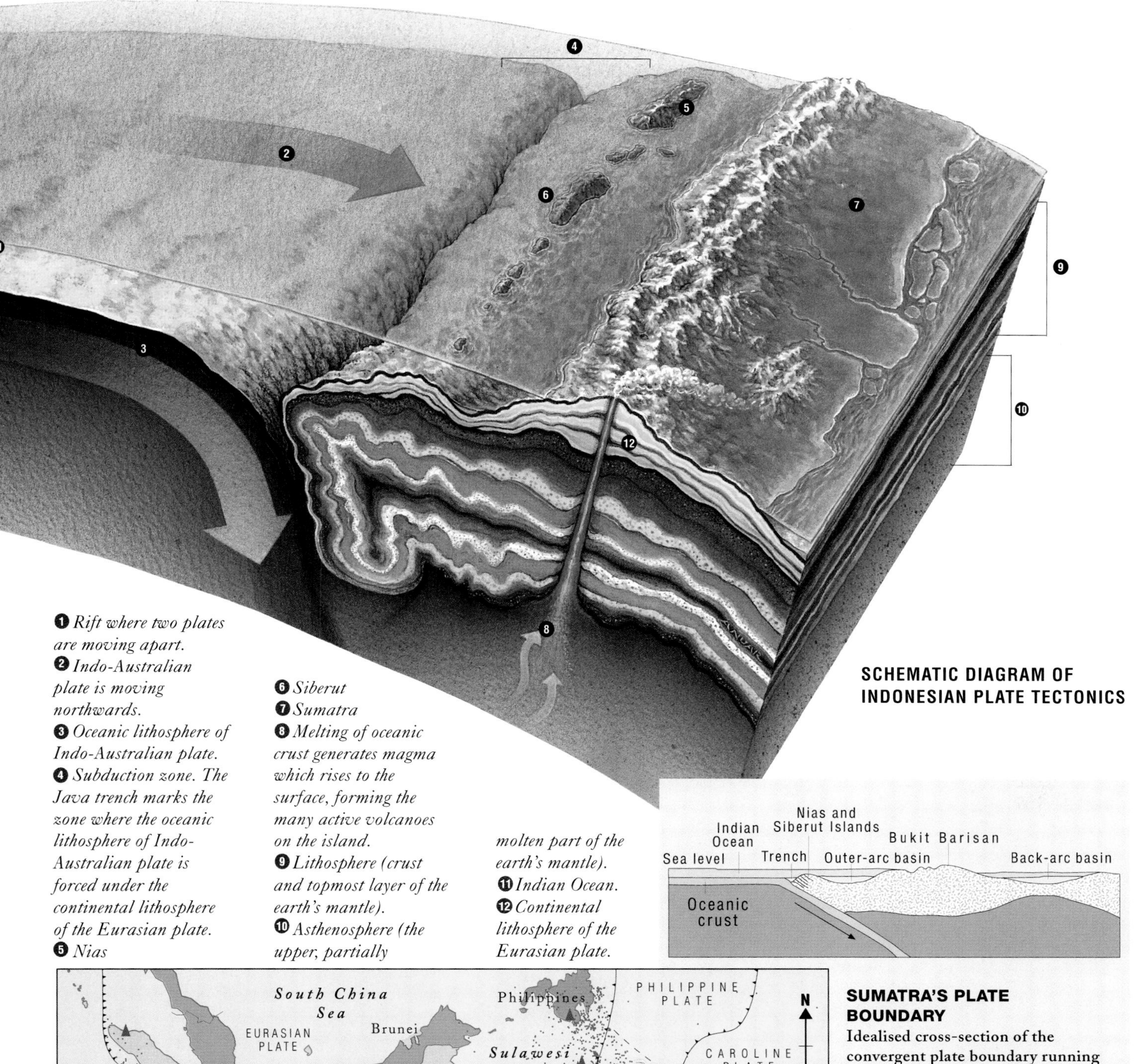

SCHEMATIC DIAGRAM OF INDONESIAN PLATE TECTONICS

❶ *Rift where two plates are moving apart.*
❷ *Indo-Australian plate is moving northwards.*
❸ *Oceanic lithosphere of Indo-Australian plate.*
❹ *Subduction zone. The Java trench marks the zone where the oceanic lithosphere of Indo-Australian plate is forced under the continental lithosphere of the Eurasian plate.*
❺ *Nias*
❻ *Siberut*
❼ *Sumatra*
❽ *Melting of oceanic crust generates magma which rises to the surface, forming the many active volcanoes on the island.*
❾ *Lithosphere (crust and topmost layer of the earth's mantle).*
❿ *Asthenosphere (the upper, partially molten part of the earth's mantle).*
⓫ *Indian Ocean.*
⓬ *Continental lithosphere of the Eurasian plate.*

Indian Ocean
Nias and Siberut Islands
Bukit Barisan
Sea level
Trench
Outer-arc basin
Back-arc basin
Oceanic crust

SUMATRA'S PLATE BOUNDARY

Idealised cross-section of the convergent plate boundary running along the west coast of Sumatra. The Indo-Australian plate (oceanic lithosphere) is forced beneath (subducted) the thicker Eurasian plate (continental lithosphere). An oceanic trench marks the point of subduction. The outer-arc and inner-arc basins tend to be filled with sediment derived from the magmatic (volcanic) arc. Magma generated from the partial melting of the oceanic lithosphere at depths of 100 to over 200 kilometres rises to produce the numerous active volcanoes on the island.

South China Sea
EURASIAN PLATE
Brunei
Philippines
PHILIPPINE PLATE
CAROLINE PLATE
N
Singapore
SUMATRA
KALIMANTAN
Sulawesi Sea
SULAWESI
MALUKU
IRIAN JAYA
Java Sea
Krakatau
BALI
Sumbawa
Lombok
Flores
Flores Sea
Banda Sea
JAVA
Timor
NUSA TENGGARA
Sumba
Arafura Sea
INDIAN OCEAN
Timor Sea
INDO-AUSTRALIAN PLATE
Subduction zone
Uncertain boundary
Volcanoes
Earthquake epicentre
0 450 km

INDONESIA'S TECTONIC PLATE BOUNDARIES

This map shows the relation between the major tectonic plates and the distribution of earthquakes and volcanoes through the Indonesian Archipelago.

Making Sense of Indonesia

Indonesia's cultural and environmental diversity means that the way Indonesia is divided–in essence how it is understood–takes on great importance. The government administers the country through a series of spatial units from the province down to the village. These divisions, however, cannot do justice to the human and environmental fabric of the country.

With the development of industry, urban areas are rapidly expanding, and more families are migrating to urban centres like Yogyakarta in Central Java.

Rural scenes, as seen in this old print, are less common now; urban expansion is absorbing many of these kinds of settlements.

Unity in Diversity

Indonesia consists of 13,677 islands that stretch out along the equator for over 5,000 kilometres. Approximately 300 ethnic groups live on these islands, speaking an estimated 583 different languages and dialects. The country has, arguably, the most diverse flora and fauna in the world with 10 per cent of the world's flowering plant species, 12 per cent of mammal species, 17 per cent of bird species and 25 per cent of the world's species of fish, and its environment encompasses a myriad of ecological zones. This diversity is reflected in the country's national motto Bhinneka Tunggal Ika which may be translated as 'Unity in Diversity'. The principles of Pancasila represent an attempt by the state to unite the divergent linguistic, cultural and religious elements of the archipelago. They comprise: 1. Belief in God; 2. Humanitarianism; 3. Nationalism; 4. Representative government by consultation and concensus; and 5. Social welfare and justice.

Inner and Outer Indonesia

Many commentators talk of 'Inner' and 'Outer' Indonesia. The Inner or Metropolitan Islands are Java, Bali and Madura, and the Outer Islands comprise the rest. This is a division of core and periphery: Java, constituting less than seven per cent of the country's land area, represents the hearth of political influence, and centre of economic power.

Even the main island of Java can hardly be viewed as an homogeneous entity. Historically, an important distinction was that between the coast and the interior. Coastal or *pasisir* states such as Banten, Demak and Surabaya owed their wealth and power to maritime trade, while the inland state of Mataram drew its wealth by extracting the surplus from peasant-based agriculture. The former were also the first to embrace Islam, while the interior kingdoms maintained their Hindu-Buddhist traditions for far longer.

Greater and Lesser Sundas

An alternative division is based on ecological factors. This contrast is between the Greater (Sumatra, Java, Kalimantan and Sulawesi), and Lesser Sundas (the islands of Nusa Tenggara and Maluku, including Bali and Timor) on the one hand, and Irian Jaya on the other. The flora and fauna of the former are largely Asian in origin, while the latter has a greater proportion of plants and animals that are of Australasian origin.

Upland and Lowland

At the level of human activity, a more pertinent division is one between settled and shifting agriculture, and more particularly between wet rice cultivation or *sawah* and swiddening. These two agro-ecosystems represent contrasting strategies of cultivation. While sawah involves a long term reworking of the environment, shifting cultivation more closely mirrors the natural environmental cycles. In contrasting irrigated rice culture and shifting cultivation, Geertz writes: 'On the one hand a multicrop, highly diverse regime, a cycling of nutrients between living forms, a closed cover agriculture, and a delicate equilibrium; on the other, an open-field monocrop, highly specialised regime, a heavy dependency on water-borne minerals for nutrition, a reliance on man-made waterworks, and a stable equilibrium.'

Upstream and Downstream

Indonesia's larger islands, especially Kalimantan (Borneo), Sumatra and Irian Jaya (New Guinea), have important river systems which have become the basis for distinguishing between different peoples. On these islands, river systems frequently became important trade and communication routes where overland travel was difficult. The relationships that developed between the different groups of people living along these watercourses usually came to be expressed in terms of their locations along the river course. They are most usually couched in terms of *hulu* (upstream) and *hilir* (downstream).

Rural and Urban Divisions

Indonesia is no longer a nation of farmers. An on-going process of structural change means that today while 54 per cent of the workforce still remain employed in agriculture, this sector contributes only 19 per cent of Gross Domestic Product (GDP). In contrast, industry and services contribute 78 per cent (40 per cent and 38 per cent respectively). It may, therefore, be more appropriate to think in terms of rural and urban areas, and, by association, in terms of agriculture and industry; in other words, the farmer and the city dweller.

Unfortunately even this division is less than satisfactory on two counts: first, many farmers and members of their families migrate to cities to work; and secondly, urban areas are rapidly expanding into the countryside, as part of a continuing process of *kotadesasi*.

Cultural and Ethnic Divisions

A cultural division which does have a greater spatial dimension is between cultural or ethnic groups: for example, the Minangkabau of West Sumatra, the Papuans of Irian Jaya, and the Sasak of Lombok. Like the other people-centred divisions, however, this imposes a static spatial categorisation on humans who are mobile. Although the area near modern Jakarta was formerly associated with the Betawi people, modernisation and economic development have attracted migrants and guest workers from all over the Archipelago (and beyond Indonesia's shores), who have contributed to the cosmopolitan nature of the city.

DISTRICT

Labuhan Batu

Rantau Prapat

PROVINCE

Langkat
Medan
Binjai
Deli Serdang
Tebing Tinggi
Tanjung Balai
Kabanjahe
Karo
Simalungun
Asahan
Dairi
Pematangsiantar
Labuhan Batu
Siki Dalang
Rantau Prapat
Lake Toba
Tapanuli Utara
Tapanuli Tengah
Tarutung
Sibolga
Tapanuli Selatan
P. Musala
Padang Sidempuan
Gunungsitoli
Nias
P. Pini
SUMATRA
P. Tanahmasa
P. Tanahbala
Special Territory Of Aceh
INDIAN OCEAN
Riau
West Sumatra
Jambi
South Sumatra
Bengkulu
Lampung

Provincial boundary
Kabupaten boundary
Kotamadya (town)

ADMINISTERING INDONESIA

Indonesia is divided into 27 provinces or *propinsi*, of which three have special administrative status: the Special Territories, or Daerah Istimewa, of Aceh in north Sumatra, Yogyakarta in Java, and the Special Capital Territory or *Daerah Khusus Ibukota* (DKI) of Jakarta. Each province is headed by a governor (*gubernur*), who administers between 20 and 50 districts (*kabupaten*). Urban municipalities, which have the same administrative status as districts, are known as *kotamadya*. Each district, in turn, is headed by a *bupati*, while under the district are arrayed a number of sub-districts (*kecamatan*) made up of individual villages or *desa*. The village head or *kepala desa* represents the lowest level of administration.

WALLACE'S LINE

The Victorian naturalist Alfred Russel Wallace was the first person to record the dramatic ecological transformation that occurs along the islands of Nusa Tenggara, and particularly between the islands of Bali and Lombok. In January 1858, in a letter to fellow naturalist Henry Bates, he wrote of the 'line' for the first time. Later, in his monumental *The Malay Archipelago* (1869), he wrote of the 'remarkable change...which occurs at the Straits of Lombock, separating the island of that name from Bali; and which is at once so large in amount and of so fundamental a character, as to form an important feature in the zoological geography of our globe.' Although the presence of such a definite 'line' is now disputed, the islands east of Bali do mark a zone of transition between the Indo-Malayan and Austro-Malayan zoogeographic regions.

The strongest contrasts in the agricultural sector are between settled, wet-rice agriculture (top), and shifting, slash and burn, or swidden agriculture (bottom).

Mapping Indonesia

Early maps of Indonesia were made by foreign traders who drew upon the knowledge of local pilots. These maps were needed to navigate the Archipelago. The Europeans' need for accuracy led to the introduction of cadastral mapping and later a General Map Index system. Today, Indonesians under the National Mapping Agency are incorporating the latest mapping technologies for systematic topographic mapping.

»Mermaids and other creatures were often used to fill the empty spaces of early maps, while characteristic landscapes provided a 'picture' of the area.

» These maps show the progressive knowledge of Asia between 1540 and 1830. In the Linschoten map the north-south axis has been substituted for an east-west axis.

Maps and 'Reality'

Maps simplify and distort the real world as the examples of map projections show. This is due to several factors: ignorance; the impossibility of representing complex, three-dimentional reality on a small, two-dimensional sheet; the difficulty of accommodating the earth's curved surface onto a flat piece of paper; and political or other views which affect map-making.

Indigenous Mapping

The absence of early maps of Indonesia drawn by Indonesians does not mean that such renowned seafarers as the Makassarese, Bugis and Madurese travelled the seas without the aid of charts. Evidence indicates that charts and maps were being produced, and used, at an early date. Alfonso de Alburquerque sent a chart drawn by a Javanese pilot to the King of Portugal in 1512, and a letter mentioned that it referred to the Cape of Good Hope, Portugal, Persia and the Red Sea, and to the Spice Islands (Maluku) and trade routes through the South China Sea. The chart was lost in the floundering of the Flor de la Mar in the Strait of Melaka in 1512.

Clearly early European maps and charts of the Archipelago drew on the knowledge of local pilots, and the charts that they used, well into the middle of the 17th century. Less clear is how far these early European charts drew upon the map-making skills of Malay, Indian, Chinese and Moorish pilots.

Early European Maps

Francisco Rodrigues charted the Spice Islands during Alburquerque's 1511 expedition but few Portuguese maps of Indonesia survive. The Portuguese guarded their knowledge jealously and only a small number of hand-drawn maps were produced. The Dutch East India Company (VOC) took control of trade in the region in the 17th century. At this time the introduction of the copper plate press

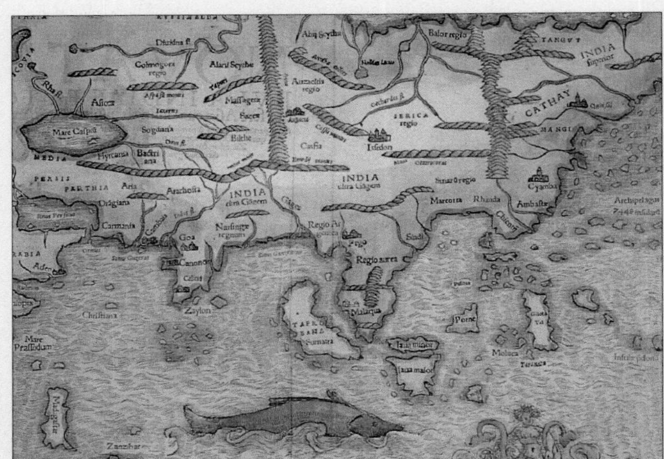

Sebastian Munster, "Asia", 1540

Ortelius, "Indiae Orientalis", 1570

Linschoten, "Indiae Orientalis", 1599

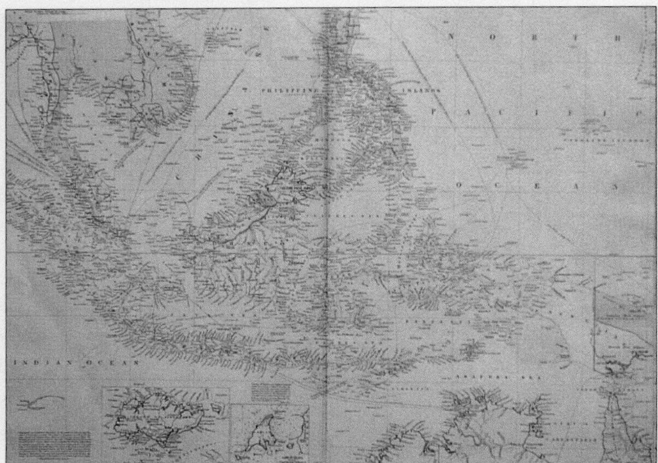
Arrowsmith, "Asiatic Archipelago", 1830

allowed larger, more detailed sheets to be printed, and maps of Indonesia became more widely available and more accurate. Batavia (now Jakarta) became the trading and map-making heart of Indonesia with a chart office being established there.

These early European maps of the Archipelago reflected the demands and interests of the Europeans at the time, primarily showing straits, islands, features of maritime importance (shoals and reefs, for example), and coastlines with important ports. As the Europeans began to build fortified settlements along the more important sea lanes, so the next generation of maps began to show more of the interior. River mouths were also charted in more detail, as were ports and their surroundings. By the end of the 18th century, administrative and economic exigencies had forced the VOC to take control of the Spice Islands, much of northern Java, and areas of Kalimantan and Sulawesi. This, in turn, required maps be made of these areas. The interest in these early European maps lies as much in their artistry as cartography, and it is significant that coordinates were usually lacking.

Developments in Mapping

When Sir Thomas Stamford Raffles was Governor-General of Java in 1815, he introduced cadastral mapping. This innovation was motivated by the need for accuracy in determining land taxes. However, the introduction of the new system was cut short by the transfer of administration back to the Dutch in 1816. It was not until 1875 that the Topographical Survey was established and charged with the task of accurately mapping the archipelago. Initially the Survey was not centrally administered and each region set its own coordinates. When the maps were finally assembled there were significant differences in the quality of the maps and gaps between the regions. As a result, the Survey was centralised, and made a branch of the Department of War, removing it from the control of the Corps of Engineers.

Soon after the centralisation of the Survey, a Permanent Commission on Surveys and Mapping was established. The members of this organisation were drawn from departments such as Public Works, Forestry, the Land Revenue Office, and the State Railways. During their meeting of 1925, the Commission decided to adopt a single General Map Index System for the entire territory, replacing the rather haphazard and confusing regional system.

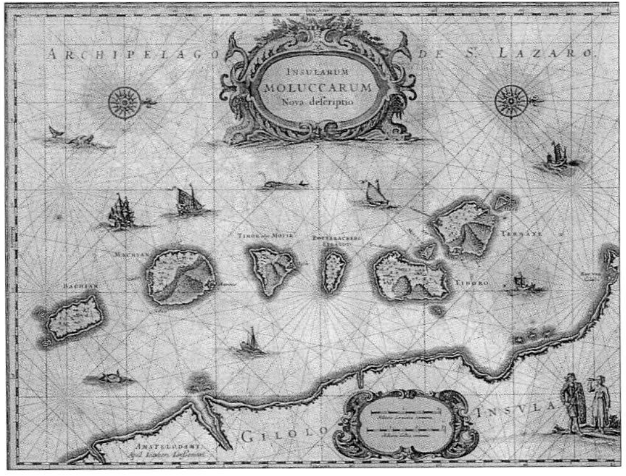

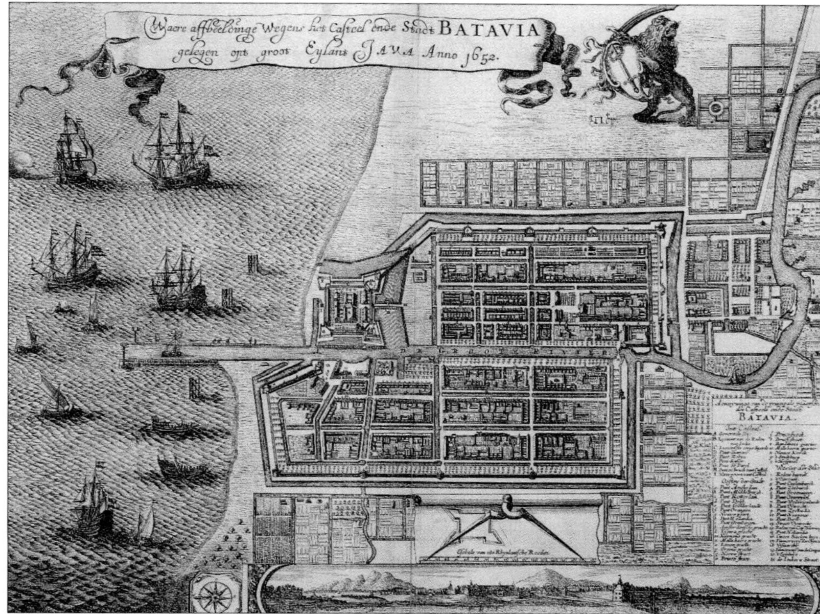

An old cadastral map of Batavia, dating from the early 18th century, in the Maritime Museum 'Prins Hendrik' in Rotterdam. The key marks out the quarters of the different ethnic groups, including the Indians from Malabar, and the Bandarese. The main buildings and streets are also named.

Given Indonesia's extent and geographical complexity, and differing levels of development, the regions were mapped at different scales and to different degrees of accuracy. Java was mapped at 1:25,000, while Bali, parts of Sumatra, Kalimantan, and South Sulawesi were mapped at 1:50,000. Less developed areas of Sumatra, Minahasa (northern Sulawesi) and elsewhere were mapped at 1:100,000. The least developed areas of the country–Irian Jaya, Kalimantan and Central Sulawesi–were mapped at 1:200,000. To provide an overview, the territory was also mapped in its entirety at a scale of 1:250,000. In 1938 the incomplete, but nonetheless fine, *Atlas van Tropisch Nederland* was finally published.

Shortly before World War II, the Topographic Survey of the Army started to experiment with aerial photographs with the aim of facilitating mapping, especially of remote areas. The first product of this was the 1:100,000 series of Minahasa, though the war meant that it did not appear until 1952.

Mapping Since Independence

By the beginning of the Pacific War, 39 per cent of the land area of Indonesia had been mapped. Systematic topographic mapping resumed in 1969 under the auspices of the National Mapping Agency, and now incorporates the latest developments in mapping technology. However, some 6,000, about a half of the total of Indonesia's islands remain unnamed. Hydrographic mapping is carried out by the Hydrographic Office of the Navy.

In addition to land maps and sea charts, some thematic maps have also been published. The Geological Survey produces charts of the country's geology. Since 1960, assisted by the United States Geological Survey, the Geological Survey has been compiling a systematic series at a scale of 1:100,000. Soil surveying and mapping in Indonesia comes under the jurisdiction of the Department of Agriculture, and the Department of Forestry.

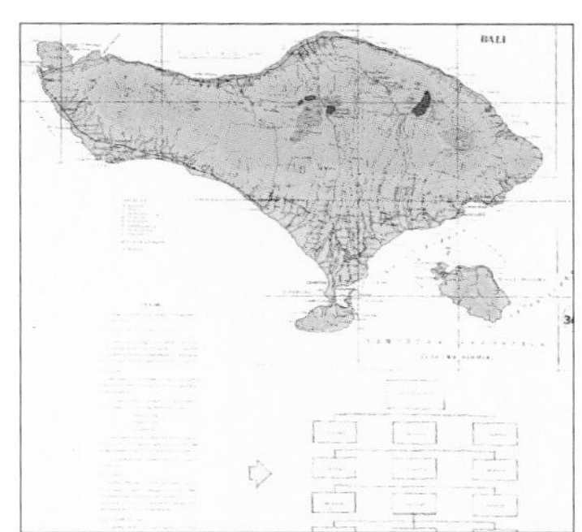

A modern thematic map from the Atlas of Indonesia showing land use and geology.

«« The Spice Islands (now Maluku) were mapped in great detail by the early European powers due to their economic importance. A 1652 map by Abbé Sanson 'd Abbeville, Geographer to the King of France.

Places of Plenty Places of Want

The Indonesian archipelago offers a wide range of environments. The uneven distribution of population, ranging from the densely settled areas of rural Java to the sparsely settled expanses of Irian Jaya and Kalimantan, testify to the differing attractiveness of places of plenty and places of want. However, these superficial divisions often belie important local-level variations in potential.

Lower rainfall levels can only sustain savanna vegetation

Village destroyed by volcanic eruption

Changing Fortunes

The superficial contrasts between places of plenty and places of want mask the fact that periodic events can decimate populations and livelihoods. Places of want are varied and changing. The historical experience of the Banda Islands of Maluku illustrates this. The European thrust eastwards in search of the fabled Spiceries of Maluku took the Portuguese, and later the Dutch, to the Banda Islands in 1512, which at that time enjoyed a virtual monopoly in the production of nutmeg and mace. The Dutch East India Company (VOC) was able to buy the spices for 1/320ths of the

value commanded in Amsterdam. Along with the other Spice Islands they represented, for some years, the focus of the Dutch presence in the archipelago. But by the early 19th century the Bandas' monopoly had been broken and the price of nutmeg and mace fell precipitously. With the fall in price, so the basis of the Islands' attractiveness to the Dutch also waned. Their remoteness from the centres of economy, dry climate and mountainous terrain precluded most other activities and people began to leave the now economically barren islands in search of livelihoods elsewhere. Now, nearly two centuries later, the population of the Bandas are contemplating the possibility of new wealth, this time based on tourism–a new industry–and fisheries–a traditional industry revitalised by new technology.

RAINFALL ZONES

The islands of eastern Indonesia generally have lower annual rainfall than the western part of the country, and are more likely to suffer drought, especially during the northeast monsoon. These two maps show the great variations in rainfall, even over individual landmasses.

Figures are not available for East Timor

Coping with the Environment

Humans transform nature to their advantage. They manipulate environments, turning forested land into productive fields, though they may also undermine these lands, creating degraded environments through over-exploitation. In the rice fields of Java and Bali, artificial ecosystems achieve enormous productivity. However, although nature has provided the rich, volcanic soils and ample rainfall on which the productivity of the wet rice system is based, farmers cultivating the slopes of Mount Merapi in central Java, or Mount Batur in Bali, work with the threat that volcanic activity may destroy their livelihoods.

In contrast, the dry and rocky environments of Nusa Tenggara seem inhospitable. The islands of Timor, Rote, Savu and Sumba in the far eastern extremity of the island arc of Nusa Tenggara exhibit some of the most marginal climatic conditions in Indonesia. They are semi-arid, with a long dry season, and annual rainfall ranging between 750 and 1,500 millimetres a year. Although total rainfall may be low, it is the irregularity of the seasons which most challenges the ingenuity of the farmers. The 'rainy' season in parts of Timor, for example, sometimes brings scarcely any rain. In other years it may be delayed or curtailed, forcing farmers to make decisions in the face of considerable environmental uncertainty. In addition, the soils of these islands tend to be infertile, impermeable and prone to erosion. It is because of these conditions that the inhabitants have maintained a diverse range of activities, spreading their risks in the knowledge that parts of their subsistence system may fail. The islanders have exploited unique environmental niches

WATER CYCLE COMPARISON:
Forest Cover And Bare Soil Surface

One aspect of manmade destruction is the disruption of the water cycle due to uncontrolled forest clearance.

1. Prevailing winds transport evaporated water from the sea to the forest where it condenses and falls as rain.

2. Water evaporates from the land and vegetation surface, a process referred to as transpiration. Some water percolates through the soil into the water table, then flows underground to the ocean or is taken up by tree roots.

3. When the area is cleared, run-off increases, the cycle is disrupted and the forest is in danger of becoming a desert.

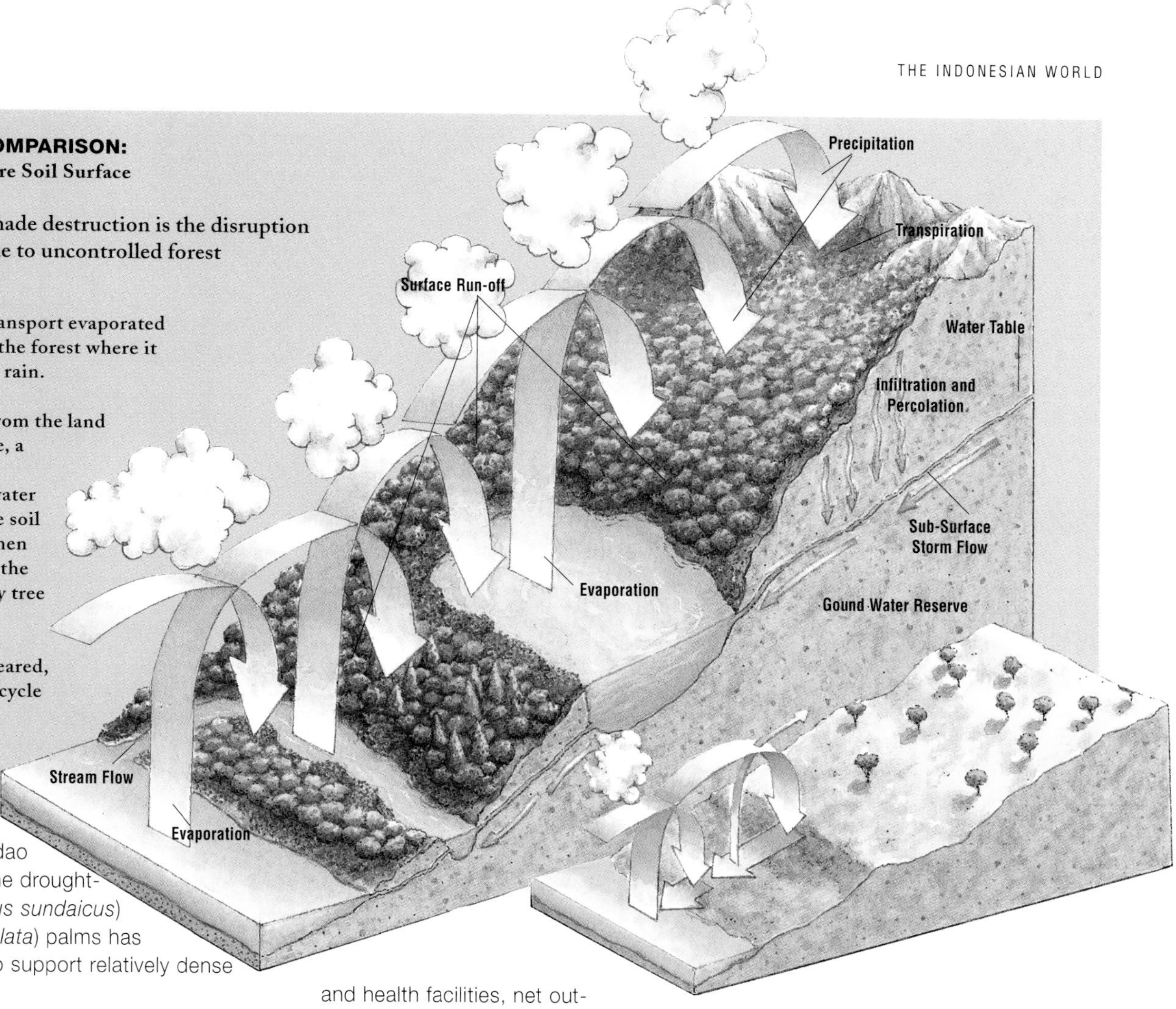

to support themselves. On islands like Savu, Ndao and Rote, the juice of the drought-resistant lontar (*Borassus sundaicus*) and gewang (*Corypha elata*) palms has enabled these islands to support relatively dense populations.

Transmigration settlers have found the forests of Irian Jaya a challenge to their agricultural ingenuity. Beneath the abundant vegetation are poor soils, heavily leached and prone to erosion when cleared. In their struggle to maintain yeilds, transmigrants have sometimes resorted to shifting cultivation, effectively surrendering to the forest. In doing this they are emulating the strategies of the indigenous people of the province, who have reaped rich rewards from the forest ecosystem.

Manmade Destruction

More gradual in turning places of plenty into places of want, are the effects of overproduction. Fragile lands with growing populations, like the province of Lampung in southern Sumatra, the district of Sikka on Flores in Nusa Tenggara, and the uplands of Gunung Kidul in Yogyakarta have all suffered from accelerated erosion, land degradation, and falling yields. Land has been abandoned and people have migrated to new areas, sometimes to clear new land from the forest in a process of pioneer settlement. Over time, however, some of these degraded, marginal areas have been 'regained' as farmers have adapted their techniques and adopted new technologies–for example, on the erosion-prone slopes of Gunung Kidul.

Unfortunately, all too often, these areas suffer from less investment in infrastructure which further marginalises them by creating a cycle of reduced production, still less investment, poorer education and health facilities, net out-migration due to a lack of opportunities, and so on. In general then, whereas investment in any, or all, of these areas, may allow an area to confront environmental constraints, more often than not the perceived or real absence of economic potential does the exact reverse.

The Role of Technology

The question of whether a natural resource can be profitably exploited depends on price and the level of technology available. Technological progress can prompt a reassessment of the viability of exploitation. This can be seen, for example, in the planned exploitation of the Natuna gas field to the north of Jakarta in the South China Sea. The Natuna gas field, discovered over two decades ago, is one of the ten largest in the world. Yet it was not exploited because the gas had a carbon dioxide content of 72 per cent. It has only been in recent years, with the development of advanced separation technology and the means to re-inject the extracted carbon dioxide into limestone aquifers that exploitation could be contemplated. Even so, the development costs that will be incurred are projected to be US$17 billion at today's prices.

Intensive land clearance on Batam has caused soil erosion on certain parts of the island.

Many Indonesians rely on the sea's bounty for their livelihood, and mangement of the ocean's resources is now an important issue.

The El Niño-Southern Oscillation

Every few years very warm waters appear in the normally cool east equatorial Pacific. At the same time atmospheric pressures drop in the east Pacific, and rise over Indonesia and the western Pacific. This signals the start of an El Niño event, the phenomena which brings droughts to many parts of the tropics, including Indonesia.

What is the El Niño-Southern Oscillation?

The term El Niño (the Spanish for 'The Christ Child') was a phrase originally coined by the fishermen along the coasts of Ecuador and Peru. They use it to refer to a warm ocean current that typically appears around Christmas and lasts for several months. Fish are less abundant along these coasts during these intervals. In some years the water is especially warm, and the term El Niño has now become reserved for these exceptional years. Various phenomena–changes in sea surface temperatures, winds and precipitation across the Pacific–are closely linked with El Niño events. When the east Pacific is unusually warm, it is relatively cool in the west equatorial Pacific and around Indonesia, and precipitation shifts eastwards into the central Pacific.

These various changes in the atmosphere have long been known as the Southern Oscillation; and the two, intimately-linked phenomena are known collectively as the El Niño-Southern Oscillation. The opposite phase of the El Niño-Southern Oscillation, is the La Niña. During this phase the whole Pacific region experiences a cool east Pacific, and a warm west Pacific. During this phase rainfall is heavy over the west Pacific and Indonesia.

These phases of the El Niño-Southern Oscillation generally last about 12 months. They often start early in the calendar year, and gradually grow in strength through the year. Their peak intensity is usually around the end of the year. They are often followed by a year with the phenomenon in its opposite phase. So, an El Niño (with drought in Indonesia), may be followed by the heavy rains associated with a La Niña.

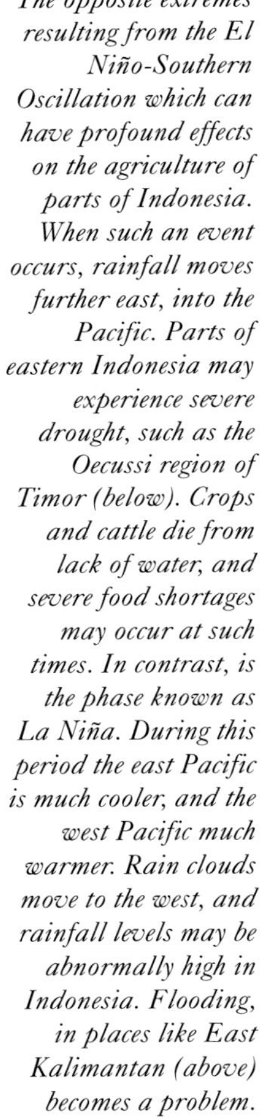

The opposite extremes resulting from the El Niño-Southern Oscillation which can have profound effects on the agriculture of parts of Indonesia. When such an event occurs, rainfall moves further east, into the Pacific. Parts of eastern Indonesia may experience severe drought, such as the Oecussi region of Timor (below). Crops and cattle die from lack of water, and severe food shortages may occur at such times. In contrast, is the phase known as La Niña. During this period the east Pacific is much cooler, and the west Pacific much warmer. Rain clouds move to the west, and rainfall levels may be abnormally high in Indonesia. Flooding, in places like East Kalimantan (above) becomes a problem.

THE SOUTHERN OSCILLATION INDEX (SOI) 1876-1995

THE SOUTHERN OSCILLATION INDEX

The Southern Oscillation Index (SOI) is a simple measure of the difference in pressure between Tahiti and Darwin. El Niño events occur when the SOI is strongly negative; when the SOI is strongly positive a La Niña event is occuring. The La Niña brings heavy rainfalls to the west Pacific and Indonesia. El Niño events occured in 1972, 1982, and 1991. La Niña events occured in the mid-1970s, and in 1988.

What Causes It?

Research in the past decade has improved our understanding of the processes causing the El Niño-Southern Oscillation. We know that interaction between the tropical Pacific Ocean and the tropical atmosphere leads to an irregular cycle of El Niño and La Niña events. Changes in the strength of the easterly surface winds along the equator induce changes in sea surface temperature, which alters the

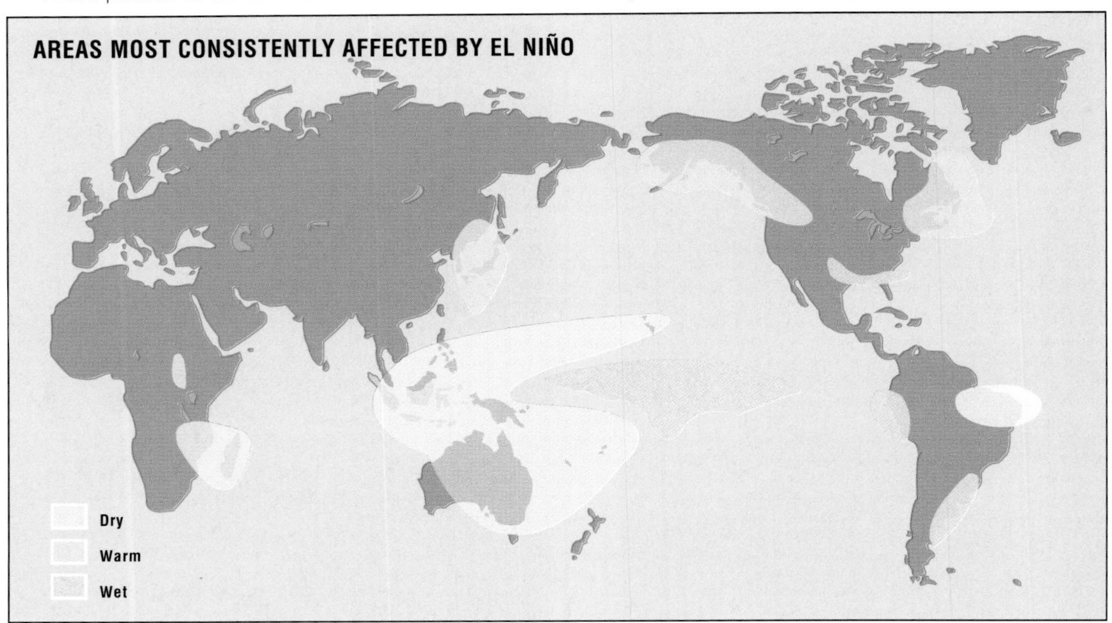

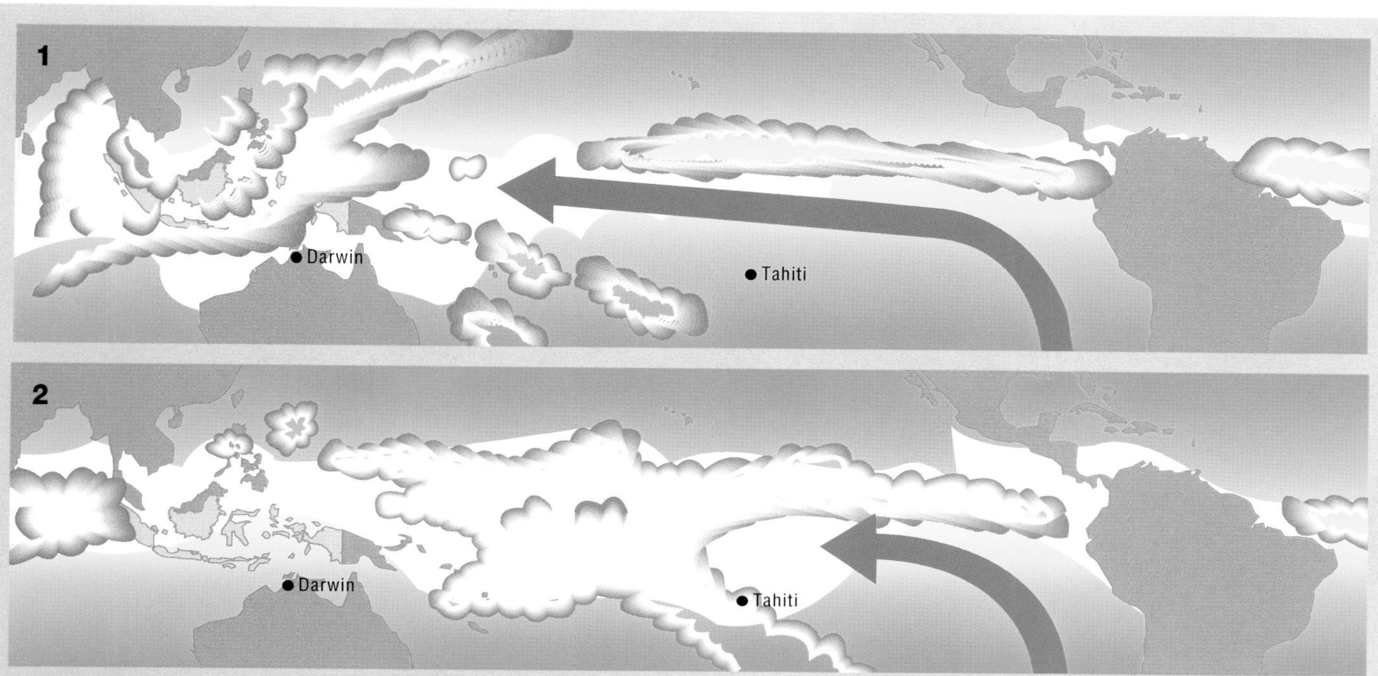

SCHEMATIC OF THE EL NIÑO-SOUTHERN OSCILLATION

1. In phase one of the Southern Oscillation, pressure is higher (darker orange on the map) in the east Pacific than further west. The east-west pressure difference along the equator causes surface air to flow westward, as indicated by the long arrow. This causes upwelling, or cool sub-surface waters to reach the surface of the east Pacific, making this region relatively cool. Precipitation (shown as clouds in the map) is heaviest over the warmer waters of the west Pacific than over the cool east Pacific.

2. When an El Niño occurs, the pressure difference weakens, and the winds also weaken and retreat eastwards, indicated by the short arrow. The upwelling weakens, leading to warming of the central and eastern Pacific. This allows the heavy precipitation areas to move east. At the same time ocean temperatures around Indonesia drop, leading to decreased precipitation.

NB. The term upwelling refers to easterly winds that blow along the equator across the Pacific, producing currents flowing from east to west. The Earth's rotation deflects these currents away from the equator. When the surface water is transported away by these currents, cooler sub-surface waters replace it, in a process called upwelling.

strength of winds, and so on. These changes and interactions can be reproduced in computer models which can simulate the operation of the El Niño-Southern Oscillation. Still unknown are the factors causing changes in the intensity and timing of the El Niño–why are some events stronger and more persistent than others?

Impact on Indonesia

Eighty per cent of the El Niño events that occurred between 1879 to 1982 were also accompanied by below average rainfall between the months of June and November. Ninety per cent of the La Niña episodes were abnormally wet in Indonesia and New Guinea between July and December. Indeed the effect of El Niño events on Indonesian rainfall is substantial enough to be observable in tree rings. Low rainfalls during the El Niño events in 1982 and again in 1991 contributed to the development of major forest fires in Kalimantan. Heavy frost and even freak snowfalls in Irian Jaya can accompany El Niño events.

In the past, El Niño events have been associated with crop failures and with, sometimes chronic, food shortages in various parts of Indonesia, but most particularly in the eastern part of the country. Heavy rains accompanying La Niña events, while having beneficial impacts on many crops, may also increase the prevalence of pests and diseases. For instance,

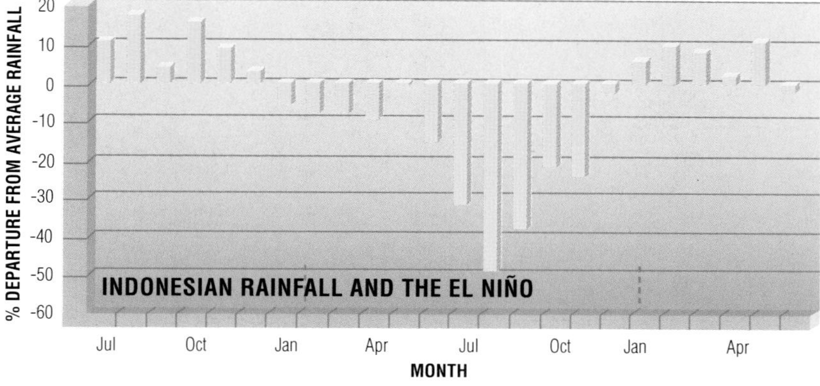

Average monthly precipitation over Indonesia is lower during El Niño episodes, especially from about June to October. In some major El Niño episodes, the low rainfall can be further prolonged, sometimes lasting up to December or January.

mosquito populations tend to increase during heavy rainfall periods. This may lead to an increased prevalence of mosquito-borne diseases.

Predicting El Niño and its Consequences

The first signs that an El Niño event is developing are usually detected by the middle of the calendar year. This means that very simple indices of the El Niño-Southern Oscillation, such as the Southern Oscillation Index (SOI) can be used to predict rainfall for the July to December period, even without a prediction of the El Niño iself. Coupled ocean-atmosphere models are currently being developed for predicting El Niño events. These may lead to forecasts of rainfall with longer lead times.

The photograph (below) is a colour composite picture taken from an altitude of 914 kilometres. It shows the northwest corner of Java, and a small part of the easternmost coast of Sumatra, visible to the left of the photo ❶

Jakarta ❷*, a city with a high population density, lies in the broad bay along the coast. The large piers along the harbour* ❸ *are clearly visible. To the east of the city is a series of mangrove swamps on either side of the Tarum river* ❹*. To the west, the bluish area is newly emerged land* ❺*, now mainly used for wet rice. Along this coast are tambak (fishponds) making up a series of connected basins that fill with tidal waters* ❻*.*

To the south of the city is a network of small streams flowing on an alluvial fan ❼ *developed by drainage from the volcanic highlands further south. This area, is a rich agricultural region supporting small plots of paddy (bluish patches), terrace rice, tapioca, banana, rubber, kapok trees, sugar, tea shrubs, and tobacco. The dark red patches are the heavily forested highlands* ❽*.*

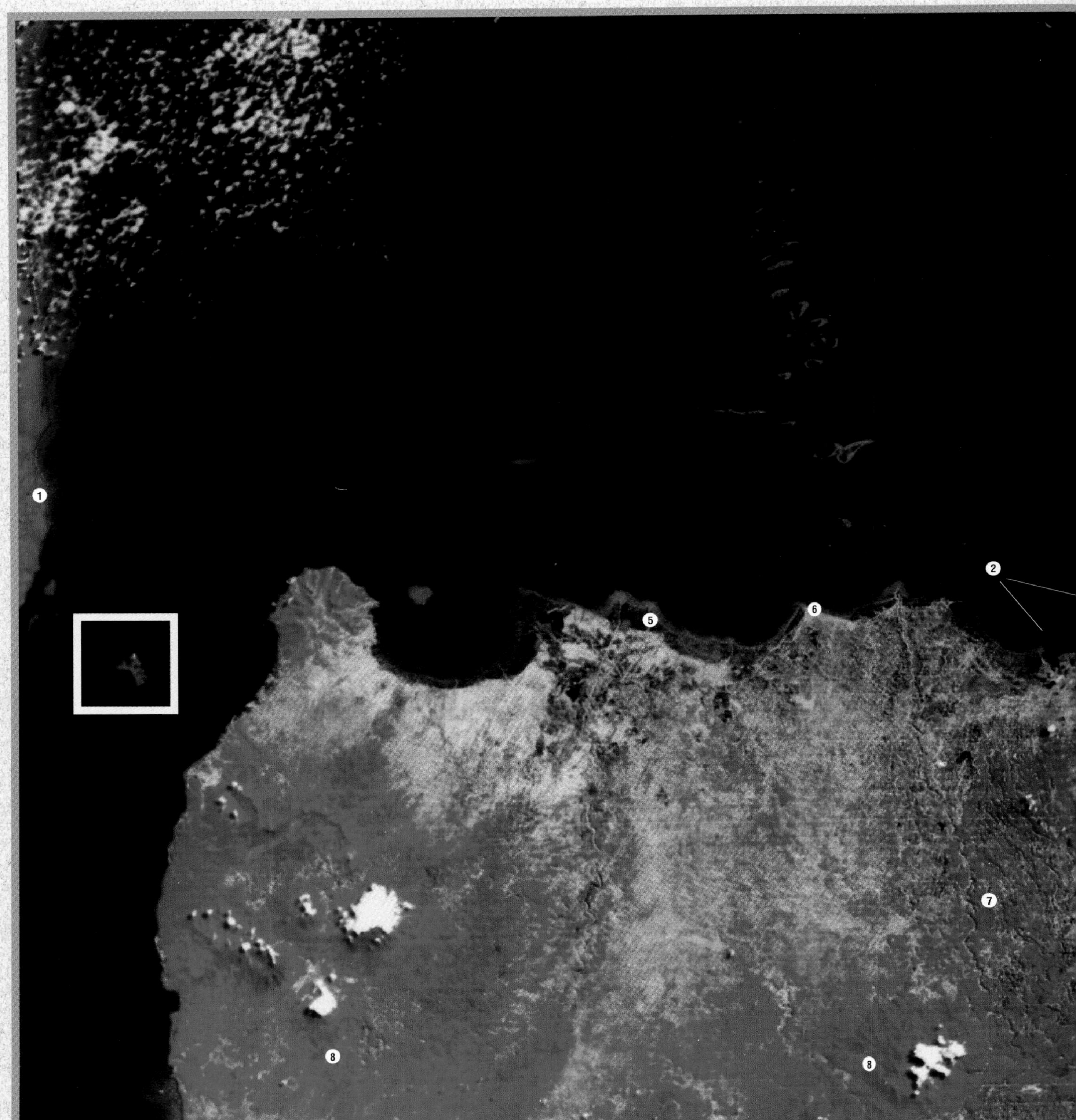

The photograph (inset) shows Anak Krakatau, the island that emerged after the eruption in 1883. It can be seen off the west coast of Java in the satellite photograph (boxed).

SENSE OF PLACE: THE ARCHIPELAGO

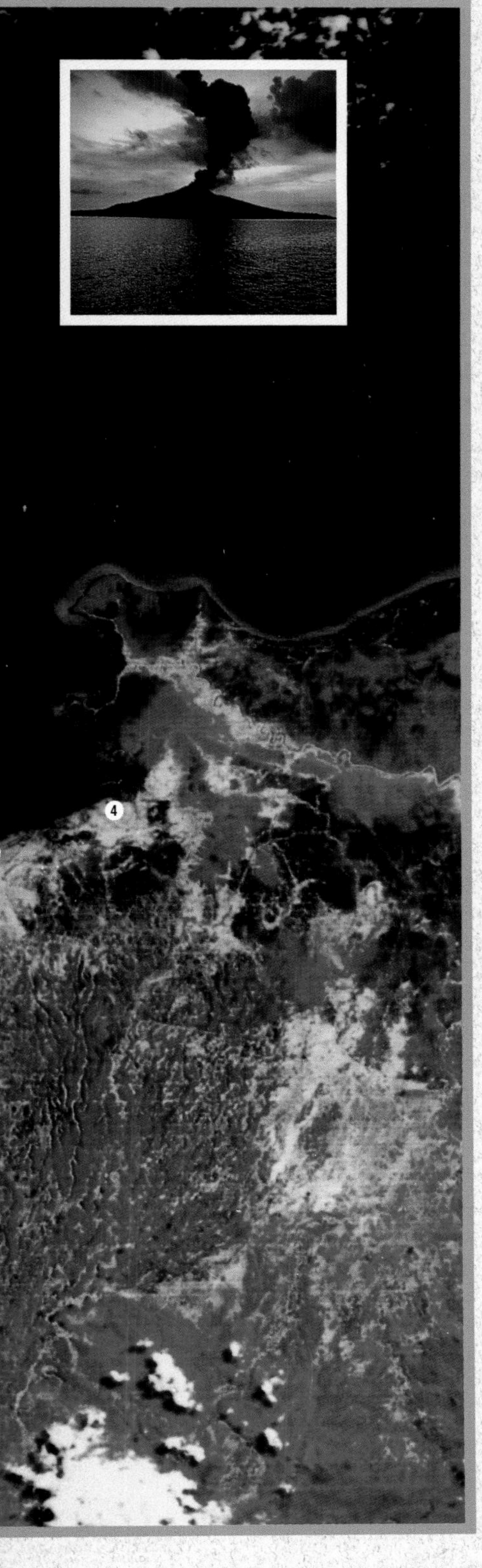

Indonesia did not exist as a nation until recently. The Dutch wrought an archipelagic empire out of a piece of tropical space that had little cultural unity, no sharply defined boundaries, and no sense of shared history. It was assembled through conquest, treaty and accident, and with little idea of where the process might end or what shape the final country might take.

Following Independence, the Dutch East Indies became Indonesia and the government of the new country had the task of building a sense of nationhood. The State used, and continues to use, various means to achieve the end of national unity: a nationwide education system, the promotion of Bahasa Indonesia, the media, groups like the Dharma Wanita (Women's Association) that have a countrywide presence, and political organisations like Golkar (Golongan Karya)–effectively the State's own political party. Important elements within regional cultures have been fused into a *kebudayaan nasional* or national culture. All this was done with the aim of forging a country into a nation. Great strides have been made in 'creating' Indonesia, and many scholars–and the government–speak of the very diversity of the country as a mark of unity.

Clearly, there is almost no limit to the degree to which Indonesia can be sub-divided, from country level down to the particularity of individual *desa* (villages). Ethnographic studies are partly based on the belief that every village, every household, is distinct and unique, offering insights into processes and structures that a household across the lane or a village on the other bank of a river, would not offer. That other household or village would, in turn, offer its own unique view of the Indonesian world. There are also numerous ways in which the country can be partitioned. On the basis of ecological factors, cultural groups or administrative divisions, for instance. For this chapter we have chosen the major islands, or island groups. They show a certain environmental and cultural coherence, that allow some generalisations to be made. This is not, however, to say that a villager in the Torajan highlands of South Sulawesi would not reveal a closer affinity with a Batak from Sumatra than with an inhabitant from another part of Sulawesi. Regional designations are generalisations that quickly reveal themselves as such if they are stretched too far, or are used in a too deterministic fashion. How Indonesia is segmented and then presented, as was made clear in the opening chapter of this volume, is dependent on the task at hand.

Java

The island of Java, about 1,000 kilometres in length, and some 200 kilometres in width, is an island of contrasts. It is punctuated by an irregular line of volcanoes running the length of the island. These include Mount Sumeru, the highest peak at 3,676 metres; Mount Merapi, the most active; and Mount Kelud, the most violent.

The smoking Mount Batur and Mount Bromo, testify to the geological instability of the island. These are only two of the chain of active volcanoes that run all the way along the central mountain ridge of the island.

Aerial view of a Javanese suburb. As more Javanese move to the cities, the differences between rural and urban culture become greater than between the different ethnic groups.

This old print depicts a traditional wedding group in Batavia (Jakarta). Ethnic dress is now worn only on festive occasions, as young Javanese adopt Western influenced clothes.

The Landscape

Nutrient rich lava and ash from Java's many volcanoes account for the fertility of their foothills and the northern plains. This contrasts with the shallow soils and soluble rocks of the limestone karst areas, the Rembang Plateau and Gunung Sewu in the northeast and southeast, and the acidic and leached soils of the southern hills. The island of Madura, which lies to the east of mainland Java, is separated by a narrow strait, and is geographically and geologically related to Java. It is a flat and dry island with infertile soils and rocky limestone slopes.

Average monthly temperatures are stable at around 27 degrees Celsius, though maximum daily temperatures can reach as high as 34 degrees Celsius. Highland temperatures be as low as four degrees Celsius, even during the day. Rain falls mainly between October and March, while April to September is dry. Parts of central Java have extremely high rainfall totals of between 3,000 and 7,000 millimetres per annum, but figures for the eastern lowlands dip as low as 900 millimetres. This is due to the fact that Java is in the transition zone between the wet equatorial region of Sumatra, Kalimantan and Malaysia to the north, and the drier southeast, of which Nusa Tenggara is part.

Many of the plant and animal species found in Java are common to the Asian mainland and to Sumatra and Borneo. When sea levels were much lower than they are today, they all formed a single land mass, the Sunda Shelf. Some species which have become extinct in Sumatra–like the Javan rhinoceros–are still found in Java. Java also has some species not found in any of the surrounding islands.

Vegetation types reflect the climatic changes that occur as one moves from west to east. In the west, the much wetter climate supports lush and diverse rainforests and the kinds of plants typically found in them, while in the east can be found deciduous forests and dry savanna grasslands. About 63 per cent of Java's land area is cultivated, and agricultural use reflects the physiographic and climatic conditions found on the island. About 24 per cent of all agricultural land is under wet rice cultivation, giving Java its characteristic scenery of flooded rice fields, rice terraces and irrigation networks. Also found are estates of tea, rubber, oil palm and cacao, and dry fields of maize, soybeans, peanuts, and cassava.

The People

Java supports over 115 million people, which constitutes some 60 per cent of Indonesia's total population, squeezed onto a mere seven per cent of the country's total land area at a density of 850 persons per square kilometre. Some 25 per cent of this population is classified as urban; in short, Java is still mainly rural.

The three main ethnic groups are the Javanese, the Sundanese in west Java, and the Madurese. The Javanese account for about two-thirds of the island's total population, with the Sundanese and Madurese accounting for about 20 and 10 per cent respectively.

The island can be divided into four main cultural areas. The *kejawen*, or Javanese heartland in Central and East Java is the seat of several powerful kingdoms, whose past glory is reflected in the monuments of Borobudur and Prambanan and the palaces of Yogyakarta and Surakarta. Islam is the main religion, and orthodox practitioners can be contrasted with those who embrace a more syncretic system of belief, which incorporates mysticism and traces of Hinduism. Christianity and Hinduism are also represented among some groups.

The northern coastal plain of Java is often considered as constituting a second cultural area with its *pasisir* culture. Here, the effects of early contact with various trading groups is evident in the mixed Javanese, Malay, Arab and other ancestry of the people. The area is characterised by a stronger adherence to the orthodox tenets of Islam.

The western Priangan highlands of Java make up a third cultural area. This region is populated mainly by the Sundanese who speak a language which is closely related to both Malay and to Javanese. Like the *pasisir* of the north coast, the Sundanese differ from the *kejawen* in their strong observance of an orthodox Islam. The rigid adherence to rank and status are less conspicuous here, however.

The fourth and final cultural area can be found in the eastern segment of Java, which is known traditionally as Blambangan, after the Hindu kingdom that existed here until the late 18th century. The indigenous people here are the Osing. They are Muslims, although a small proportion of the area is populated by Hindu Tenggerese. Large numbers of Madurese have also settled in the area, mainly on the north coast of this area.

While the Javanese can generally be distinguished along these lines, such differences are not entirely clear-cut. There are important variations in characteristics in each area, and an urban culture has recently evolved, built on the influences of mass education and mass media, such that a general contrast has arisen between the urban and rural peoples. Urban Javanese, Sundanese, and Madurese therefore have more in common with one another than with their rural counterparts. Java has received Madurese migrants, but those remaining on Madura tend to be more traditional than their Javanese counterparts, with older islanders still wearing the *destar* or headcloth. Both groups retain their own distinctive language.

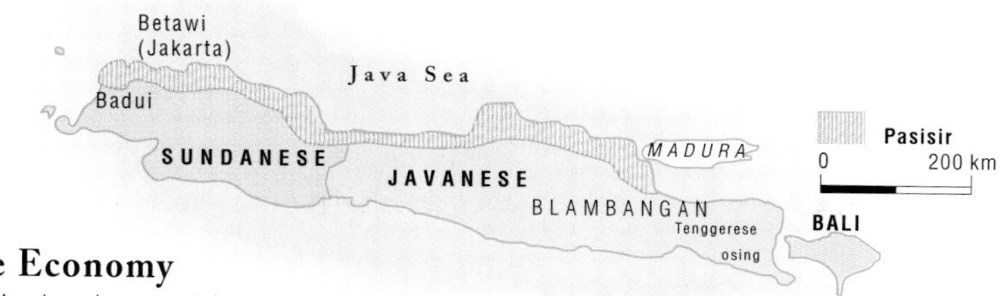

The map shows the regional variation of Javanese culture. In the eyes of the Javanese, their culture does not constitute a homogenous unity, rather it reflects diverse differences extending over the whole island, and the island of Madura.

The Economy

Java's development is unevenly distributed, being biased towards the north west. The imbalance between the north and south is primarily due to geography. The north is accessible via almost continuous coastal plains, and the sea to the north is calm, allowing for the development of ports. The southern coast, by way of contrast, is for the most part rocky and very inhospitable. Here, the sea is rough and dangerous to shipping. The limestone karsts and the acidic, leached soils along the southern edge of the Island have also rendered the area infertile and at points the land is inaccessible.

In turn, the imbalance between the east and west of the island has been created with the centralisation of political and economic functions in Jakarta. With the concentration of foreign financial and industrial investment in the west, many of the island's workers also congregate in and around Jakarta, so much so that the northwest corridor has superseded the old industrial region at the other end of the island, centred on Surabaya.

Area :		132.187 km^2
Population in 1990 census :		107.6 million
Population density in 1990 :		814 people/km^2
Population growth (1980-1990) :		1.66%
Forested area in 1990 :		3,013,000 ha
Total arable land 1990 :		7,653,000 ha
	SEASON	
Dry	**Wet**	**Rainfall**
Jun-Aug	Dec-Feb	West: 2,360 mm Central: 2,400 mm East: 1,660 mm

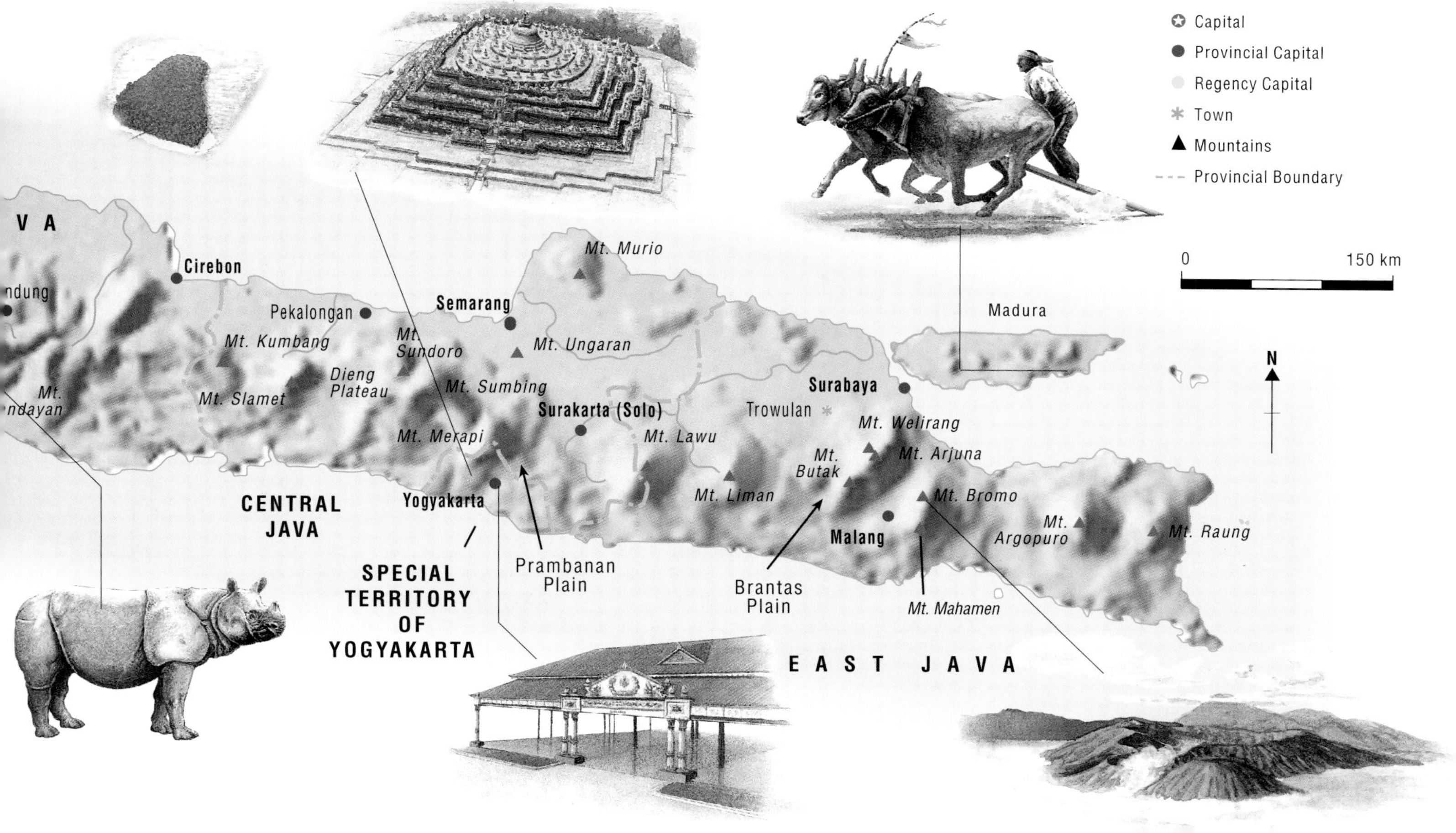

Bali

Bali is one of Indonesia's smallest provinces, covering just 5,561 square kilometres, or 0.3 per cent of the country's total land area. It is separated from Java to the west by the Bali Strait and from Lombok to the east by the Lombok Strait. The island lies over two overlapping tectonic plates, and as a result, is an area of geological instability. Earthquakes and volcanic eruptions occur often, and indeed the island itself is dominated by a series of volcanic peaks over 2,000 metres in height, the highest of which is the active Mount Agung at 3,140 metres.

Bali's spectacular terraced rice fields are an important attraction for its thriving tourist industry.

Planners have tried to focus tourist development near the south coast of Bali; this aerial view shows the coastline and tourist resorts of Nusa Dua.

The Landscape

To the south of Bali's central mountain core is the main expanse of foothills and lowlands in Bali. Most of the rivers on the island flow from the central highlands into the Indian Ocean through these foothills and lowlands and their rich and fertile soils are cultivated with rice.

The most distinctive feature on the mountain slopes is the terraced rice field, efficiently irrigated by a traditional water management system based on the *subak*. The *subak* is an irrigation society that is set up to ensure the equitable distribution of water amongst farmers. At least two crops can be produced from these fields per year. Villages, which are sustained on rice cultivation, are often located on the ridges that divide the various river systems.

To the north of the island, the mountains drop steeply to the sea, with only a narrow coastal lowland strip. The climate is drier here than in the southern lowlands and many of the rivers only flow during the wet season. As a result, rice is not widely cultivated in this area, and where it is, just one crop per year is harvested. Instead, dryland agriculture is more common, with the cultivation of citrus fruits, coffee and cloves. Like the north, the west is comparatively arid and the soils also lack the fertility of those in the south.

Bali is hot and humid, with temperatures at sea level averaging 26 degrees Celsius. In the highlands, average daily temperatures are lower at about 20 degrees Celsius. The dry season in Bali extends from about May to October, with August and September being the driest months. In turn, the wet season is from November to April, with December and January being the wettest months. Total annual rainfall averages 2,150 millimetres.

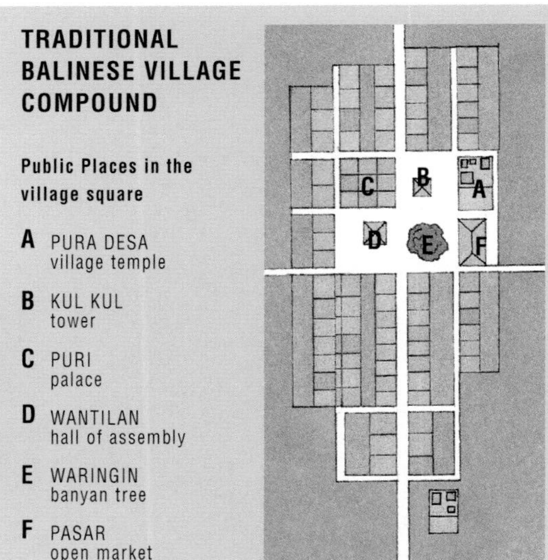

The People

Bali's total population of three million includes a majority Hindu element and a minority Bali Aga component. The latter claim to be the original inhabitants of Bali; their minority status is a result of the in-migration of Javanese since the 10th century. Today, small communities of Bali Aga can be found mainly in the eastern part of the island.

The majority of Balinese (95 per cent) are Hindu, although it is Hinduism of a syncretic kind. Combining Buddhism, Hinduism and animist beliefs, Balinese religion is known as Hindu Dharma or Agama Hindu. Worship of spirits, ancestors and natural elements is therefore combined with a belief in the tenets of Hinduism. One of the more important religious rituals in Bali is that of cremation. During this rite of passage, gamelan music, dances and offerings accompany a procession in which a decorated tower is carried from the home of the deceased to the cremation ground. The elaborate practices have become somewhat eroded through the years, though they still serve to attract tourists.

The legong is a classical dance of the palaces. Legong dancers were chosen from among a villagers' most attractive young dancers.

Balinese Hinduism combines Sivaism, Buddhism and traditional beliefs from the Indonesian Archipelago.

The village is the predominant settlement type in Bali, with each housing anything from 200 to several thousand inhabitants. Around a central courtyard are clustered family compounds (*kuren*) enclosed by high walls. Each *kuren* supports several families, which worship, cook and eat communally. The central courtyard is the place of congregation for villagers who use it for their cultural activities, marketing, meetings and so forth.

Balinese society is stratified in two ways. The first–*wangsa*–is based on descent, in which each individual is born either into the nobility or the *sudras* (also known as *jaba*, literally, the outsiders of the

Area :	5,561 km^2
Population in 1990 census :	2.8 million
Population density in 1990 :	500 people/km^2
Population growth (1980-1990):	1.18%
Forested area [including Nusa Tenggara] in 1990 : 3, 418, 000 ha	
Total arable land [including Nusa Tenggara] in 1990 : 3, 318, 000 ha	

SEASON		
Dry	**Wet**	**Rainfall**
May-Oct	Nov-Apr	Average 2,150 mm

court). The nobility, in turn, are divided into three castes, the priests (*brahmanas*), the ruling nobles (*satriyas*) and the warriors (*wesyas*). The majority of the population belong to the *sudras*. The second social 'indicator' is based on one's place of residence, and the *banjar* system forms the backbone of this structure. Within each village, there may be several *banjars*, each drawing members from a particular neighbourhood within the village. It is a male-focused system and every Balinese male is required to belong to a *banjar*; women are excluded from membership. Within each *banjar*, a member is elected as head and he enjoys some minor privileges such as additional rice during festivals. In effect, the *banjar* functions like a cooperative, with common funds and even communal ownership of ricefields.

The Economy

Agriculture is an important source of livelihood for the bulk of Bali's inhabitants. The most important crop is rice, and at least two crops are produced from three-quarters of Bali's riceland each year. Since the mid 1960s, farmers have adopted high-yielding varieties of rice which are usually cultivated using large amounts of chemical fertilisers. Cloves, fruit, vanilla, and vegetables are also cultivated, and livestock reared.

Tourism makes up the second major element of Bali's economy. In 1992 nearly one million tourists arrived by air and by sea from Java and Lombok. This accounts for almost half of the total visitors to Indonesia, underlining the importance of Bali in Indonesia's overall tourism sector. The thriving tourist industry has led to a boom in the construction sector. From 1984 when there were 9,000 hotel rooms, the number has now increased to 20,000. While most of the tourist resorts have hitherto been confined to the far south and southeast coast, there are currently various plans to develop other parts of the island by extending the road system and tourist information centres. Indeed, this kind of development illustrates how tourism can benefit the Balinese in general, and not just those directly involved with the industry, by improving and expanding transport facilities, telecommunications, and electrical power supplies. Part of the potential for future growth also lies in developing ecotourism, which will harness the island's natural and cultural landscapes.

While tourism holds much promise as a revenue-generator, it has nevertheless created some problems. In particular, the drawbacks of the tourist influx include environmental degradation, the erosion of traditions, inflation, and the growth of crime and drug abuse. In order to counter some of these problems, the Tourism Guidance and Counselling Service has been set up to encourage respect for the island, its culture and history. Even so, environmental protection and guarding against the adulteration of traditional social and cultural practices remain challenges for the future.

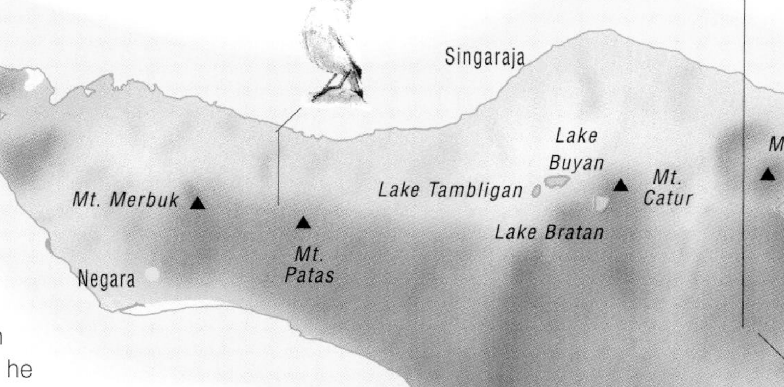

The manufacture of arts and crafts, and garments is also important in terms of employment and revenue potential. Craft items of silver, wood and shell, as well as paintings and clothing, constituted 70 per cent of the total value of Bali's exports in 1989. A large proportion of this was through direct sales to tourists although foreign partners with knowledge of the international market have also helped to open up opportunities for the export of Balinese products.

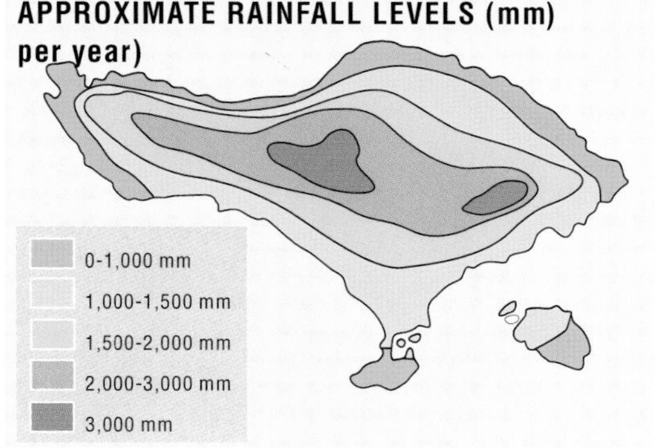

Sumatra

Sumatra has a land area of 475,000 square kilometres, and is the world's fourth largest island. It runs parallel to the Malaysian peninsula, and is separated from it by the Strait of Melaka. The Bukit Barisan mountains run down the western edge of the island, many of the 93 peaks exceeding 2,000 metres. Mount Kerinci (3,805 metres) is the highest.

Formed as a result of a huge volcanic explosion, Lake Toba, with Samosir Island in the middle, is the largest lake in Southeast Asia. Some scientists believe it may have triggered the onset of the last ice age by lowering northern temperatures by three to five degrees Celsius a year.

» Minangkabau society in the western highlands of Sumatra is based on matrilineal descent

The Landscape

Like the island of Java, Sumatra lies over a major fault line and is geologically unstable. In the north of the Bukit Barisan range is a crater lake, Lake Toba, formed after a massive volcanic eruption 75,000 years ago and said to have been the most powerful explosion in the last million years. To the east of the Bukit Barisan, the foothill region gives way to extensive swampy lowlands, traversed by some of Indonesia's largest rivers–the Musi, Batanghari and Rokan, for example. To the west of the Bukit Barisan, the coast is narrow, and seldom exceeds 20 kilometres in width. A few fishing and agricultural villages, as well as the towns of Padang and Bengkulu, have developed on this narrow stretch of land. Offshore to the west are Nias and the Mentawai islands.

Sumatran soils are generally not very fertile. In the east, waterlogging poses a problem while the foothills of the Bukit Barisan tend to be very heavily leached. Once the land is cleared of forest for agriculture, the fertility of the soil declines rapidly without fertilisation.

The equator dissects Sumatra, and monthly temperatures average between 26 and 27 degrees Celsius. In contrast, rainfall is more varied, and is highest in the western plains and foothills of the Bukit Barisan. Here, rainfall averages about 4,000 millimetres per year, though it can climb as high as 6,000 millimetres per year in the town of Bengkulu. In the central, eastern and northern portions of Sumatra, rainfall averages between 2,500 and 3,000 millimetres per year. While rain falls throughout the year, it is heaviest between October and April for places north of the equator, and between October and January south of the equator. June and July are, by comparison, drier months.

Sumatra has a larger diversity of wildlife than any other Indonesian island. Amongst the best known mammals are the Sumatran rhinoceros, Indian elephant, orang utan and Sumatran tiger. Other species include the slow lori, the subalpine grey shrew and honeybear, for example. Few species are endemic and the ranges of many species include Malaysia, Java and Borneo.

The Sumatran rhinoceros is one of 176 mammals that can be found in Sumatra. It is the smallest of the rhinoceros family, and lacks the tough hide of other species, having a soft, hairy hide.

The People

For an island of Sumatra's size, its population is comparatively small, being about 37 million people. However, areas like the province of southern Lampung with a population of six million, are beginning to suffer the effects of overpopulation. In terms of distribution, while the highlands of the Bukit Barisan range generally do not encourage human habitation, the plateaus and upland lake areas have nevertheless been settled by various groups. For example, the Batak inhabit the volcanic plateau around Lake Toba in the north, and the Minangkabau have settled in the western highlands. Settlements have also developed in the foothills and river basins.

The Minangkabau are a matriarchal society, though at the same time staunch adherents of Islam. The Batak and the Acehnese in the north, and the people of Lampung in the south constitute the other major groups. In addition there are smaller populations of, for example, the Sakai in Riau Daratan and the Kubu in the south, as well as more isolated peoples of Nias and the Mentawai islands, such as the Sakkudai. Many of these small groups are hunter-gatherers. Although generalisation is always difficult, the Acehnese tend to live by rice cultivation and cattle-rearing while the Batak cultivate rice and grow vegetables. The Orang Laut, on the other hand, rely on fishing, and have settled along the swampy shores of east Sumatra and on the multitude of islands that constitute the Riau Archipelago.

Javanese transmigrants have also made their presence felt, particularly in the southern parts of Sumatra, although some have also settled on the west coast and in the reclaimed swamps of the east. In fact, Sumatra is the most important transmigration destination, with about 60 per cent of Indonesia's transmigrants settled here. The majority of migrants from Java can be found in rural centres cultivating crops such as rice, whether in swidden fields, on swamplands, or in irrigated fields, rubber (mainly along the rivers), and coffee.

Urban Centres

While the majority of Sumatra's population lives in rural areas, there is also a handful of fast-growing urban centres. Medan in the province of North Sumatra with two million inhabitants is the largest Indonesian city outside Java. It is a cosmopolitan centre, with a large population of Chinese descent, and also smaller Indian and Arab communities. Sumatra's second city is Palembang in the province of South Sumatra. It is located on the site of the capital of the once great Sriwijayan empire. Today it has a total of about one million inhabitants.

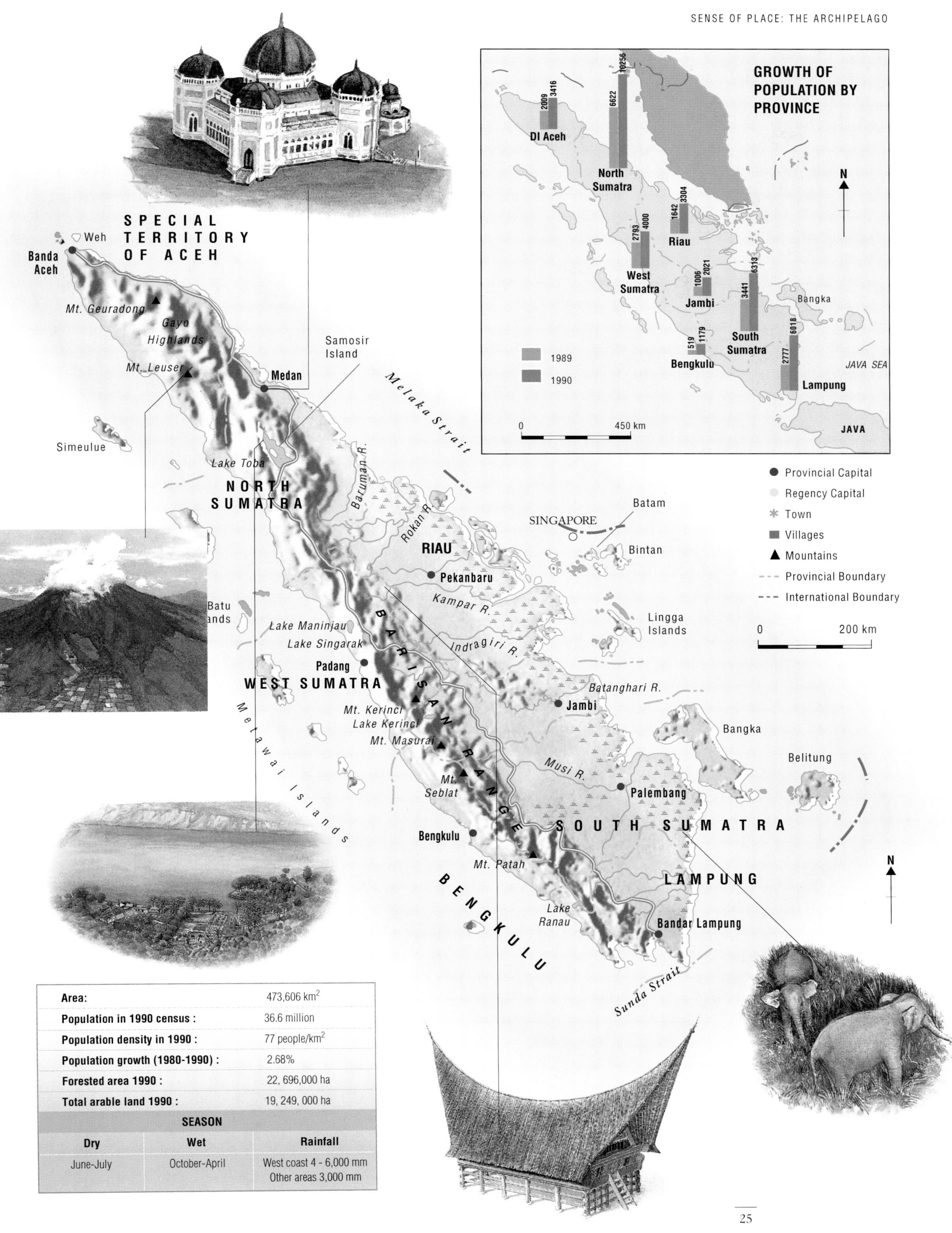

Area:	473,606 km^2	
Population in 1990 census :	36.6 million	
Population density in 1990 :	77 people/km^2	
Population growth (1980-1990) :	2.68%	
Forested area 1990 :	22, 696,000 ha	
Total arable land 1990 :	19, 249, 000 ha	
SEASON		
Dry	Wet	Rainfall
June-July	October-April	West coast 4 - 6,000 mm Other areas 3,000 mm

Kalimantan

Kalimantan, or Indonesian Borneo, embraces the south-eastern two-thirds of the island, with Brunei and Malaysia's Sabah and Sarawak making up the rest of the area. The highest mountain ranges run roughly from Sabah in the north, to the southwest where they diverge towards the east and west.

Bahau Dayak woman from East Kalimantan performs one of the traditional dances of her people. She is holding hornbill tailfeathers, and is dancing on top of a gong.

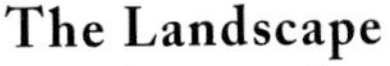

The Landscape

With the exception of the Meratus Mountains in the south-east of the island, and limestone outcrops in the west (the highest, Mount Mulul, is 2,377 metres), much of Kalimantan's land area is barely above sea level. Kalimantan is dissected by a network of rivers that originate in the central mountain core. The two largest are the east flowing Mahakam and the west flowing, and longest, the Kapuas. Numerous other large rivers drain north to south.

Kalimantan has a monsoon climate bringing dry winds from the southeast from May to September; and moisture-laden winds from the north-west between October and March. Most rain falls during the months of November, December and January, whereas July, August and September remain dry. The total annual rainfall averages 3,000 millimetres on the coast, while inland it is somewhat higher. The reverse is true of temperatures, those on the coast being hotter, reaching 37 degrees Celsius, whereas further inland the mean annual temperatures range between 24 and 26 degrees Celsius. In the interior highlands temperatures drop still lower with increasing altitude. A degree of unpredictability has crept in as far as Kalimantan's weather patterns are concerned in recent years. Some experts have attributed these events to large-scale deforestation.

Kalimantan's rainforest is a valuable timber resource. Here a logging road has been cut through the forest to transport the logs out.

The People

The interior tribes of Borneo are collectively termed Dayak (Dyak, Daya and Dya). As a generic term it masks the cultural and linguistic diversity contained within a population consisting of 200 or so ethnic groups (*suku*). Many of these groups share common cultural traits. The origin of the term is the subject of some dispute. Some scholars believe it means 'interior' or 'inland' peoples; others argue that it simply means 'native'. Whatever its origins, however, the term does distinguish the Dayak from the other main population group, the Muslim Malays.

The Malays are mostly coastal-living, dominating the main cities of Kalimantan. Their livelihoods are usually based on trading, settled agriculture–particularly swamp rice farming, and coastal and estuarine fishing. The Dayak, in contrast, are interior-living, swidden cultivators, who also hunt and gather forest produce, and fish the rivers. More recently immigrants from Sulawesi, Sumatra and Java, and from the Malay Peninsula have settled in the coastal areas. The transmigration scheme has provided a further transfusion of Muslim Malay immigrants. It is very difficult to provide accurate figures for the population of Kalimantan by ethnic group. Some scholars, however, argue that the Dayaks are now in a minority and are outnumbered by Malays.

Despite the diversity of Dayak groups, there are some common linking threads between them. Firstly, most Dayaks are found in the interior of Borneo, usually along rivers. Many live in large communal dwellings (not always the longhouse that is more common to the north of the island) raised on stilts. Second, the characteristic subsistence strategy is the shifting cultivation of dry rice, although hunting and gathering remain important among some groups (this allows a sub-division between settled agricult-uralists and 'nomads'). Thirdly, in terms of religion, there are also similarities in terms of cosmology, ritual and symbolism. For example there is a wide-spread belief in an upper and underworld, and most Dayak groups practice some kind of secondary

MAIN DAYAK GROUPS IN KALIMANTAN

Name(s)	Main Distribution	Estimated Numbers	Livelihood/Ecological Criteria	Sociological Criteria
Punan (also Penan, Ot, Basap, Bukit, Bukat, Bekatan)	Central Kalimantan	12,000	Hunter-gatherers	Egalitarian society
Kayan (also Bahau,Busang)	Central and East Kalimantan (Kayan basin, near the Mahakam and Mendalam Rivers)	27,000	Settled agricurallists	Stratified society: *aristocrats *ordinary villagers *slaves
Kenyah	Central and East Kalimantan	40,000	Settled agricurallists	Stratified society
Ga'al (also Segai, Long Glat, Modand, Menggai)	Central and East Kalimantan	5,000	Settled agricurallists	Stratified society
Kelabit-Murut (also Apo Duat, Lun Dayeh, Lun Bawang)	Northeast Kalimantan	40,000	Shifting cultivators, rice cultivators	Stratified society
Meloh (also Memaloh)	West Kalimantan (Kapuas Basin)	12,000	Shifting cultivators	Egalitarian society
Iban	West Kalimantan (Kapuas Basin)	500,000 - 550,000	Shifting cultivators	Egalitarian society
Bidayuh groups (Land Dayaks)	West Kalimantan	100,000	Settled agriculturalists	Egalitarian society
Malayic Dayaks	West and South Kalimantan	—	Settled agriculturalists	Egalitarian society
Barito groups	South Kalimantan	350,000	Shifting cultivators	Egalitarian society
Kadazan (also Dusun)	Border areas of East Kalimantan	400,000 (including the majority in Sabah)	Settled agriculturalists; cattle raisers; shifting cultivators	Egalitarian society

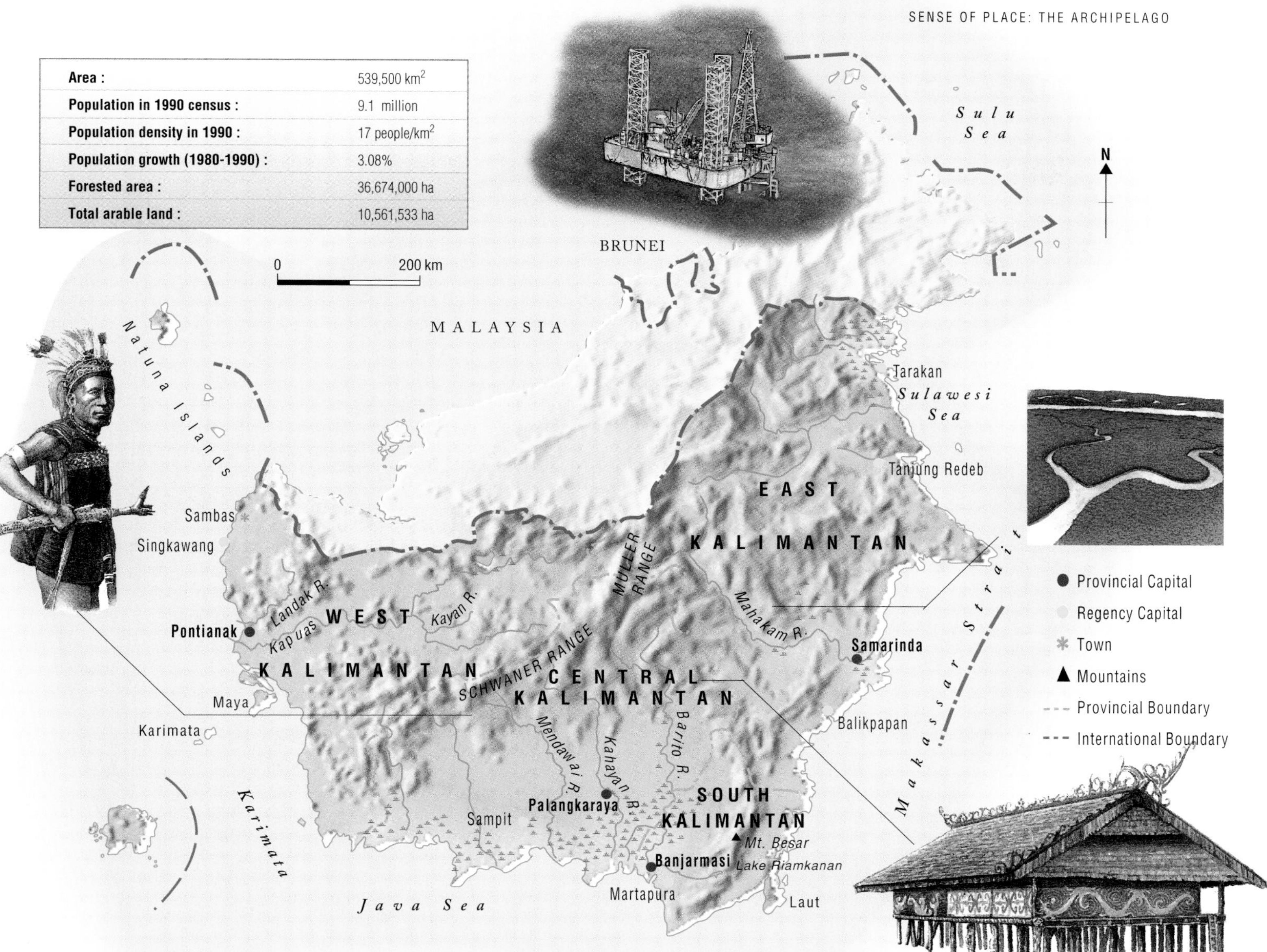

Area :	539,500 km^2
Population in 1990 census :	9.1 million
Population density in 1990 :	17 people/km^2
Population growth (1980-1990) :	3.08%
Forested area :	36,674,000 ha
Total arable land :	10,561,533 ha

mortuary rituals. Formerly the practice of head-hunting was also widespread among the Dayak. The material culture of the Dayak also shows common roots. Their artistic expressions also display remarkable similarites, sharing certain symbolic motifs such as the hornbill and the naga for instance. However, given that various processes of both socio-cultural fission and fusion have taken place in Borneo for many centuries, it would be a grave mistake to examine any one Dayak group in isolation from the others. By the same token it would be equally wrong to try and study and understand the coastal Malay community in isolation from the interior Dayak.

The Economy and Development

Compared to other regions of Indonesia, Kalimantan still has a low level of industrialisation. Its basic infrastructure, such as community services, health provision, piped water and education is limited. The poverty level is also high, associated with low incomes, subsistance agriculture such as rice farming, smallholding rubber and coconut cultivation and artisanal fishing.

Kalimantan is, however, rich in resources, and its economy is based on their exploitation. Apart from gold and diamonds, large scale coal mining began in the late 19th century, followed by a series of oil booms. East Kalimantan has produced oil since the beginning of the 20th century, and liquefied natural gas is an important export. Kalimantan's forests also provide valuable timber; large-scale lumber operations which began in 1967 continue today at alarming rates. Recently, uranium has been discovered.

Naturally some of Kalimantan's communities have benefitted from economic opportunities. Such benefits, though, tend to be fairly localised, generally at a few places around the coast. For example the petroleum industry is concentrated on the east coast round Balikpapan. Many of the oil workers, moreover, come from other parts of Indonesia, and few locals have found alternative economic opportunities.

There are other ways in which Kalimantan is being developed, and is, to a large extent, related to the destruction of the rainforest. In recent years large-scale resettlement programmes have led to the relocation of Indonesians to different areas in Kalimantan. Forests have been cleared to make way for cash-crop estate cultivation of oil palm, cocoa and rubber, and many Dayak have been encouraged to give up their traditional shifting cultivation practices to go and work on these estates.

Sulawesi

Sulawesi is easily distinguishable by its unusual orchid shape. Formerly known as the Celebes, the island has a total land area of 189,216 square kilometres. Even though the total area is comparatively large, no place is more than 40 kilometres from the sea.

Ancient stone burial chambers (waruga) from Sawangan, North Sulawesi.

The Landscape

Geologically, Sulawesi consists of two halves, an eastern and western, which collided 18 million years ago due to continental drift. Apart from a narrow coastal strip, there are few areas of lowland. Most of the island is above 500 metres, a fifth over 1,000 metres. There are 11 active volcanoes, in the Minahasa region of north Sulawesi. Deep valleys dissect the uplands, and fast-flowing rivers run through them–the Lariang is 200 kilometres long. The difficult terrain makes much of Sulawesi inaccessible. Soils are generally poor because of high levels of magnesium and heavy metals, the exception being the region of Lompobatang in the extreme south, where volcanic ash has contributed to fertile soils.

There are significant variations in rainfall between different areas. Manado in the north and Ujung Pandang in the south are wet with an annual rainfall of over 3,000 millimetres, while Palu in the centre only has about 700 millimetres as it remains in the rain shadow for most of the year. Western Sulawesi receives its heaviest rain in December, while on the east coast, the wettest month is May. There are also great temperature variations between areas because of altitudinal differences. While average temperatures in the lowlands generally do not range beyond 25 to 27 degrees Celsius, temperatures in higher altitudes often dip to below 10 degrees Celsius at night.

The People

Sulawesi's population of about 13 million, comprises numerous ethnic groups, with varied cultures, languages and religions. The best known and the largest groups are the southern lowland coastal peoples: the Bugis, the

↗ The Toraja have become well-known, and despite their conversion to Christianity have maintained their distinctive culture, drawing large crowds of tourists to their lavish funeral celebrations

Makassarese and the Mandarese; the Toraja highlanders; and the northern Minahasans. The Bugis and Makassarese are traders and seafarers who have settled across Eastern Indonesia, Borneo and Malaysia. The Toraja are interior-living agriculturalists, brought under Dutch administrative control in the early part of the 20th century. Even within groups there is linguistic diversity–the Minahasans and Mandarese each speaking half a dozen different languages, for example.

About 80 per cent of the inhabitants of Sulawesi embrace Islam, though this is interlaced with local practices of ancestor and spirit worship. A further 17 per cent of the population are Christians, mainly concentrated in the north (Minahasa and the Sangir-Talaud islands), in the Poso district in Central Sulawesi, and in the Toraja highlands in the south. The Christian Minahasans were perhaps more influenced by, and identified with, Dutch colonial culture than any other group in Indonesia.

The Economy

North Sulawesi produces 30 per cent of Indonesia's clove output and is also an important producer of coconuts and nutmeg. A rice surplus is produced in the south and exported to other parts of the country. This emphasis on rice is the result of government initiative, prompted by its concern to ensure Indonesia's self-sufficiency in rice in the 1960s and 70s. Other important crops are coffee in South Sulawesi, and cacao and soybeans in western Southeast Sulawesi. South Sulawesi is also the third largest cattle-producing province in the country.

SULAWESI'S UNIQUE FLORA AND FAUNA

Sulawesi has a diverse flora and a unique fauna. Many of the plant species are closely related to those found in other dry parts of the archipelago. However, Sulawesi's fauna also shows a remarkable degree of endemism. That is the species are found naturally occuring nowhere else on earth. Of the 127 mammal species found on the island, 79 are not found anywhere else, even within Indonesia. These include the dwarf buffalo or anoa (*Bubalus depressiornis* and *B. quarlesi*) and the babirusa or pig-deer (*Babirousa babyrussa*). Of the 328 species of bird, 88 are endemic. This high level of uniqueness makes the conservation of Sulawesi's wildlife particularly important. Nineteen species are currently classified as endangered. In adddition, the island's rugged terrain has made variation within Sulawesi itself highly pronounced as in other islands in the Indonesian archipelago. There are, for example,seven species of macaques occupying different parts of the island.

ENDEMIC FAUNA

1. Red knobbed hornbill (Rhyticerous cassidix)
2. Crested black macaque (Macaca nigra)
3. Babirusa (Babirousa babyrussa)
4. Maleo (Macrocephalon maleo)
5. Anoa (Bubalus depressicornis)
6. Spectral tarsier (Tarsius spectrum)
7. Bear cuscus (Phalanger ursinus)

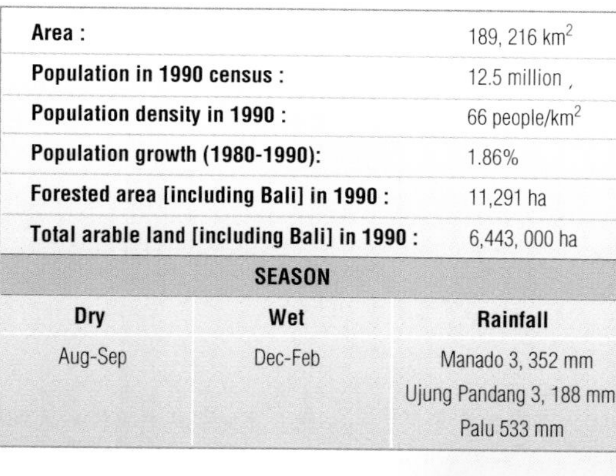

Area :		189, 216 km^2
Population in 1990 census :		12.5 million ,
Population density in 1990 :		66 people/km^2
Population growth (1980-1990):		1.86%
Forested area [including Bali] in 1990 :		11,291 ha
Total arable land [including Bali] in 1990 :		6,443, 000 ha
SEASON		
Dry	**Wet**	**Rainfall**
Aug-Sep	Dec-Feb	Manado 3, 352 mm Ujung Pandang 3, 188 mm Palu 533 mm

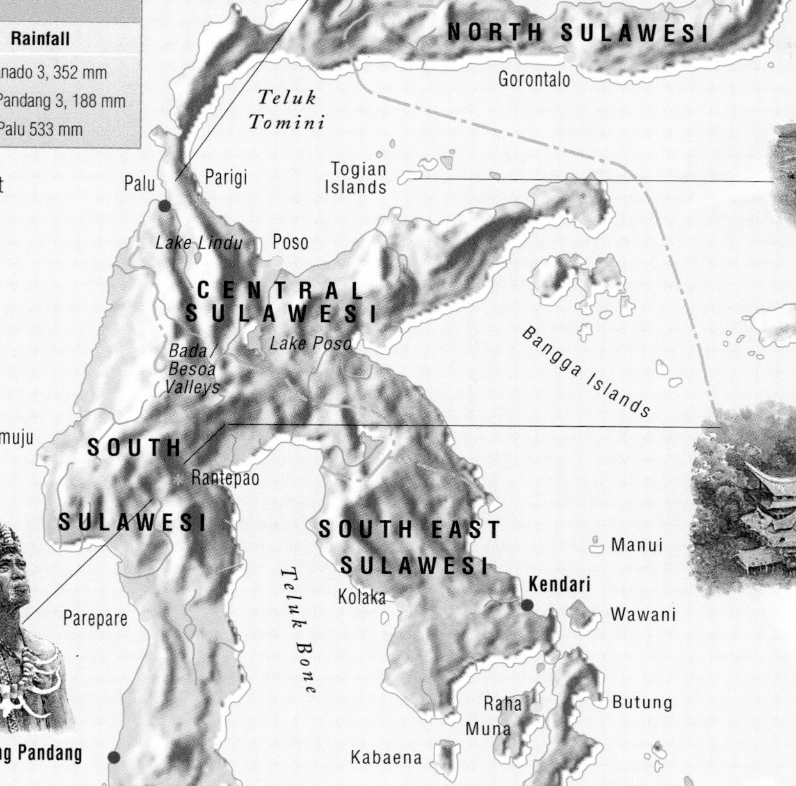

While agricultural wealth is an important arm of the economy, most production is conducted on small-scale, family-owned farms.

Sulawesi also has potential for growth from fishing and related activities. Much current coastal fishing is based on traditional techniques, though modern technologies and facilities are now being introduced and adopted, including the establishment and expansion of coastal fish and shrimp ponds. Japan's demand for frozen shrimp may well provide the market for a thriving industry.

Forest products currently constitute an important source of revenue for Sulawesi. Central Sulawesi exports hardwoods; Southeast Sulawesi produces teak. Rattan is also exported. In the past, many products were exported unprocessed. Recently, however, government legislation has stipulated that processing must occur before export. This should add value to the timber industry, auguring well for future growth in terms of employment and value.

Another primary industry, mining, also offers prospects of development. While nickel mining is well-established in South and Southeast Sulawesi, and asphalt mining on the island of Buton, it is gold and copper in the north and iron ore in the central region of the island that promise to be major future revenue generators. Oil has also been discovered, as has natural gas, and production may well lead to significant economic benefits.

Even though there is a range of manufacturing activities (cement plants, a paper mill, and sugar mills), they remain small in scale and contribute little to overall economic development. This is because they are remote from the main domestic markets and suffer from high labour costs. Indeed, it is tertiary activities that hold more promise for Sulawesi's development. Transportation and tourism are areas with great potential. Sulawesi already accounts for a large proportion of inter-island and local shipping. Ujung Pandang, South Sulawesi, is a hub for air and sea transport, and would benefit from improved port infrastructure. Its main competitor as the centre for regional growth is Surabaya in East Java. The government has pinned hopes on tourism, although existing infrastructure is probably only adequate in the far south, and to a lesser extent, in the far north. For this service industry to take off, rapid attention has to be paid to infrastructural development.

Sulawesi is a major source of cloves; here in Minahasa, North Sulawesi, harvested cloves are being dried.

«« Bugis schooners moored at South Sulawesi's thriving port and capital of Ujung Pandang.

Nusa Tenggara

Administratively, Nusa Tenggara is divided into three provinces: West Nusa Tenggara (Nusa Tenggara Barat), East Nusa Tenggara (Nusa Tenggara Timur) and East Timor (Timor Timur). The province of West Nusa Tenggara comprises the islands of Lombok and Sumbawa. In turn Nusa Tenggara is made up of major islands, namely Flores, Sumba, Timor and Alor. In addition, there are another 562 smaller islands, of which 320 are not even named. The third province of Nusa Tenggara–formerly the Portuguese colony of East Timor–became part of Indonesia in 1975.

A traditional village in Hato Builico, East Timor.

The Landscape

The islands stretch over 1,300 kilometres, divided into two arcs. The longer northern arc is volcanic in origin and comprises Lombok, Sumbawa, Komodo, Flores and Lembata. The shorter southern one consists of Sumba, Savu, Rote and Timor, formed from raised coral reefs and sedimentary rocks. The volcanic soils of the northern arc are fertile, though some are too ashy and porous to hold water well, while others have become weathered and infertile. In the east, the lack of reliable rain also renders the soils less productive than they might otherwise be. The alluvial plains of the north, built up by river sediments, are generally fertile. The islands of the southern arc comprise barren limestone plains and sparse savannas.

The southern islands have irregular coastlines. The northern islands on the other hand, have much more regular coastlines, alternating between cliffs and narrow sandy beaches. The northern island arc is dominated by volcanoes of up to more than 3,000 metres, (Rinjani, Tambora, Sangeang, Kimang and Ujolewung). The caldera of Mount Tambora in Sumbawa is seven kilometres in diameter. On all islands, there are few permanent water courses, with rivers and stream beds filling up and disappearing as and when the rains come.

As a whole, Nusa Tenggara is the driest area of Indonesia. The central mountainous zones tend to be wetter than the coastal zones. For example, total annual rainfall in the higher reaches of Lombok, Sumbawa, Flores and Timor exceed 3,000 millimetres while the coasts receive under 1,500 millimetres. In fact, in some areas such as parts of Flores' north coast, rainfall is only between 500 and 750 millimetres. The wetter months for the south facing slopes are from May to July, while December to March brings more rain to the north-facing slopes. Lowland temperatures are high all year round, with only minor variations. The hottest months of October and November have monthly averages of 28 to 29 degrees Celsius, while the cooler months of July to August experience only slightly lower temperatures at 25 to 26 degrees Celsius.

Bearing the Christ coffin in the Easter procession, Larantuka on Catholic Flores. This practice is a remnant of Portuguese influence derived from an earlier settlement on the island of Solor, which then transferred to Larantuka.

Nusa Tenggara supports its own distinctive fauna. One of the most notable creatures of the region is the Komodo dragon. Well known as the world's largest lizard, the Komodo dragon is found on Komodo, Rinca and in parts of western Flores. Another 56 species of animals are thought to be endemic to the region, and many of these are endangered. Plant life is nowhere as rich and luxuriant as on other islands in the archipelago. Most vegetation is sparse, with a mountainous terrain on the islands of Flores and Alor and more open savanna in Sumba and Timor. Timor is particularly noted for its drought resistant trees consisting of acacia, casuarina, eucalyptus, Borassus and Corypha palms.

In contrast to the terrestial flora and fauna, the coral reef ecosystems of Nusa Tenggara are extremely rich and diverse, making them one of the richest diving areas in the world. Aquatic species range from large, pelagic fish (whale sharks, reef sharks and manta rays) to aquarium fish (angelfish and butterfly fish) and mammals (sperm whale and dugong).

The People

As with many other Indonesian islands Nusa Tenggara is characterised by diversity of ethnic and linguistic groups. There are well over 50 different languages spoken in Nusa Tenggara and many of these languages consist of various dialects. The Dutch East India company contributed to the process of local differentiation by recognising numerous local rulers. The most important of these rulers was the Sultan of Bima on the island of Sumbawa, and the sacred ruler of Wehali in west Timor, whom Company officials referred to as 'keizer' or 'emperor'. On the island of Rote, the Dutch recognised no less than 18 autonomous 'raja' or 'regents'. Throughout the colonial period, Nusa Tenggara remained a region of indirect rule where administration was mediated via the local raja. Most of the languages of Nusa Tenggara belong to the Austronesian language family, but a number of languages spoken on Alor, Pantar and in central and west Timor belong to the Trans-New Guinea phylum of languages.

Portuguese influence is most evident today in East Timor, but this influence is also evident in Flores and west Timor. The first Portuguese-speaking settlement which had a diverse, mainly local, population was on the island of Solor. From there the population transferred to Larantuka on Flores, which still maintains a Portuguese tradition in its liturgical rituals, especially at Easter, and to Lifao, in the present enclave of Oekussi on the north coast of west Timor.

Lombok and Sumbawa are predominantly Muslim with a small number of Hindu

The northern arc of islands in Nusa Tenggara are volcanic in origin. On Lombok, Mount Rinjani, some 3,726 metres high, is the third highest mountain in Indonesia, and dominates the northern part of the island. In the crater is a beautiful mineral lake, called Segara Anak (child of the Sea)

Balinese in West Lombok and adherents to what is known as Wetu (Waktu) Telu, mainly in settlements on the north coast of Lombok. Nusa Tenggara Timur is divided between Catholics and Protestants. Catholics predominate in Flores; Protestants in Sumba, Alor and the islands of Rote and Savu. West Timor has both Catholics and Protestants whereas East Timor has become overwhelmingly Catholic. Muslims form a minority and are located mainly on coastal settlements where they are heavily involved in marine activities and in trade. Both on Sumba and on Savu and in parts of Flores and Timor, adherents of ancestral traditions continue their rituals.

Most of Nusa Tenggara is dry. Where environmentally feasible, wet rice cultivation is the favoured form of agriculture. Lombok is a major producer of rice, and efforts have been made to increase rice production elsewhere in the region. The predominant form of agriculture remains dryland cultivation, primarily of maize. Many farmers rely on the intercropping of sorghum, millet, mung beans, cowpea and other beans, in addition to maize. Cassava, sweet potato, yams and taro also play a part in local subsistance. Tobacco, onions and shallots are grown for local consumption and for sale. Cattle-raising is especially important on Timor and Sumba. Throughout the region, farmers raise chickens and goats. In Nusa Tenggara Timur and East Timor, farmers also raise pigs, sheep and waterbuffalo.

In this region, especially from Sumba through to Timor, there exists the possibility that the monsoon rains may fail–an occurence that is part of the El Niño cycle. When this occurs, there is always the threat of famine. This defines a major difference between this region and the rest of Indonesia.

The Economy

There are few modern industries in Nusa Tenggara and unlike other peripheral areas, such as Kalimantan and Irian Jaya, there are also few commercially valuable natural resources. Even white sandalwood, once Timor's major export, only occupies a small proportion of the land today, although there have been recent governmental efforts to encourage the replanting of this species. Most of the population relies on fishing or subsistence agriculture. Tourism is generally not as important as in Bali, although it is rapidly growing in Lombok and Maumere (Flores).

Area :		82,927 km^2
Population in 1990 census :		7.5 million
Population density in 1990 :		81 people/km^2
Population growth (1980-1990):		2.07%
Forested area [including Bali] in 1990 :		3, 418, 000 ha
Total arable land [including Bali] in 1990 :		19,249,000 ha
	SEASON	
Dry	**Wet**	**Rainfall**
Apr-Oct	-	East Flores & Sumba 8-9,000

Maluku

Maluku (formerly the Moluccas) consists of over 1,000 islands, varying in size from small uninhabited atolls, to Seram, the largest island of the province, which covers 18,400 square kilometres. The entire province, including both land and sea, covers 851,000 square kilometres, only ten per cent of this being land. The islands are widely dispersed, with Morotai in the north, more than 1,000 kilometres from Tanimbar in the south.

The active volcano Mount Gamalama dominates Ternate Island.

» The nutmeg and mace of Maluku were one of the major spices that first attracted foreign traders to the region.

A dance performance on the Tanimbar Islands, in the southeastern region of the province.

The Landscape

The northern and central islands have dense tropical forests and active volcanoes. Others, like the Arus in the southeast, are made up of mangrove swamps, tidal salt marshes and seagrass. The town of Ambon, with a population of some 250,000, on the island of the same name, in Central Maluku is the provincial capital. To the east of Ambon are the Lease Islands (Saparua, Haruku and Nusa Laut). Saparua, the largest, has a population of about 50,000 people. Clove and nutmeg plantations are found here. To the northeast of Ambon is Seram. Its highest peak, Mount Binaiya or Mount Manusela (3,019 metres) is also the highest point in Maluku. Most of Seram's population live on the coast, the forested interior being sparsely settled, mainly by the Naulu and Bati–whose traditional life-styles and beliefs remain strong. To the southeast of Ambon is the Banda archipelago–six small islands–totalling 60 square kilo-metres. The island of Banda Neira, with a population of 15,000, includes Bandaneira, the capital. Nutmeg and mace are grown here. West of Ambon is Buru, the third largest island in the Banda archipelago.

To the north of the province lies Halmahera, the second largest island in Maluku, covering about 18,000 square kilometres. Much of the island remains forested. Halmahera's interior is inhabited by tribal groups whose lifestyle has not changed very much over the last century. The main settlement is the town of Tobelo, with 15,000 people. North of Halmahera is Morotai, some 1,800 square kilometres, and the northernmost island in the Maluku archipelago. Moratai's capital Daruba has a population of 5,000. Ternate and Tidore lie to the west of Halmahera and were also important sources of spices in the past. Yet both are only about ten kilometres in diameter. Ternate is dominated by the active volcano Mount Gamalama (1,720 metres), and Tidore by Mount Kiemtabu (1,740 metres). Ternate's main town goes by the same name, and the island has a population of about 80,000. Tidore's population is half the size at 40,000.

Southeast Maluku covers 25,000 square kilometres. Among the larger islands are Kei, Aru, Tanimbar, Babar, Wetar and the Kisar Islands. Some local trade takes place with other ports of Maluku as well as with South Sulawesi. The total population is about 275,000. Missionaries have been active in this area, and the local population has converted in large part to Christianity although beneath its veneer, traditional beliefs and forms of worship still persist.

The climate of Maluku varies. North and central Maluku receive rain throughout the year though it tends to be concentrated during the period of the east monsoon between May and October. For example, the island of Ambon in central Maluku has over 3,000 millimetres of rain per year, with June and July (577 millimetres and 513 millimetres respectively) being the wettest months and November the driest (61 millimetres). Similarly, Ternate in the north has about 2,400 millimetres of rain per year, with most falling in June. Such a climate has allowed forests to thrive in the northern and central islands. Average monthly temperatures are fairly constant between 26 and 27 degrees Celsius. In contrast, in south-east Maluku, a long dry season extends from December to March during the the west monsoon. Average annual rainfall is about 1,400 millimetres. Here savanna vegetation dominates.

Maluku has a range of unique animal species, reflecting its transitional position between the Asian and Australian faunal realms–marsupials like the dwarf tree kangaroo and the cuscus. Species of butterflies, birds and insects are also diverse, with several being endemic to the islands.

Maluku's indigenous population is diverse and this diversity reflects the province's complex history. The majority of languages of the region are Austronesian, but some of the historically most important languages, such as the language of Ternate, along with many languages in Halmahera belong to the West Papuan family of languages which are also found in the northwest of Irian Jaya. A distinct form of Malay has been used as a lingua franca for hundreds of years. The region has attracted traders from all over the world. Chinese and Arab minorities, along with individuals claiming Portuguese, Dutch or even Spanish ancestry, form part of a complex mosaic. Also prominent are groups such as the Butonese who have come as traders from Sulawesi, or fishing peoples such as the Bajau Laut who live in small settlements on many islands.

The Economy

Maluku was once called the Spice Islands, after the spices such as cloves and nutmegs which were cultivated there and which generated such wealth. Indeed, it was the spices of Maluku which first drew Europeans to this part of the world. The Portuguese and the Dutch in turn enjoyed monopolies in the Banda Islands and Ternate, extirpating any trees from islands not under their firm control. The Dutch

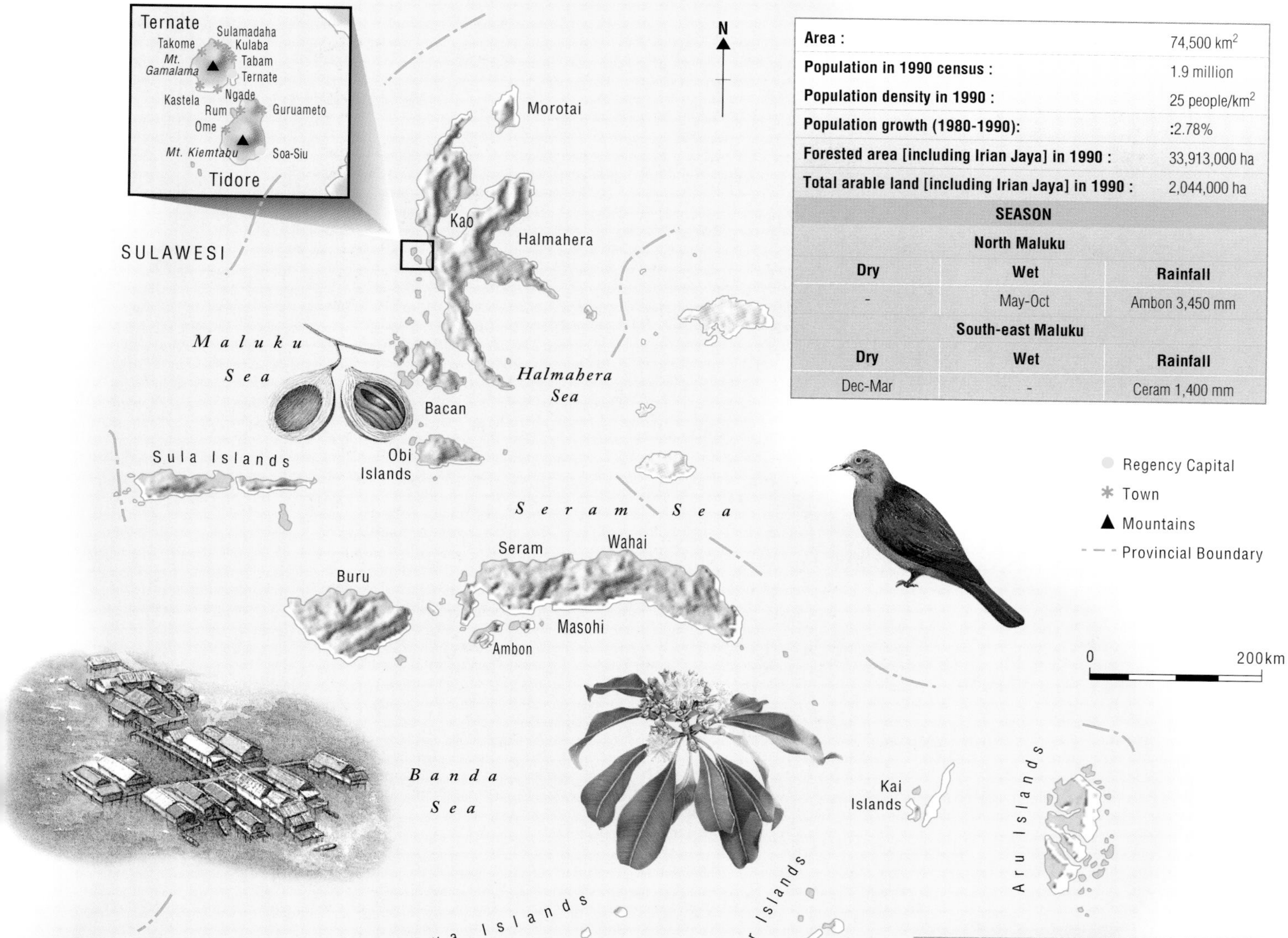

Area :		74,500 km^2
Population in 1990 census :		1.9 million
Population density in 1990 :		25 people/km^2
Population growth (1980-1990):		:2.78%
Forested area [including Irian Jaya] in 1990 :		33,913,000 ha
Total arable land [including Irian Jaya] in 1990 :		2,044,000 ha
SEASON		
North Maluku		
Dry	**Wet**	**Rainfall**
-	May-Oct	Ambon 3,450 mm
South-east Maluku		
Dry	**Wet**	**Rainfall**
Dec-Mar	-	Ceram 1,400 mm

Ternate
Sulamadaha
Takome
Kulaba
Mt. Gamalama
Tabam
Ternate
Ngade
Kastela
Rum
Guruameto
Ome
Mt. Kiemtabu
Soa-Siu
Tidore
N
Morotai
SULAWESI
Kao
Halmahera
Maluku Sea
Halmahera Sea
Bacan
Sula Islands
Obi Islands
Seram Sea
Seram
Wahai
Buru
Masohi
Ambon
Banda Sea
Kai Islands
Aru Islands
Tanimbar Islands
Barat Daya Islands
Leti Islands
EAST TIMOR

Regency Capital
Town
Mountains
Provincial Boundary
0 200km

monopoly was to last until the late 18th century when the French and subsequently the British succeeded in propagating nutmegs and cloves elsewhere. The price of nutmeg and mace dropped dramatically and Maluku suffered an economic downturn.

Today, Ambon, Ternate and the Bandas are the most important islands economically. The fishing industry has grown in recent years exploiting large resources of tuna, shrimp, crab and sea cucumber. Forestry is also important, with mills on all the largest islands–Buru, Seram and Halmahera. Ambon's plant processes logs into plywood for export to Japan, Singapore and Hong Kong. Important crops include the sago palm, coffee, copra and coconut. Spices such as cloves and nutmegs continue to be cultivated.

The Bandas have also begun to develop tourism as a new industry to revive the economy and stem out-migration. This industry is being built on the diving and snorkeling possibilities in the surrounding waters and the rich history of the islands. Indeed, there are plans afoot to develop the island for ecotourism. Unfortunately, the same cannot be said of Ambon, where the reefs have been destroyed by dynamite fishing, to be used for building material, or have been killed by pollution. Halmahera is also being developed and its infrastructure upgraded as it has been targeted as a transmigration destination. At the same time, forestry is likely to grow in importance here too.

Modern Ambon Town, the capital of Maluku province.

Sorting nutmeg on Banda Neira.

«An old copper engraving of Fort d'Amboine, 1607.

Irian Jaya

Ecologically, the province of Irian Jaya can be divided into three main geographic regions: a mountainous zone; the coastal lowlands; and the interior lowlands. The mountainous zone is made up of a range running from north-west to south-east, with 11 peaks exceeding 4,800 metres. The highest of these is Mount Jayawijaya which at 5,030 metres is also the highest mountain in Indonesia.

Jayapura, the provincial capital of Irian Jaya. Many urban areas in the province are expanding rapidly as people migrate from other parts of Indonesia. Jayapura now has a population of about 100,000.

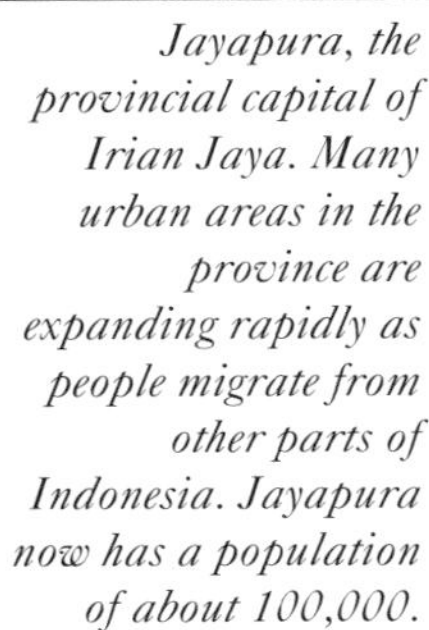

» An Asmat craftsman works on a carving. This ethnic group is famous for carving, and make their living selling their work to tourists.

Irian Jaya has become a tourist destination, and cruise liners regularly stop along the coast so that travellers can visit Asmat villages.

Many Irians need to work for cash in order to buy imported goods.

The Landscape

Irian Jaya, Indonesia's most eastern province, makes up the western half of the island of New Guinea, with the state of Papua New Guinea making up the eastern half. The shape of the island resembles a cassowary bird with its head looking westwards and for this reason New Guinea is sometimes called Pulau Cassowary or Cassowary island.

The peaks of the central mountain range ensure that Irian Jaya is the consistently highest part of Southeast Asia. The higher peaks are permanently covered with glaciers and snow. In addition to this central range, the mountainous zone also includes a smaller range to the north known as the Coastal Range or the Van Rees Mountains. These mountains form a natural barrier between the north and south of the island, being broken only by the fertile Grand Baliem Valley, the interior lowlands.

The coastal lowlands are thinly distributed between the narrow strips of land that lie to the north and south of the coastal mountains, and in the east. To the north of the central mountains, a large swampy depression (the Lake Plains Region) pushes the northern plain in to a thin belt along the coast. To the south of the central range, where the descent is steep, there are a few plains before the mountains reach the sea. In the east, large coastal swamps separate the mountains and seas, crossed by huge meandering rivers.

Irian Jaya is hot, wet and humid with only minor seasonal variations in the generally high levels of rainfall, though there can be marked spatial variations. For example, rainfall can reach up to 8,000 millimetres per year in the highlands, but on the north coast, the figure is only about 2,500 millimetres, while in the southeast it can drop to below 1,500 millimetres. Except at high altitudes, average monthly temperatures are fairly constant at 26 to 28 degrees Celsius.

A range of vegetation types are found in Irian Jaya: lowland rainforests, montane forests, coastal mangrove swamps and alpine grasslands. Some species found in one part of Irian Jaya may not be found in another due to the differences in rainfall and temperature. The flora and fauna of the province reflect Asian and Australasian origins–for example, northern latitude oaks can be found along with southern latitude beeches. Irian Jaya's most distinctive fauna are the 26 species of bird of paradise, once hunted for their plumage which are now both rare and protected.

The People

The majority of indigenous Irian Jayans are Melanesians and, more specifically, Papuans. They still dominate the interior despite the considerable settlement of 'western' Indonesians in Irian Jaya, especially in the cities and towns of the north coast of the province. Most of the Papuans in the central mountain zone are isolated not only by terrain, but also by their languages and customs. Physically, linguistically and culturally, they differ from the western Indonesians, and even among themselves there is tremendous diversity. For example, there are over 700 distinct languages, with some spoken by as few as 2,000.

The total population of Irian Jaya is about 1.7 million, that is roughly four persons per square kilometre. The population, however, is not evenly distributed, and some areas are completely uninhabited. The difficult terrain, means that many areas are inaccessible and contact is minimal between different groups. Catholic missionaries (mainly in the south), Protestants (in the north) and American evangelists have all sought to make converts of the indigenous population.

The main urban centres such as Jayapura, Biak and Merauke, have experienced a tremendous increase in their population in recent years due to the movement of population from other parts of Indonesia to Irian Jaya. This movement is likely to be paralleled in the rural context as the Indonesian government encourages transmigration to this under-populated province.

In the interior, both lowlanders and highlanders cultivate food crops, especially sago and taro. The Dani of the Baliem Valley have developed a sophisticated system of irrigation allied with intensive pig-rearing and the containment of malaria to make this valley the mostly densely populated rural area in Irian Jaya. In coastal regions, sago and taro are cultivated alongside coconuts, with the diet supplemented by raising pigs and catching fish. Maritime trade has led to coastal groups, such as the Asmat, acting as intermediaries between overseas traders and the highland and lowland peoples of the interior. In recent years the Asmat have achieved worldwide renown for their accomplished wood carvings.

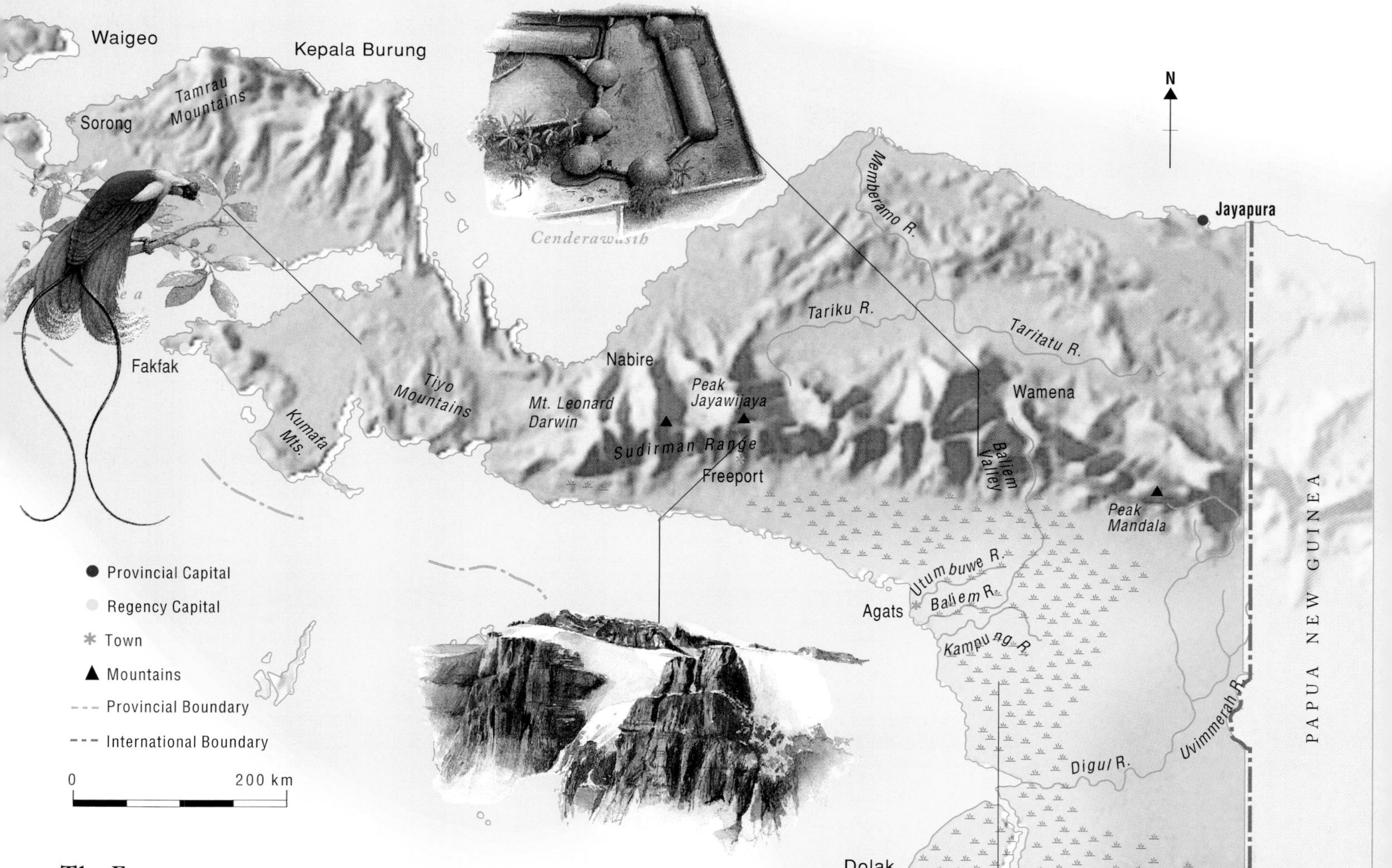

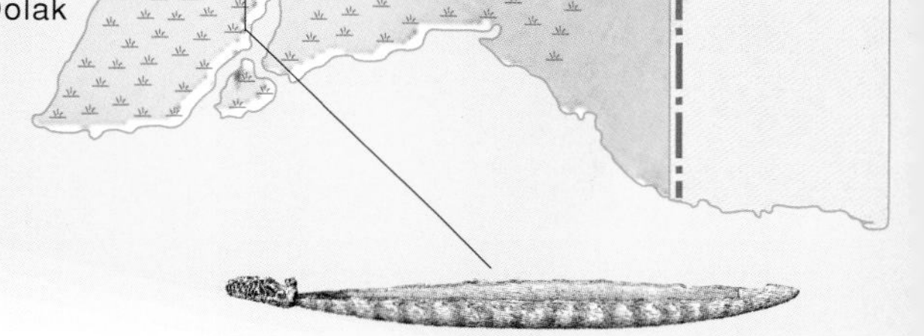

Waigeo
Kepala Burung
Sorong
Tamrau Mountains
Fakfak
Tiyo Mountains
Kumafa Mts.
Nabire
Mt. Leonard Darwin
Peak Jayawijaya
Sudirman Range
Freeport
Memberamo R.
Tariku R.
Taritatu R.
Jayapura
Wamena
Baliem Valley
Peak Mandala
Utumbuwe R.
Baliem R.
Agats
Kampung R.
Digul R.
Uvimmerah R.
Dolak
PAPUA NEW GUINEA
N

● Provincial Capital
Regency Capital
* Town
▲ Mountains
--- Provincial Boundary
--- International Boundary
0 200 km

The Economy

Irian Jaya is largely undeveloped and offers great potential for agricultural development, especially important in the light of land-scarce conditions in other Indonesian islands such as Java. Irian Jaya has thus been earmarked as a major transmigration destination, but to offer promise to transmigrants the infrastructure must be improved. The development of other industries may also help oil the wheels of economic progress. Although copper was found in Irian Jaya in 1936, it was only in 1950 that the ores were exploited, and 1972 before copper was exported. This was because the ores are 3,500 metres above sea level, and difficult conditions had to be overcome. Today, over 90 per cent of the value of Irian Jaya's exports comes from copper, gold and oil, and reserves exist for further exploitation. Once again though, this will be possible only with improvements to the physical infrastructure of the province, and in recognition of this, the Indonesian government has invested heavily in such improvements.

Finally, there is considerable development potential in the exploitation of the immense forest reserves of Irian Jaya. The province has some of Indonesia's finest timber reserves, for example, hardy, weather- and borer-resistant ironwood. The potential has not been fully realised though, because marketing and logistical problems have not been resolved.

While Irian's resources have been exploited to some extent, most of the benefits have not accrued to the indigenous Irians. Many of the senior positions in both the public and private sectors are filled by outsiders and Irianese are generally engaged in the less skill-intensive jobs. If development of Irian Jaya and its population are to be achieved, this imbalance will need to be addressed.

Area :		421,981 km^2
Population in 1990 census :		1.6 million
Population density in 1990 :		4 people/km^2
Population growth (1980-1990):		3.95%
Forested area [including Maluku] in 1990 :		33,913,000 ha
Total arable land [including Maluku] in 1990 :		2,044,000 ha
SEASON		
Dry	**Wet**	**Rainfall**
-	-	North Coast 2,,500 mm Interior 5-8,000 mm Merauke 1,500 mm

«« *The Baliem Valley is one of the most fertile areas of Irian Jaya. The rivers leave the flat upland plain through a series of narrow gorges.*

West Sumbanese village showing linear layout.

A village in Bali

Traditional Sasak village layout, Lombok

Village layout in Flores.

THE HUMAN CONTEXT

Nature and space are not abstract concepts in traditional Indonesian eyes. All space is filled with life-giving and life-taking energies that need to be ordered and managed to maximize benefit and avoid harm. Therefore settlements are situated and constructed with careful attention to their position and orientation. To ignore the power of place, space and orientation is to court disaster. The kraton of Yogyakarta faces the life-giving Mount Merapi, and the population of the city used to settle as close to the walls of the royal palace as possible, so that they might bathe in the radiated, life-enhancing energies of the Sultan. Here, geography, cosmology, nature and power combine to give meaning to space, and to provide spaces with hidden meanings.

Interior space is also manipulated to maintain harmony. So, just as in a social sense every Indonesian occupies a place in a hierarchy of living, spatially houses and communities also have their order. Often the two combine so that the social and the built environments mirror one another, and they in turn are linked to the natural and spiritual environments. People may trace their lineages through houses, and terms for parts of the house may ape those for parts of the body. Indeed, houses may be imbued with life just as humans.

For administrators, steeped in modern education, these traditional views of the significance of space have been displaced by a concern for such things as the spatial distribution of people, population growth, and migration. It is these, latter-day issues which are the concern of the last four spreads in this chapter. In some senses, the traditional focus on the management of space has been replaced by an emphasis on the management of people in space. Where populations are perceived to be too great–for example in parts of Java and Bali–villagers are encouraged to join the transmigration programme and be resettled in 'empty' areas of the archipelago. Most dramatically perhaps, the government has been instrumental in reducing fertility through a highly organised and well-financed family planning programme. Indonesians have always been mobile–most famously, perhaps, the Minangkabau of West Sumatra–but since Independence mobility has become far more prevalent. Improvements in communications and widening spatial disparities in incomes and opportunities have driven people to move in search of wealth and advancement. This can take myriad forms from daily commuting, to weekly circulation, seasonal migration, permanent migration to an urban area, and officially sponsored land settlement.

The Cultural Mosaic

Culturally Indonesia appears extremely diverse. Each community has its own culture and follows its own customary adat. Some 250 different languages are spoken and over 300 distinctive ethnic groups have been recognised. Yet there are also remarkable similarities between cultures across the Archipelago. Common culture elements appear to be ancient, with differences in geography, economy, religion and history producing the present cultural variations.

The vibrant commercial and trading sectors in the coastal cities have attracted people from diverse ethnic backgrounds, like those shown in this old print of Batavia. Cities were formerly spatially divided by ethnicity.

Changing Subsistence Base

Indonesia may have been inhabited first by hunter-gatherers who relied on the forests for their sustenance. Fishing and horticulture developed, followed by animal husbandry and rainfed cultivation of cereals. There developed the widespread mastery of fibres still evident in basketry and textiles. Wet rice became the staple crop for the most fertile areas. Trade developed in various goods, and cities appeared. Later, plantation agriculture was promoted by large scale trade in various crops. Mining and logging increased along with all the trappings of modern industrial society. These livelihood strategies–some still practised today–help to demarcate important distinctions between cultures. For example, coastal communites are often fishing specialists, trading their catches in the markets. They also trade with the specialised hunter-gatherer groups of the interior like the Orang Kubu of Sumatra or the Penan of Kalimantan.

Foreign Cultural Influences

The coastal regions have always been open to new cultural influences through migration and trade. The forested and mountainous interiors were less accessible, and have provided secure havens for some local cultures to develop in relative isolation for long periods. Only in the 20th century have isolated cultures been brought under a central administration, and animistic religions based on ancestor worship and spirit belief remain more prevalent among the interior peoples. The arrival of Buddhism and Hinduism early in the first millennium AD led to some urbanisation in the western regions of Indonesia, and the formation of state societies. The spread of Islam and Christianity along the trade routes saw the Hindu-Buddhist states reduced to Bali alone, though Hindu beliefs are still present in parts of Java.

Indians, Chinese, Arabs and Europeans have all brought their cultures to Indonesia's many islands. Many of these visitors settled, so that there are few towns today without some of their descendants. The Chinese comprise an important ethnic minority, and they contribute significantly to the economy. The immigrant cultural influences have been variously absorbed, so while Aceh in North Sumatra is strongly Islamic, the neighbouring Minangkabau of West Sumatra, though Muslim, retains a matrilineal *adat*. Catholic Flores contrasts with the Protestant Toba and Karo Batak. Today the cities are the strongholds of world religions, the countryside of ancient faith. In the cities too, the signs of western acculturation are most obvious. Urban activities everywhere are mainly concerned with manufacturing, trade, commerce and administration, and with health, education and religious services. The growth of modern industries is particularly marked in the port towns of Java and Sumatra.

In general, there have been three major cultural forms in Indonesia. Firstly, there were the great stratified state societies based on irrigated rice cultivation, notably those of the Javanese, Sundanese and Madurese. Secondly, there were the smaller coastal states, based on a combination of trading and fishing as well as irrigated rice. These two cultural forms were strongly influenced by their ancient courts, with refined and elaborate music, dance, art, architecture, literature and artisan crafts. Lastly, there are the shifting cultivators inhabiting the zone between river and forest, with village-based societies, such as the Dayak of the provinces of Kalimantan.

SPREAD OF ISLAM AND CHRISTIANITY

Pasai ☾1290
Aceh ☾1400
Patani ☾1520
Trengganu 1303?
To Champa
Barus
Nias
Pariaman
Melaka ☾1410 ✝1511
Brunei ☾1500
Mindanao
Sulu ☾1460
Sulawesi Sea
SUMATRA
KALIMANTAN
Ternate ☾1460
MALUKU
SULAWESI
IRIAN JAYA
Ambon ✝1544
Makassar ☾1605 ✝1641
Java Sea
Gresik ☾1410
Banten ☾1525
Buton 1580
Flores Sea
Banda Sea
Arafura Sea
JAVA
Cirebon ☾1525
Demak ☾1480
Sumbawa
BALI
Flores
Timor
Sumba
Timor Sea
NUSA TENGGARA
N
☾ Islam
✝ Christian
0 450 km

Yogyakarta Man, Java

Dani Tribesman, Irian Jaya

Dayak Boy, East Kalimantan

Nias warrior

Balinese dancer

Topeng Dancer, Cirebon,Java

Old Rato Priest, Sumba

Timorese Girl

Adat

Each community in Indonesia follows its own customs, commonly known as its *adat* (from the Arabic, *ada*, custom). *Adat* is the locally accepted code of behavior, a set of norms and rules deriving their legitimacy from tradition. The term covers a wide range of injunctions about proper behavior in all aspects of life ranging from etiquette to criminal law. Hence it can include the principles for being a good citizen and a dutiful relative, the ideal organisation of the community, the correct procedures in ceremonies and rituals, and customary law concerning crime, property, succession, inheritance, adoption, marriage and divorce. The Minangkabau of West Sumatra have managed to maintain their traditional matrilineal social structure in the face of modernisation. Here conformity is maintained largely by participation and example, but a wide range of sanctions can be invoked, from gossip to cursing, through fines through to the exile of the offender.

Adat is a body of knowledge which binds and harmonises social relations. It is seen by the people as essential for group survival; unchanging, the rock on which society is based. In practice it has always been pragmatic and flexible. Much of it is in the form of verse, easily remembered in the days when it was transmitted orally from generation to generation. While a comprehensive grasp of *adat* is considered necessary wisdom for traditional community leaders, everyone is familiar with the injunctions of their *adat* through the common proverbs and aphorisms of their language and their general upbringing.

A Minangkabau wedding. The Minangkabau are famous for their traditional matrilineal social structure, even though they are strong adherents of Islam.

Though each community has its own unique *adat*, there are broader patterns across the nation. This was recognised by the Dutch authorities, who selected some aspects of *adat* to be codified as customary law. This was then locally administered as the lowest tier of the evolving national legal system. So diverse were the *adat* recorded that they could only be consolidated as distinct customary law codes for each of the 19 different major *adat* areas. Even then, some areas were recognised as containing considerable variations.

Today whole *adat* differences are still recognised in customary law. At the same time, however, much progress towards a national culture has been made through education, particularly by establishing the national language. Essentially the state philosophy of Pancasila (The Five Principles) encourages the evolution of an increasingly Indonesian (national) identity for every citizen. As a result of these changes, the importance of adat is now in decline.

««Man from Dili Market, East Timor..

Concepts of Space: Settlement Patterns

Traditional settlement patterns among Indonesian peoples were more than simply a question of providing shelter from the elements, or refuge from wild animals and enemies. They were conscious attempts to reflect cosmological concepts and social relationships on the ground.

This old photograph of a Toba Batak village was taken by Modigliani in 1892. Ideally, Toba Batak houses stand side by side with the front gable facing the village 'street'–this common, open area being called the alaman. *Karo Batak villages are grouped around a central rice pounding house and assembly hall, and although the houses face each other, their axis is determined by the flow of the nearby river.*

Ordering Space

In theoretical terms the organisation of many traditional Indonesian societies can be linked to cosmological ideas. These ideas are frequently reflected in religious rituals so that the sacred and the profane are incorporated into a single conceptual framework. In these traditions, important relationships between natural elements, as well as relationships between social units are generally understood in terms of a binary scheme of complementary opposites. Important examples of these oppositions include such pairs as: male and female, uphill and downhill, east and west, left and right, sun and moon, gold and silver, and weapons and cloth, for example. Within this social and cosmological scheme these two opposite poles are linked by relationships of exchange (most commonly goods and wives through marriage arrangements) which mediate between the two extremes. The pre-eminent natural world expression of this relationship is the mountain to the sea polarity mediated by the river traversing hills and plains in between, and creating a suitable dwelling place for humans.

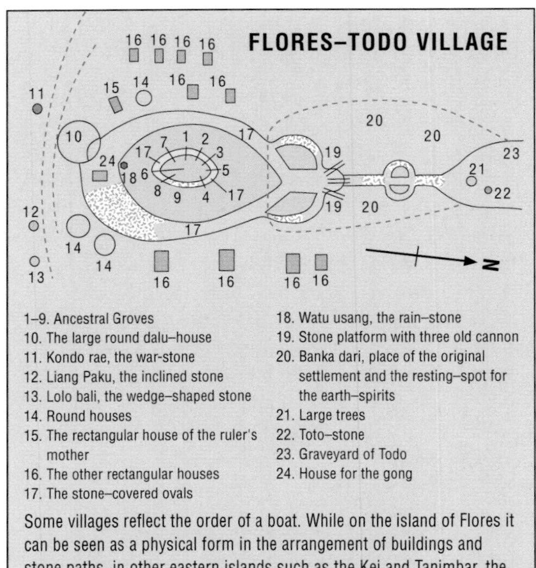

Some villages reflect the order of a boat. While on the island of Flores it can be seen as a physical form in the arrangement of buildings and stone paths, in other eastern islands such as the Kei and Tanimbar, the meeting place of the elders is in the form of a boat. Boat symbolism also reflects this unity, co-operation and order of a social unit working together as crew of a boat an aspect reflected in terminology for social roles and positions.

Dwelling Places Fit For Humans

Indigenous settlement patterns are derived either from local, topographical and cosmological features, or idealised relationships. Often the two are linked together in a single ordered scheme.

For example, the traditional Bali Aga village of Bali is based on an idealised mountain-sea polarity. Their society is divided into two halves who construct their villages so that people live in rows of dwellings which face each other across an open space. In South Bali the actual axis is one that runs from north to south, but it is conceived as a mountain-sea polarity. The village half that is situated to the east is identified with, and responsible for, matters related to the village temple of origin which is located above the

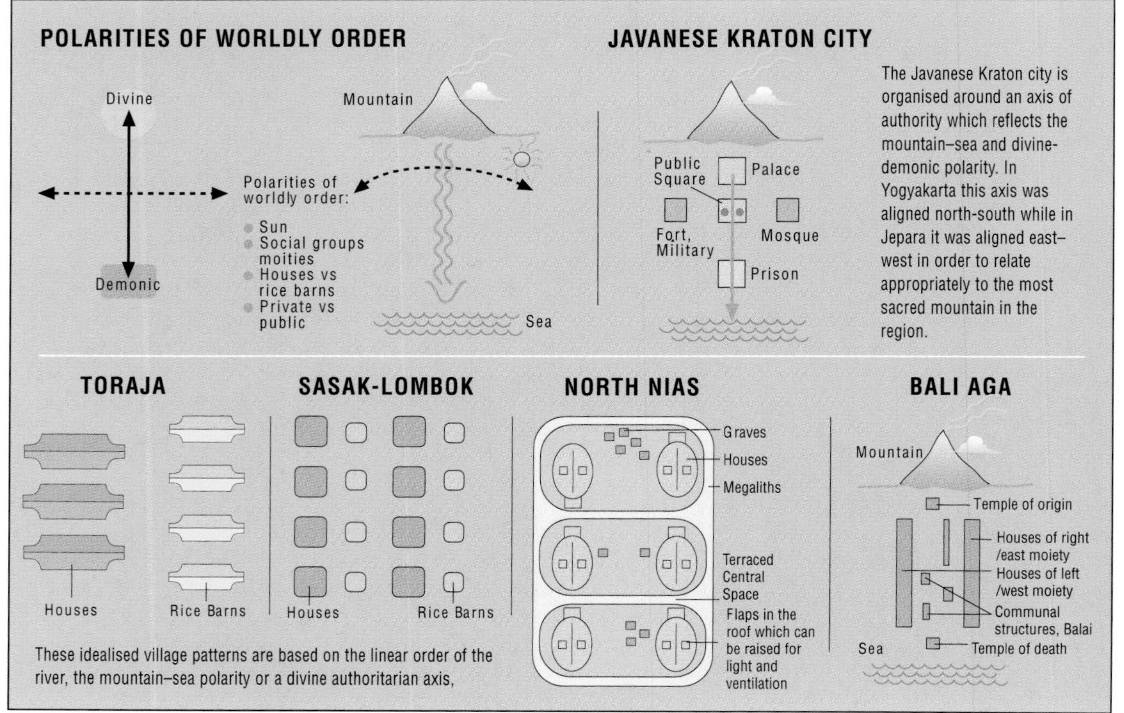

These idealised village patterns are based on the linear order of the river, the mountain–sea polarity or a divine authoritarian axis,

village, and towards the mountain. The village half situated to the west of the axis is responsible for the temple of death and cremation ceremonies.

On the southern half of the island of Lombok, the Sasak, who have a similar world view, adopt a more prosaic attitude towards their settlement patterns. While preserving the dual nature of the village, they follow local land contours, wrapping their alternating rows of houses and granaries around small hillocks, leaving the flat land free for agriculture.

Typically, physical landmarks such as mountains, rivers and trees, and even rocks, were drawn on to organise the layout and orientation of settlements. Spiritual oppositions are also perceived within this natural order. Thus mountains and high places are regarded as divine and the sea or other low lying places are regarded as demonic. The river is often seen as a mediating element between these extremes. For example, the Ngaju Dayak of Central Kalimantan build their villages on the banks of the river, which is conceptualised as flowing between the upperworld and underworld, also conceived of as lying along a mountain-water axis. Good spirits are said to come from the upriver direction, while disease bearing spirits are said to arrive from downstream. Ideally these polar opposites are not merely balanced but harmonised, a process requiring continuing effort and cyclical renewal. Hence, during religious ceremonies the good spirits who are invited to attend will arrive in their celestial boats, while offerings to the evil spirits are floated downstream to keep them at bay.

Various expressions of this order and its embodied dynamic processes emerge in the settlements of the diverse island cultures of Indonesia. Most physical ordering patterns involve an anchored centre mediating between opposites. This is expressed either as a linear order or as a centric order with a central focal element such as a building or space. The Toba Batak village of Simanindo, for example, follows these principles with a linear central space flanked by houses on one side and rice barns on the other. Within this space are a sacrificial pillar and a sacred tree, both of which figure in village ceremonies. Likewise the linear villages of South Nias create or recognise a central node by the placement of a special, circular 'navel stone' signifying the village's origin. The location of the chief's house and megalithic monuments add presence to this area. Sumbanese origin villages, on the other hand, reflect a more centric order, similar to the Toda village of Flores. Sumbanese clan origin houses are arranged around a central space occupied by ancestral memorial structures.

The basic ordering pattern is typically mediated by secondary ordering notions which may overlay a cyclical pattern on, or establish diagonal or reflective relationships within the basic order. This is visible in the organisation of the Hindu Balinese village and house, which distribute structures according to a nine square mandala reflecting both the mountain-sea and rising and setting sun polarities. These mediating patterns are often expressed in the *adat* or traditional customs and rituals associated with spaces or elements within the basic pattern. In this way, natural, divine, human and demonic order and energies are harnessed and harmonised in the settlement traditions of Indonesia to create an order which identifies and expresses cultural values and reminds humans of their place in the cosmic order.

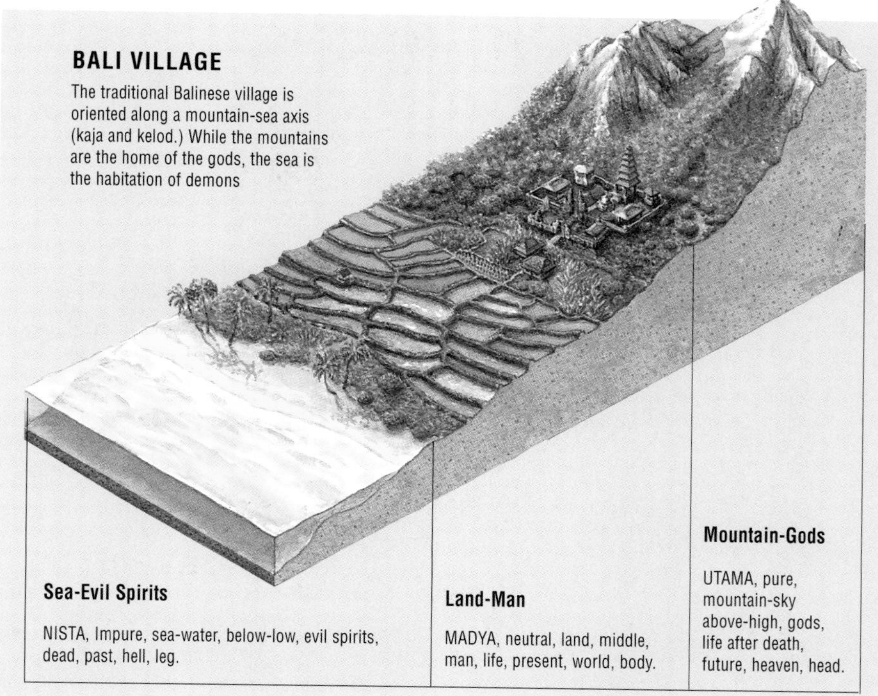

BALI VILLAGE

The traditional Balinese village is oriented along a mountain-sea axis (kaja and kelod.) While the mountains are the home of the gods, the sea is the habitation of demons

BALINESE VILLAGE

An aerial view, facing seaward, of the Balinese village shown in schematic form above. Note the village's location along the mountain ridge. This traditional Balinese village is orientated along the mountain-sea axis.

Living Houses

Indonesia's indigenous cultures share an animist world view which to varying extents has been integrated with the newer world religions like Islam and Christianity. Many objects and aspects of nature which others might regard as inanimate have a subjective personality. Ideas about nature, religion and cosmology have all been major influences shaping vernacular architecture and the meanings invested in spatial arrangements.

Bawomataluo village, South Nias showing the chief's house raised on pillars.

Living Architecture

In a universe in which everything can be potentially communicated with, humans must strive to maintain harmony with their environment. Houses must be built properly and with the appropriate rituals to ensure that they will not cause harm to their owners. People tend to trace their ties to each other through houses which may be related to each other as 'trunk' to 'tip'. Images of the growth of trees or bamboo are used to speak of the development of kinship groupings. The house itself may be made sacred by the presence of ancestors, and is the store for powerful heirlooms.

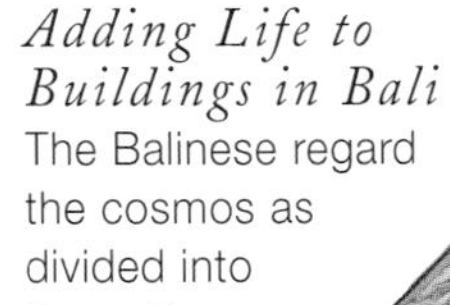

Adding Life to Buildings in Bali

The Balinese regard the cosmos as divided into three: the upper, middle and lower worlds. Orientation is usually towards the mountain and away from the sea. The layout of villages and house compounds reflects this pattern, also echoed in the division of the body into head, trunk and legs. The most sacred direction in the house compound is the north-east (associated with the head), where the family shrines are located; the next most important building, the enclosed sleeping room of the householders, is to the north. The centre or 'navel' of the compound is an empty space, used for daily activities. To right and left (like the arms of the body) are open pavilions, and the kitchen and granary are to the south (the legs). The gate is associated with the sexual organs, the rubbish pit in the backyard with the anus. This

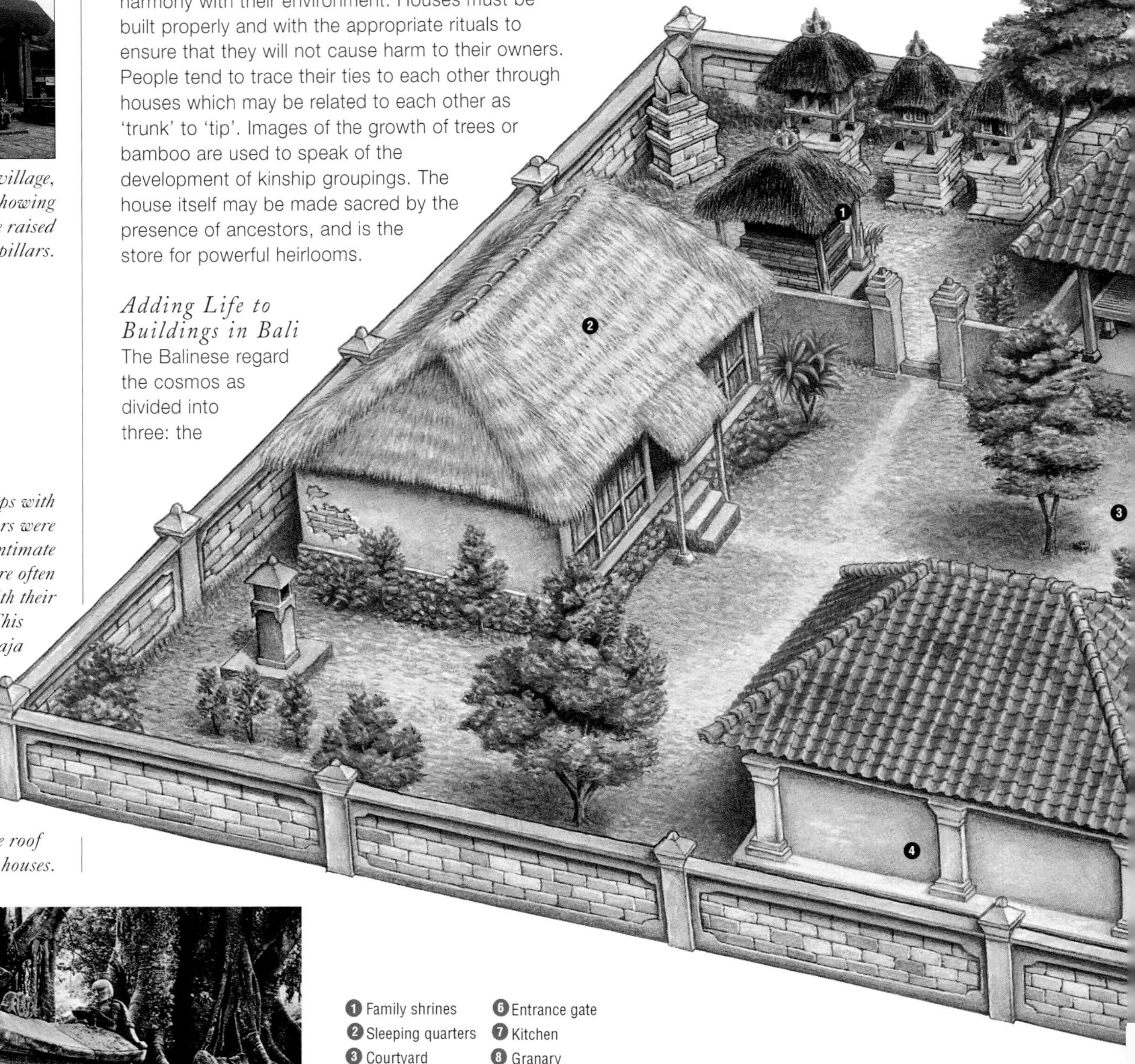

Relationships with the ancestors were traditionally intimate and the dead are often provided with their own 'houses'. This stone tomb of Raja nai Batu Sidabutar on Samosir Island, Lake Toba has a curved lid which resembles the roof shape of Toba houses.

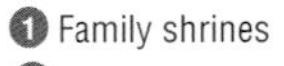

1. Family shrines
2. Sleeping quarters
3. Courtyard
4. Pavilion
5. Pavilion
6. Entrance gate
7. Kitchen
8. Granary
9. Rubbish pit/Pig sty
10. Pavilion

overlay of organising metaphors–house, body, cosmos–used to be quite typical in many Indonesian societies. All buildings in Bali must be 'brought to life' through construction rituals and by the 'adding on' of a certain additional amount to each measure, called the 'soul of the measure' or the 'life' (*pangurip*). Measurements for a house are based on dimensions of the householder's own body. An incorrectly measured compound will be *embet* (blocked), and may cause death to the inhabitants.

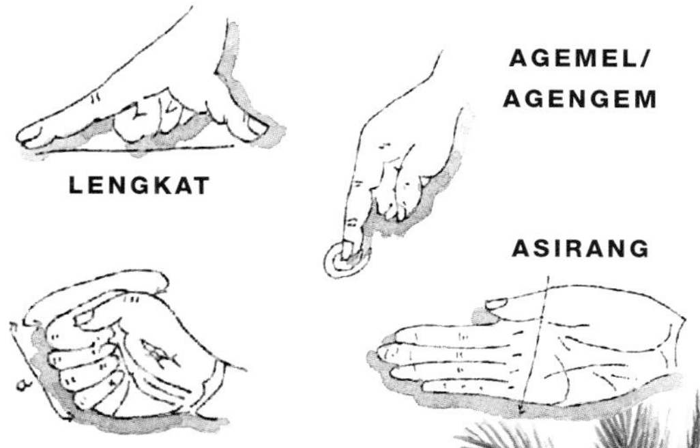

LENGKAT

AGEMEL/ AGENGEM

ASIRANG

AHUSERAN

Cosmology and Politics in Nias

The chiefs of south Nias grew rich and powerful during the 19th century by trading slaves to Aceh in exchange for gold. Houses became impressive and huge. An elaborate set of ideas seems to have developed in the village of Bawomataluo, identifying the chief's house (22.7 metres tall and raised on giant ironwood pillars) with the body of the chief as well as with the earth and the cosmos. Chiefs appear to have exploited these symbolic ideas, as well as the material structure of the house, as a means of enhancing their own position and power.

Rice barn in Sasak village of Sade, Lombok. Often the house as a whole, as well as its inner portion, seems to be symbolized as 'female', being associated with positive images of life, prosperity and nourishment.

In Tana Toraja, people trace ties to origin houses (tongkonan), the birth-places of their parents, grandparents and more distant ancestors. The 'face' of the house must always be to the north, the direction associated with Puang Matua, the 'Old Lord' of the cosmos, an important creator deity. The 'rump' of the house is to the south, the direction of the land of the dead. East - west is the most important axis of orientation. East is associated with life, the deities, and the rising sun, west with the setting sun and ancestors in their deified form.

The Population Issue

With an estimated population in 1995 of 195.3 million people, Indonesia is the fourth most populous nation in the world and accounts for 40 per cent of Southeast Asia's population. Population issues have been a major concern to governments in Indonesia both during the colonial era and since Independence.

Indonesia's labour force is growing at a more rapid pace than the population as a whole.

Population Growth

Indonesia's population has risen dramatically in the last two centuries, especially in Java. A high priority has been given to population reduction. For several years after Independence lower rates of growth occurred due to the disruption caused by the Japanese occupation and War of Independence. Improvements in mortality in the 1960s and 70s led to an increase in the annual growth rate. The 1980s, however, saw a decline in the growth rate that has continued into the 1990s. The success in reducing population growth has been achieved mainly through a significant reduction in fertility over the last two decades, and mortality levels have been greatly reduced. Life expectancy at birth has also increased from 47 in 1971 to 52 in 1980, and is now around 59 (58 for males and 61 for females). Indonesia is now well advanced in the demographic transition and it is anticipated that fertility will reach replacement level early in the next century.

» A crowd of Indonesians in a street in Kalimantan.

Population Density and Distribution

The three islands of Java, Bali and Madura have very high population densities in comparison with other regions. This contrast reflects the actual variation in resource endowments and ecological situations between the nation's provinces. Throughout most of the 20th century, Java's population has been growing at a much slower rate than that of the islands of Outer Indonesia. Hence the proportion of Indonesians living in Java has declined from around two thirds at the time of Independence to 60 per cent at the 1990 census. In the late 1970s and early 1980s some 1.29 million families (around four and a half million people) were moved under the transmigration programme. The goals of the programme are however, predominantly articulated in terms of regional development in the Outer Islands rather than demographic redistribution. The shift in government policy in the late 1980s to facilitate investment and industrialisation, however, is tending to favour growth in Java. Between 1985 and 1990 the number of people moving into Java (773,789) was almost as great as the number moving in the opposite direction (973,340).

Indonesia's Changing Age Structure

It is important to realise that certain age groups in Indonesia are growing more quickly

The figure (below) shows the number of Indonesians recorded in each five year age group at the 1980 and 1990 censuses. The 1980 population pyramid has a broad base, with each older five year age group tending to have fewer members than the one directly below it. This is because for any birth group mortality will gradually erode their numbers as they age 'up' the pyramid. Hence if fertility is more or less constant, each older age group will have less than the one immediately below it and more than that immediately above it.

If there is a significant continuing improvement in mortality, however, it will mean that as a group moves into an older age category the numbers in that age category will–relatively–increase. This is because although the group may have started off around the same size as that of the slightly older group leaving that age category, more of its members have been 'saved from death' by improved mortality. This is the situation in Indonesia.

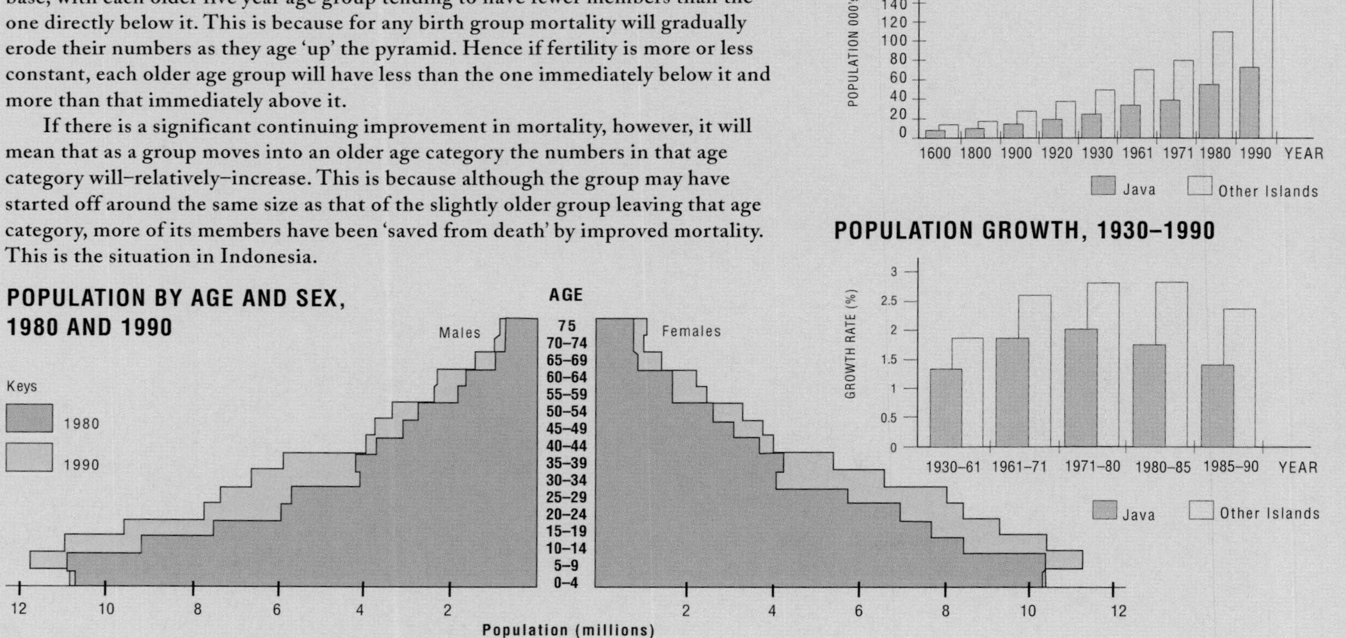

THE DEMOGRAPHIC TRANSITION

Social change and development in a society is accompanied by a sequence of changes in birth and death rates. The Demographic Transition model identifies this sequence. A fall in fertility is ascribed to an increase in the burden of rearing children in an urban industrial society and the improved survival rates of infants, supported by improved methods and practice of contraception.

The generalised descriptive model was developed from observation and description of the experience of Western developed countries in the early part of this century. The model, however, is not accepted as being universally applicable.

Stage 1 High Equilibrium
Stage 2 High Expanding
Stage 3 Low Expanding
Stage 4 Low Equilibrium
Crude Birth Rate
Natural Increase
Crude Death Rate
BIRTH AND DEATH RATES
TIME AND DEVELOPMENT

• *Stage 1.* The first phase is of a 'traditional' society where there is a high level of fertility and high but unstable mortality rates caused by famines, wars and infectious disease epidemics.

• *Stage 2.* The model suggests that the transition begins in response to 'modernisation', better living conditions, and disease control. A decline in death rates occurs, while fertility rates stay high. There is a great population growth.

• *Stage 3.* Stabilisation of death rate at low levels, a reduction in the birth rate levels off population growth and death and birth rates converge in this stage. Indonesia is well into this phase in which natural increase is falling as the nation is moving towards 'low equilibrium'.

• *Stage 4.* The final phase, is of slight growth, as in the initial stage. Both birth and death rates are however, low, with some fluctuations in fertility due to changes in economic and, to a lesser extent, social trends.

than the population as a whole. This is due to a degree of uneveness in the age structure. The age structure reflects past trends in both fertility and mortality in Indonesia. Continuing significant improvements in infant and child mortality have resulted in each age group growing substantially as a more recently born group replaces an older group. Therefore the numbers of males, for example in the age group 10-19, were substantially larger in 1990 than the number of males aged 10-19 in 1980. Between 1980 and 1990 there has been a very large increase in population aged between 10 and 40. Hence Indonesia's labour force is currently growing more quickly than the population as a whole. It also means that the numbers of women in the childbearing age groups are also increasing rapidly so that, even while the number of births per woman is decreasing, the total number of births will remain large for some time.

Indonesia, like many countries in the Asian region, faces a massive growth of its elderly population. At present Indonesia has some 11.5 million people aged 60 years and over but this will increase to 16 million by 2000 and will reach 29 million in 2020. Over this period they will increase from 6.4 per cent to 11.4 per cent of the total population in 2020. This represents a considerable challenge to policy makers since the present availability of support for the dependent elderly is almost totally from family sources. Contemporary changes in the Indonesian family and society may mean that this source will not be so readily available in the future.

Future Trends

Indonesia's population growth still remains one of the greatest challenges facing policy makers and planners. Few countries in the world have been more active in seeking to influence their population growth and distribution, and in the case of the family planning programme, few have been more successful than Indonesia.

Nevertheless the demographic momentum built into the Indonesian age pyramid will ensure that substantial population growth will continue well into the next century, even if fertility continues to decline. It appears that the national population will increase to 210 million by the year 2000, 235 million in 2010 and 254 million in 2020 and will peak at 354 million. Finding ways to provide jobs and education, for example, for this substantial net increment to its population, while improving the quality of living of the total population, as well as preserving the natural endowment of resources through using them in sustainable ways, presents a huge challenge to policy makers and the Indonesian nation.

One method of incorporating the huge population into the national system is by providing various organisations such as the Dharma Wanita, that allow them to participate in wider aspects of nation building.

POPULATION DENSITY, 1990

Dua Anak Cukup

Contemporary Indonesian women are having only half as many children as their counterparts in the 1960s. This massive change is the result of a number of interrelated factors. The government's strong commitment since the 1960s to the goal of significant fertility reduction and the impact of a dynamic and effective family planning programme have been important elements in the decline.

Dua anak cukup promotion at desa post near Sangiran, Java. The sign suggests that the coil is considered to be the most practical method of contraception.

Fertility Decline

The Total Fertility Rate (TFR) is the number of children on average that women would have if they went through their whole childbearing period conforming to the age specific patterns of fertility of a given year. If current patterns were frozen Indonesian women would, on average, have around three children. Fertility levels in Indonesia two decades ago were high; in the late 60s the TFR was around 5.7. Few would have predicted that within two decades women would be having only half as many children.

There are, though, substantial variations between different regions. Fertility is much lower in Java and Bali than the other provinces. In 1991 the TFR in Java and Bali was 2.7 compared with 3.5 in the provinces of Aceh, North, West and South Sumatra, Lampung, West and South Kalimantan, North and South Sulawesi, West Nusa Tenggara, and 3.8 in the other provinces. At the same time, there are also considerable variations within these broad regions.

Fertility rates also increase from lower to intermediate levels of socio-economic status then decline for higher socio-economic status groups although Indonesia may now be moving away from this pattern toward a more direct relationship between fertility decline and level of education. Other important longstanding differences in fertility are those relating to religion. Some Protestant groups have quite high fertility rates while the Hindu Balinese and Buddhist Chinese have very low fertility rates. Women who work outside the home also have lower fertility than those who do not. Among those who work outside the home, those working in agriculture have the highest fertility rates and those working in modern sector activities the lowest.

These mothers are waiting in line for a check-up at a primary health centre in Bumi Sari, Lampung, Sumatra. The stress is now on better health care for smaller families.

CONTRACEPTION USE BY RURAL-URBAN RESIDENCE AND EDUCATIONAL LEVEL, 1991

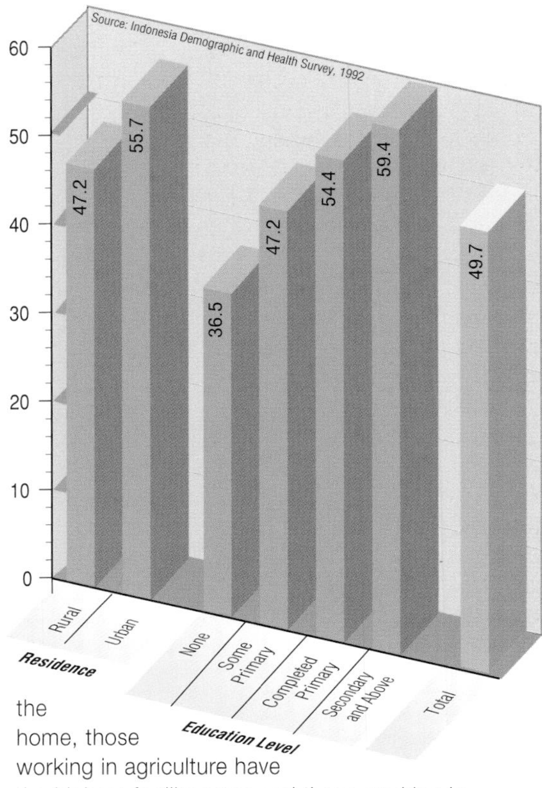

Why the Fertility Decline ?

Vast social changes have taken place in Indonesia over the last two decades altering the structure and functioning of Indonesian families, and have been conducive to fertility decline. One of these has been a significant increase in the proportion of young women who have never been married. This reflects an increase in the average age of marriage and a reduction in exposure to pregnancy in those earlier years in which previously almost all Indonesian women began childbearing. Some estimates put the contribution of increased age at marriage to the fertility decline at 20-25 per cent. By far the main factor which has intervened to reduce fertility, however, has been the increase in the use of contraception. Almost certainly factors like prolonged breast feeding and abstinence, which in the past kept fertility down to some extent, are no longer as significant as they were more than two decades ago. There has been a dramatic increase in the use of contraception. In 1972 only 400,000 couples were practising some form of family planning whereas in 1993 there were 21.3 million.

There are, however, also considerable variations between different parts of Indonesia in the extent to which they have accepted contraception. In 1991, Bali had the highest contraception rate (71.9 per cent), Irian Jaya the lowest (20.6 per cent). While the overall acceptance rate of family planning has been fairly stable over the last decade or so there has been a steady increase in the proportion using modern contraceptive methods for birth control.

Family Planning Programme

The high level use of contraception by Indonesian couples has been due in significant part to the success of the nation's Family Planning Programme. With strong government commitment and backing to bring down the alarming rate of population growth, the National Family Planning Co-ordinating Board (BKKBN) was formed by 1969, and the National Family Planning Programme initiated as part of Repelita 1. Although concentrated initially in Java and Bali, it was progressively extended first to cover a group of larger Outer Island provinces and later to the remaining provinces.The programme gained strong support not only from government but also influential Muslim leaders.

Trained fieldworkers were employed to recruit acceptors, and distribute pills and condoms through village-based volunteers. Key village leaders were also involved in achieving local support for the programme. This has led to the family planning programme gaining a great deal of acceptance and support at grassroots level. Also at the community level approximately a quarter of a million acceptor groups have been formed and the BKKBN has been able to help them with resources for income-generating and other development activities. In this way, and in others, the programme has focused not just on reduction of family size but improving the quality of life of families. Another key to the success of the programme has been the highly developed logistics system which has generally ensured delivery of supplies in a timely way in often difficult geographical circumstances.

An important element in the Family Planning Programme has been the priority given to, and effective implementation of, its Information, Education and Communication (EC) component. This has involved innovative and vigorous activity using all forms of mass media as well as more traditional channels to get across the family planning message. The programme's slogan '*Dua anak cukup, perempuan atau laki-laki sama saja*' (Two children are enough whether they are a boy or girl) is ubiquitous.

Until recently there was a 'target' system in operation which periodically drew criticism because it was alleged that in some circumstances it led to excessive pressure being put on women to become acceptors to achieve targets. This is a difficult area and the BKKBN maintain that there are important cultural differences between Western countries and Indonesia which need to be recognised in assessing what is acceptable and unacceptable, and in assessing the extent and nature of social pressures exerted to gain acceptance of family planning. In 1993, however, the target system was abandoned and a new system based on 'demand' is now being developed.

Another important element in the programme is an attempt to increase private sector involvement in the delivery of services. This is a difficult task since the BKKBN have provided such services largely free of charge up to now. However, budget pressures have meant that it is important to reduce the costs of the programme. Moreover some success has been achieved in the KB Mandiri (Self Sufficient Family Planning) Programme and the BKKBN aims to have half of users supplied by private sources by the year 2000. Assessment of the quality of services is also becoming an issue of increasing importance in the programme.

The family planning programme still faces many challenges in achieving the national goal of reducing fertility levels to replacement level by the year 2005. There is still a substantial need for family planning and it is estimated that if all currently unwanted births could be prevented by using contraception the TFR would decline from around 3 to 2.5. This need is highest in East Timor, Irian Jaya, Aceh, West Nusa Tenggara, North Sumatra and Southwest Sulawesi–generally the most remote and peripheral provinces of Indonesia. It is higher in rural than urban areas and among low socio-economic status women than higher status social groups.

WOMEN USING CONTRACEPTION (%), 1991

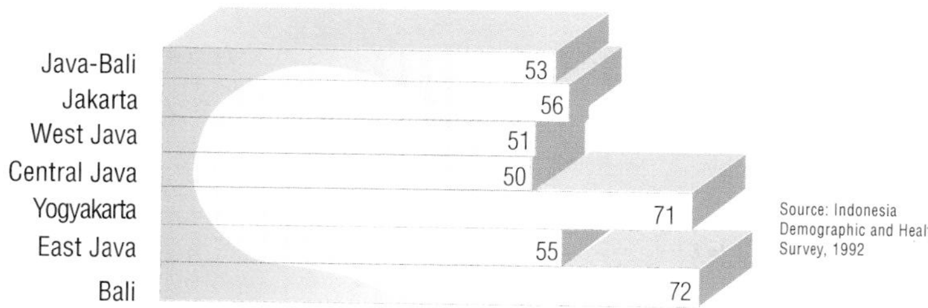

TOTAL FERTILITY RATES, 1955-1991

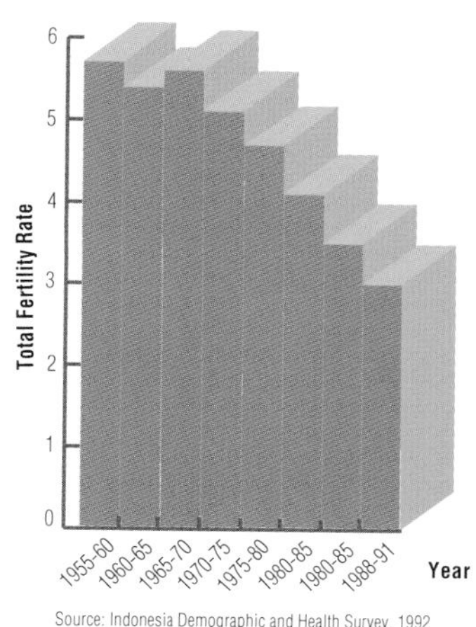

Source: Indonesia Demographic and Health Survey, 1992

TOTAL FERTILITY RATE DIFFERENTIALS 1988-1991

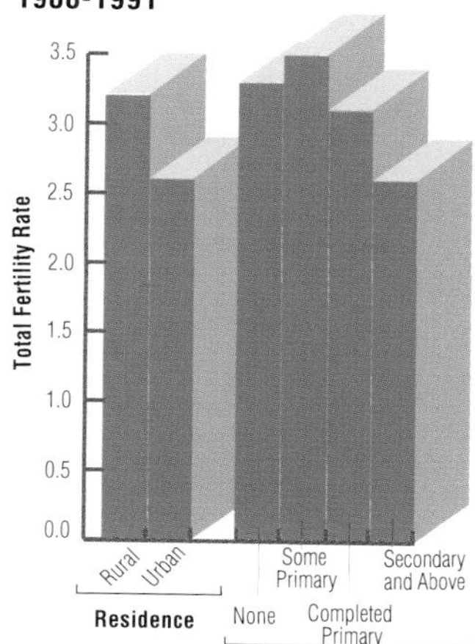

The graph (above left) shows the decline in the total fertility rate, and (above right) the lower birth rates among urban women, and those with higher educations.

Promotional poster from Pasir Putih, East Java. It reads: "Let's be succesful. The National Family Planning Movement. Two children are enough, whether they are a boy or a girl".

«« A model of the "Two children is enough" family, Bondowoso, East Java

Moving People, Changing Lives

Rural-urban migration became an important component of population change from the 1930s and still remains so. Today, short term circulatory movements between rural and urban areas are increasingly the predominant form of migration. Such movements are sometimes a continuation of traditional migration flows. Economic opportunities have also fuelled migration to other parts of Asia and the Middle East.

Increasingly, large numbers of Indonesians are going abroad to seek their livelihoods, like these Indonesians working in Brunei.

Internal Migration

The movement of people between contrasting locations, typically between the countryside and the city, occasionally across provincial and ethno-linguistic 'boundaries', can cause tensions and difficulties for migrants, and for the families they leave behind.

The pattern of migration in Indonesia has changed over the last 50 years. During the peak of economic activity under Dutch colonial control, the predominant flows of migration were towards North Sumatra and the Riau Islands, mostly from Central and East Java. These flows principally comprised the movement of rural people from parts of Java where poverty, land pressure and ecological marginality were greatest towards those areas beyond Java being colonised and developed by the Dutch for plantation agriculture, where they worked as contract coolies.

As early as the 1930s migration flows towards the capital city, Jakarta (Batavia), were already in evidence. With increasing industrialisation, the search for a source of livelihood became a major factor in influencing the incidence and pattern of migration. Land scarcity and ecological marginality continue to affect migration decisions. Today rural-urban migration has tended to supersede rural-rural movements as the main response to this situation.

Ignoring the large volume of movement towards southern Sumatra, much of which is associated with the transmigration programme, we find that movements within the island of Java have come to dominate mobility patterns in Indonesia, with Jakarta the overwhelming focus for movements from Central, West and, to a much lesser extent, East Java. Flows from the other islands (especially Sumatra) towards Jakarta have also taken on some significance in recent years.

As the national census only picks up movements across provincial boundaries and which span a relatively long time period, a whole host of short-distance movements are overlooked in the official

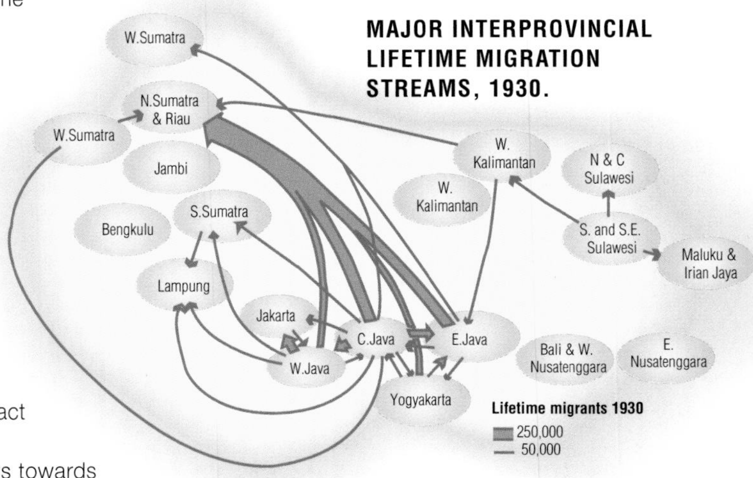

MAJOR INTERPROVINCIAL LIFETIME MIGRATION STREAMS, 1930.

POPULATION DENSITY AND CURRENT MIGRATION FLOW BY ISLAND, 1991

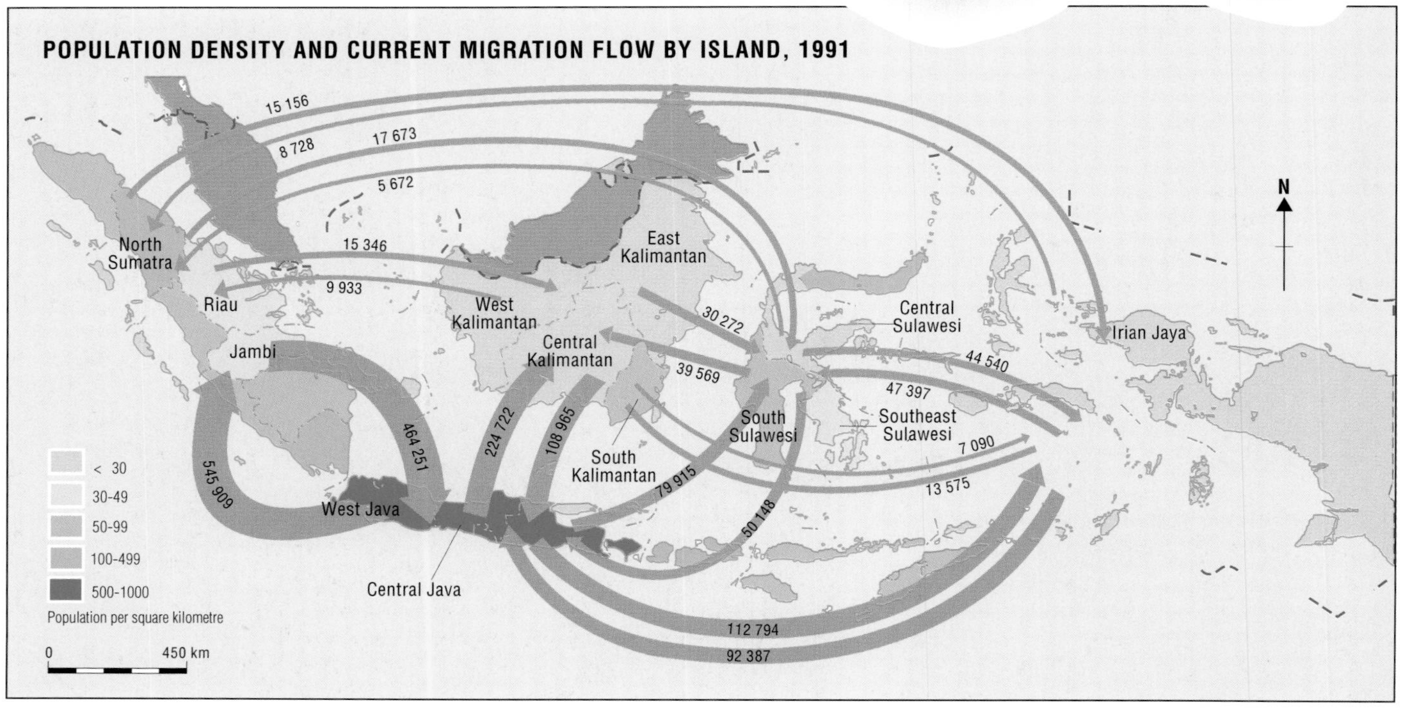

CIRCULATION IN WEST JAVA

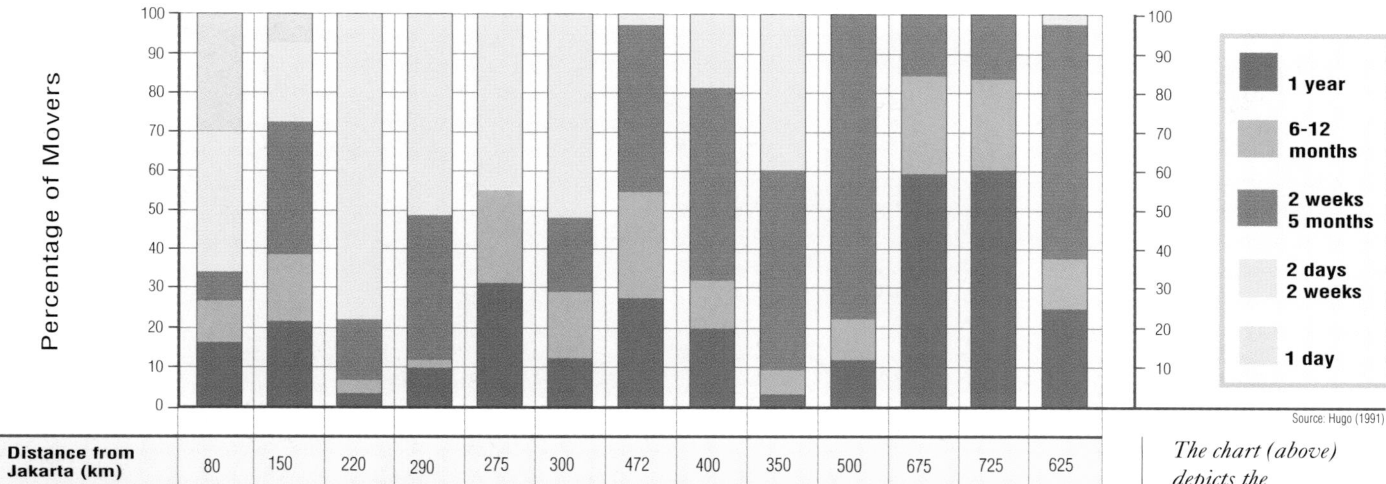

Distance from Jakarta (km)	80	150	220	290	275	300	472	400	350	500	675	725	625
Travel cost (Rp)	50	65	100	100	120	112	185	200	229	260	310	330	360
Travel Time (hrs)	1.5	1.5	3	2	5	3	6	5	9	6	12	9	12

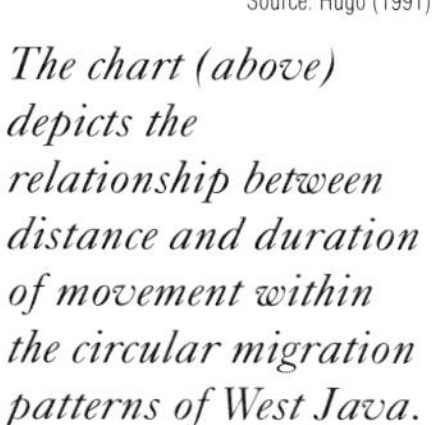

The chart (above) depicts the relationship between distance and duration of movement within the circular migration patterns of West Java.

figures. A series of micro-level studies have suggested that short-term circular movements (circular migration) are in fact the main form of mobility in Indonesia today, at least for people living in rural areas which are in quite easy reach of major metropolitan centres. Temporary and circular migration occur even though, for many Indonesians, an attachment to family and place of origin is an important socio-cultural trait.

By engaging in circular migration, migrants are able to take advantage of the opportunities the city has to offer whilst at the same time seeking to minimise the disruptive effects their absence may have on their families, the village economy, and upon themselves. The prospect of return, however forlorn it may be in reality, also helps to ease the psychological tensions which, to a rural migrant at least, may be associated with life in the big city. Furthermore, retaining a stake in the home village provides a degree of insurance should they fail to settle or achieve their objectives in town.

Traditional Movements

A rather different interpretation of circular migration sees it as a continuation of traditional forms of population movement, at least among certain of Indonesia's ethnic groups. For the Minangkabau, Batak, Bugis and Acehnese, the temporary migration of males has become almost institutionalised as a way of demonstrating their preparedness for the responsibilities of adulthood. This practice is very old. Indeed, quite powerful social pressures could be brought to bear upon those who did not undertake such movements. Some authors have attributed male migration or *merantau* among the matrilineal Minangkabau as an outcome of the inhospitable environment for men. Others see *merantau* as a product not of matrilineality, but of egalitarianism where migration is the only means by which a man can gain status in a society where everyone is equal. Today the pressures are rather more obviously economic in nature, but the traditional predilection for mobility whilst maintaining a strong attachment to one's natal village appears to persist in many modern forms of migration in Indonesia.

One consequence of the growing incidence of rural-urban migration in Java, and also some of the other islands, has been a growing dependence of villages on the external metropolitan economy. Studies in Central Java have shown that periodic moves to find work in the burgeoning urban informal sector yield considerable economic benefits to participant households to the extent that remittances brought back from town have displaced farming as the main source of livelihood in some villages.

International Migration

Not represented in these figures is the quite sizable number of Indonesians who migrate temporarily to other countries. These movements are usually in response to real or perceived economic opportunities there. In contrast to other Asian countries, the flow of Indonesians to find work in the Middle East was quite small until very recently, largely because Indonesia was enjoying the same windfall benefits of the oil price hikes which led to massive infrastructural investment programmes in the Gulf states. With falling petroleum revenues Indonesia faced a growing imperative to diversify employment opportunities, and by the late 1980s there were some 100,000 Indonesian workers in the Middle East, the majority of them women employed in domestic service. Unofficial figures suggest that there are also as many as one million Indonesians in neighbouring Malaysia, drawn there by the higher wages and better employment prospects. Because the vast majority are there illegally, it is difficult to put an accurate figure on their presence, but they may constitute as much as one-tenth of Malaysia's total labour force, with much higher proportions in the East Malaysian states of Sabah and Sarawak.

The development of the Growth Triangle has led to migrant movement towards the Riau islands like Batam. In this rapidly expanding growth area, the official workforce on Batam rose from 9,600 to 16,300 between 1988 and 1990. Construction work needs large numbers of migrant labourers.

Transmigration: A New Future

Transmigration is the government-sponsored transfer of people from the overcrowded parts of Java and Bali to new agricultural settlements established in less densely populated parts of Indonesia. Transmigrants are given free transportation to the settlement and two hectares of land as well as planting materials and foodstuffs for the first 12 months. They have, however, met with varying economic success.

A transmigration poster to attract potential migrants to the scheme.

Balinese transmigrants have brought their religious practices to their new home in East Timor. Note the wooden plank-built transmigrant house in the background.

Early History

Planned resettlement in Indonesia began when the Dutch colonial government introduced a scheme called 'colonisation'. Under this programme 200,000 people were moved from rural Java between 1905 and 1940. After Independence in 1945 the scheme was continued, and renamed 'transmigration', and national development planners tried to increase the scale of the programmes, thinking that poverty and unemployment in Java could be solved through resettlement. Although only 425,000 people left Java and Bali as government-financed transmigrants between 1950 and 1968, three times as many moved as spontaneous transmigrants, that is, people who moved of their own accord, settled wherever they pleased and received no government assistance of any kind.

Recent Transmigration

During the First and Second Five-Year Development Plans (Repelita I and II, 1969-1979), when some 700,000 people were resettled, the transmigration programme was regarded as a means to encourage regional development outside Java. It also aimed to provide new homes for natural disaster victims and for farmers whose land was needed for reservoirs and other public works.

After 1979 the main objective of transmigration once again became population reduction in Java. The scale of the programme was greatly expanded, but with the emphasis on high numerical targets the

LOCATION OF TRANSMIGRATION SETTLEMENTS (PRE- AND POST-1974)

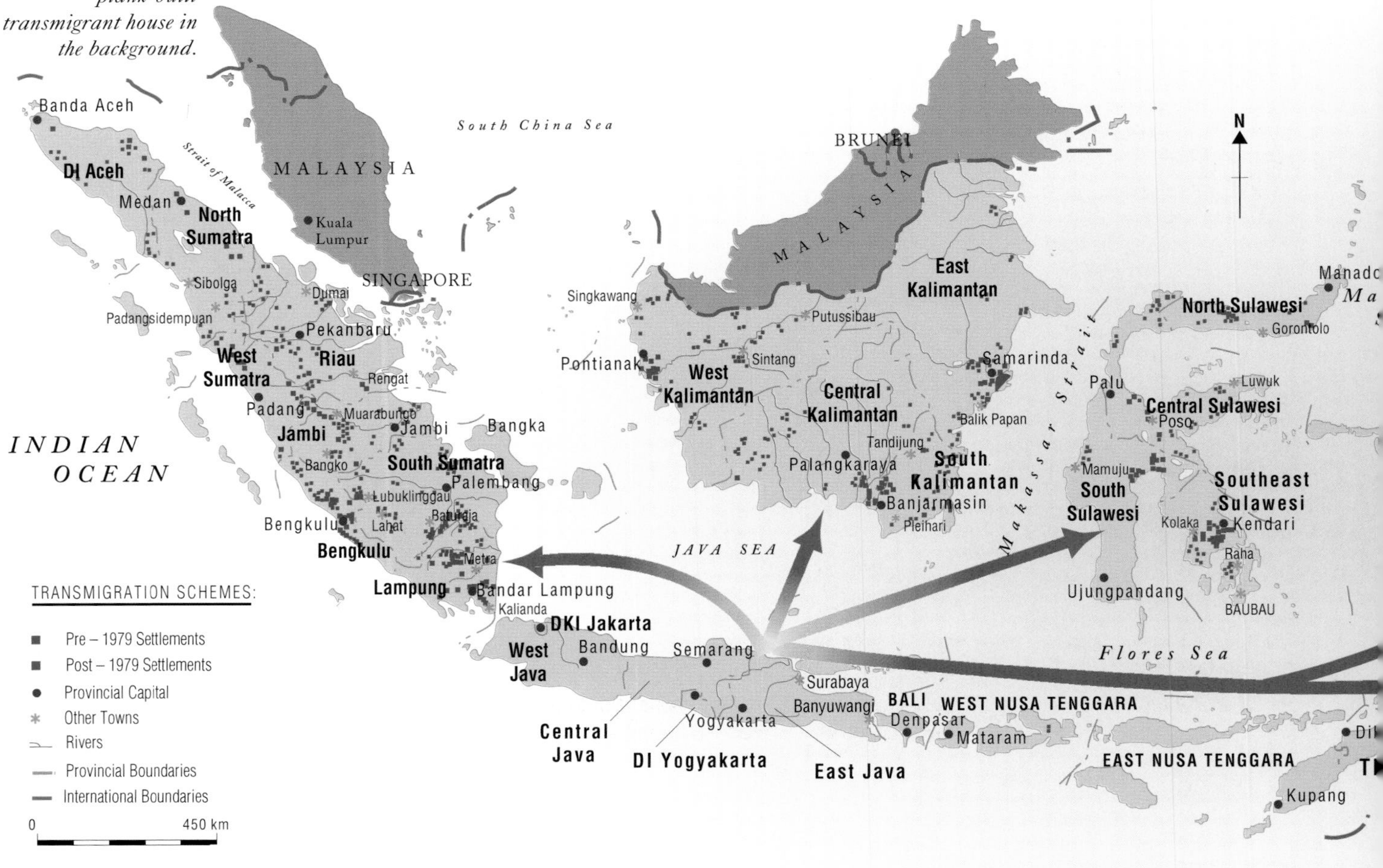

TRANSMIGRATION SCHEMES:

- Pre – 1979 Settlements
- Post – 1979 Settlements
- Provincial Capital
- Other Towns
- Rivers
- Provincial Boundaries
- International Boundaries

0 450 km

quality of resettlement work suffered. Settlement sites were often badly selected in terms of soil and topography while land preparation and house construction were inadequate. Between 1979 and 1988 almost 4.5 million people, including spontaneous transmigrants and local people from the same province, were resettled. Since 1988, there has been a considerable reduction in government-funded transmigration as a consequence of declining oil revenues and of the difficulty of obtaining suitable land for agricultural purposes.

Government-sponsored settlements were originally based on traditional wet-rice cultivation but the construction of irrigation networks proved very expensive in most regions because of unsuitable relief and limited water resources. To avoid this expense, settlements were sometimes established on large estuaries where the tidal influence extended some distance inland and was sufficient to lift river water on to rice-fields. However, so many problems were encountered because of acidic swamp soils and poor drainage that this type of settlement has been discontinued.

In most of the settlements established since the mid 1970s transmigrants depend on rain-fed food-crop cultivation for their livelihood. With rising population densities in the other islands, the sparsely populated land still available for new settlements usually has soils of extremely marginal quality. Furthermore, much of the land is already degraded because of the past activities of shifting cultivators.

The productivity of soils used for food crops is so low in some areas that transmigrants frequently have to find off-farm work to supplement their farm income. The nucleus estate and smallholder system has been introduced to overcome this problem. Transmigrants cultivate tree crops like oil palm on a smallholder basis, with guidance from a nearby estate, which processes and markets the crops. More recently, transmigrants have been resettled on softwood timber estates where they provide labour for the planting and care of trees on deforested land.

The economic success of transmigration settlements, the sustainability of the new forms of land use and the incomes of settlers vary widely from place to place, depending on soil and water resources, the extent of initial inputs, the amount of guidance given to new settlers and the year in which they were resettled. While some transmigrants have failed to prosper and have returned to Java, transmigration has on the whole provided a better life for a large number of landless and near-landless families (see case study below).

GOVERNMENT-SPONSORED FAMILIES

1 Colonisation, **2** Replita I, **3** Replita II, **4** Replita III, **5** Replita IV, **6** Replita V, Figures for 1993/4 are target figures.

	Period	Families
1	1905-41	135,006
	1950-68	91,656
2	1969/70-1973/74	27,878
3	1974/75-1978/79	65,474
4	1979/80-1983/4	371,668
5	1984/5-1988/9	228422
6	1989/90-1993/4	77485

INDEPENDENT FAMILIES

1 Colonisation, **2** Replita I, **3** Replita II, **4** Replita III, **5** Replita IV, **6** Replita V, Figures for 1993/4 are target figures.

	Period	Families
1	1905-41	8,994
	1950-68	370,548
2	1969/70-1973/74	18,390
3	1974/75-1978/79	17,485
4	1979/80-1983/4	163,806
5	1984/5-1988/9	521,728
6	1989/90-1993/4	138,555

Life on a Transmigration Settlement

Transmigration settlement in timber plantation, Kalimantan. The plantation offers employment for transmigrants.

Pak Tono migrated from East Java to one of the large projects established in southern Sumatra in 1978 with his family. From his youth he had been an agricultural labourer on the rice and sugar-cane fields of the village where he was born. As the city spread, the owner of the land sold it as a factory site. With no skills to equip him for any occupation other than farming, Tono decided to register at the district transmigration office.

The first years were difficult ones. Tono often left the project to work as a wage labourer in local sawmills to support his family. Since he had only the labour of his own household, he was able to bring all of his holding under cultivation only when draught cattle were distributed to settlers some years later. Even then, unanticipated problems arose, as when his crops of rain-fed rice, corn and cassava were destroyed by wild pigs. Meanwhile, Tono's wife purchased seedlings and young coconut and fruit trees from transmigrants living in long-established settlements in the same region to start a home garden. She was soon able to provide additional food for household consumption. Later she began raising chickens and goats. Today the settlement is prosperous, largely because it was well planned. A paved road facilitated marketing and good agricultural extension services were provided.

Rice Terraces in Bali.

Harvested rice is tied into bales for drying.

Aerial view of flooded rice fields, with other crops growing in between.

Harvesting rice using the finger knife (ani-ani).

PADI AND SAWAH: RICE IN INDONESIA

The mere statement that rice is the staple crop of Indonesia masks the degree to which rice and its production intrude into the geography of the country. The physical demands of wet rice production have created entirely new landscapes in the terraced rice fields of Java, Bali, Sulawesi and Sumatra. Irrigation schemes in Bali have transformed the hydrology of river basins, in some cases transferring water from one basin to another through ancient tunnels. At the scale of the individual field, wet rice culture fundamentally alters a soil's characteristics, including its drainage and chemical characteristics, creating a distinctive *padi* soil.

In cultural terms, rice became not just the major part of the diet of most Indonesians, but also an important medium of exchange, and a symbol of mystical and ritual importance. From an economic standpoint, rice was historically one of Java's major exports as well as the key element of production in most household economies. More recently, the need to support the rice economy became a guiding policy initiative for the Indonesian government.

In this way, rice can be seen as a 'linking' commodity, binding different spheres of life. It links nutrition with symbolic and ritual meaning, household economies with government action, and the changing landscape with political and social organisation.

The danger lies in assuming that because the visual landscape of rice production appears so unchanging, the substance of production in other ways is similarly immutable. Almost any conversation with any farmer will emphasise the degree to which–although they may be producing the same crop as their forebears, possibly in the same field–production processes have changed. New technologies encapsulated in the term the 'Green Revolution' have altered the production process, raised productivity, and in many instances brought the 'state' into the village through its role in disseminating technology and advice, and assisting in the production and marketing of the crop. Occasionally, new technologies have been rejected by farmers in favour of existing local methods and then abandoned by the government bodies concerned with dissemination as they have realised their inappropriateness.

Nor is Indonesia a 'rice growing society' in the way that it used to be characterised. Few families depend only on rice for the well-being and occupational multiplicity is often the only way to meet rising aspirations even, in some cases, to survive.

Rice in Indonesia

Rice, the staple crop of many Indonesians, was first cultivated more than 6000 years ago. Large-scale production and trade were occuring by the 15th century. Although wet rice is predominant, dry rice is grown also, especially in islands other than Java and Bali.

Both buffalo and people work the fields to form an impervious soil layer that retains water before wet rice is transplanted.

Rice as Staple Food

Rice (*Oryza sativa*) is cultivated throughout the Archipelago. No meal is complete without it, and no guest can be honourably fed without rice. In many Indonesian languages the word for 'rice' means 'food' in the wider sense–for example in the case of the Samosir Batak word *indahan*. Rice stores well and has a high weight to calorie value. This makes it attractive as a trade good. In short, rice is more than just a 'crop'. it had mystical and ritual value and still does in more remote communities, it is an important medium of exchange, and also a staple food.

Spread of Rice Cultivation

Rice was introduced into Indonesia by the Austronesians during the first thousand years BC, the earliest evidence being found in Sulawesi. It was probably first cultivated on Java in the early centuries of the first millennium, to begin with probably as a dry-field crop and only later, perhaps during the 8th century, in flooded conditions. As early as the 10th century, Java was a large scale exporter of rice and in the 15th century, the Chinese adventurer Ma Huan reported that rice in north-east Java 'ripens twice in one year' indicating the practice of double cropping. Ports such as Jepara on Java's north coast were shipping thousands of tonnes of rice to other parts of Southeast Asia just prior to the arrival of the Europeans.

DEVELOPMENT OF THE RICE PLANT

105-120 DAY VARIETY
Vegative Phase
Reproductive Phase
Ripening Phase
Plant height
Dying and non-bearing Tillers
Tiller Number
Panicle Length
emergence
seeding
panicle initiation & internode elongation
maximum tiller no.
anthesis
maturity

150 DAY VARIETY
Vegative Phase
Reproductive Phase
Ripening Phase
Plant height
Dying and non-bearing Tillers
Tiller Number
Panicle Length
emergence
seeding
maximum tiller no.
internode elongation
panicle initiation
Lag vegetative growth
anthesis
maturity

Rice Today

Over the centuries farmers have chosen rice varieties suited to a wide range of environments. Globally, there may be as many as 120,000 different kinds, with about 8,000 in Indonesia. Wet rice or *sawah* can be irrigated or rainfed. In irrigated wet rice culture, the farmer has artificial means of controlling water supply to the field, so that water can be pumped or channelled to the ricefield even when there is no rain. In rainfed systems, the farmer relys on rainfall to inundate the field. Water can be channelled off a field and the water supply between contiguous fields balanced, but additional water cannot be channelled into the ricefields unless it rains. In rainfed systems the farmer is rain dependent while in irrigated systems he is usually rain independent. The heartlands of rice culture are Java and Bali, accounting for two-thirds of total production and half the harvested area. Here irrigated and rainfed systems are found. In the Outer Islands, dry rice may be grown. In 1991, production of rice totalled over 44 million tonnes, an average yield of 4.35 tonnes per hectare.

CYCLE OF RICE CULTIVATION BATAK, SAMOSIR, SUMATRA

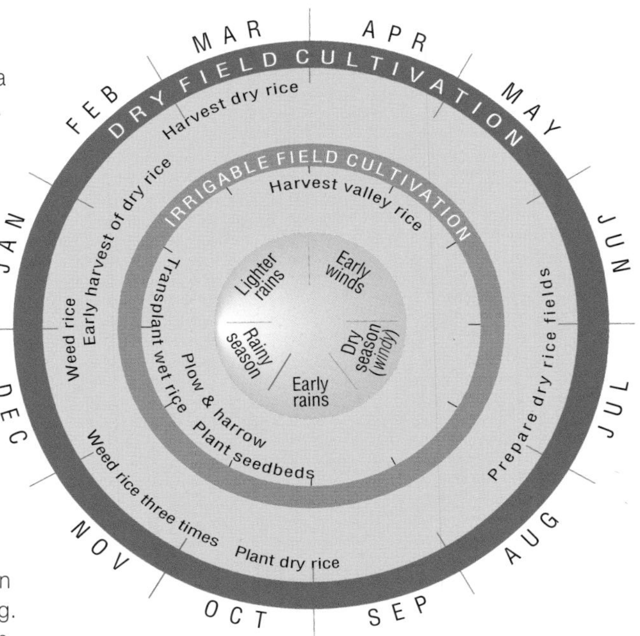

The Rice Cycle

More than any other staple crop, wet rice culture is dependent on a stable and relatively plentiful supply of water. Where possible, farmers have engineered elaborate systems of irrigation and flood control to overcome the vagaries of climate. But where rice is grown in rainfed conditions–as it is on over 30 per cent of *sawah* in Java and 40 per cent in the Outer Islands–the seasons strongly determine the cycle of cultivation. Because wet rice demands flat land, hill sides are terraced and often subdivided into small fields, each field 'bunded' by mud banks. Sluices at the up-slope and down-slope sides bring water and water-borne nutrients into the plot, and drain excess water away, usually into a neighbouring rice field.

West Javanese farmers who cultivate modern varieties of irrigated rice begin by preparing a small seed or nursery bed, two weeks before transplanting. The seed is broadcast on to the finely tilled soil and sometimes covered with straw for protection. After three to four weeks the seedlings are ready to be transplanted to the main fields. During this period,

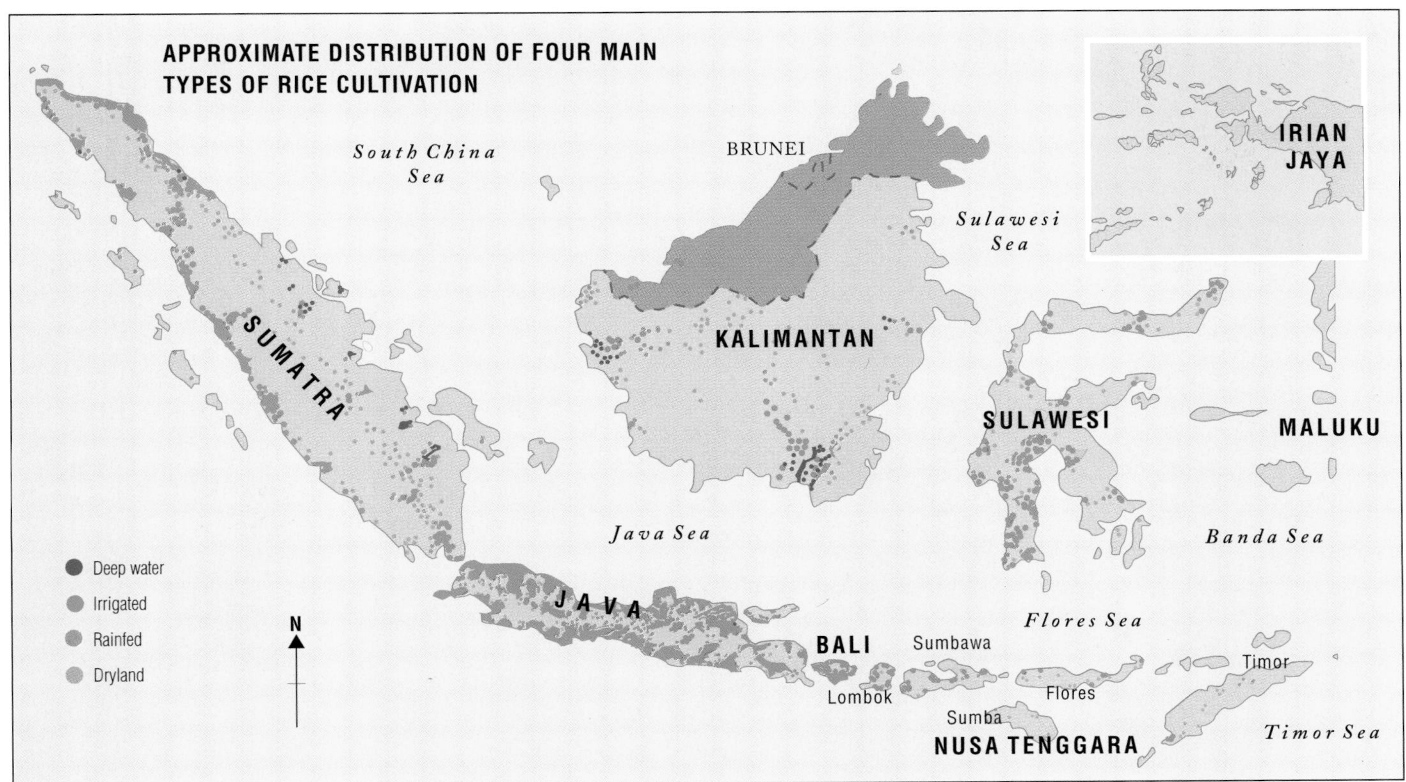

farmers prepare the rest of their land. This is the time of the heaviest work. Bunds are repaired, stubble from the previous crop either burnt or hoed into the soil, the land is ploughed, usually with buffalo-drawn ploughs, although tractors are becoming increasingly common, harrowed and finally rolled.

All these operations are designed to produce a fine tilth (cultivated soil) where the rice plant can flourish. The field is then marked into lines with a rake and the seedlings transplanted from the nursery bed. The first application of fertiliser may be made one to two weeks after transplanting and the field is drained beforehand to gain maximum benefit. Not long after the first application, the first weeding is undertaken–the chemicals promoting the growth of the rice plant and also of weeds. A second dose of fertilisers may be applied a month later, followed a week or ten days after that by a further weeding. While the rice plant is maturing, careful control of the water level in the field is vital in ensuring a good yield. Finally, after between 100 (for modern varieties) and 150 (for traditional varieties) days from the date of transplanting, the rice crop is ready for harvest.

Harvesting rice in Lawang in East Java. Here a sickle is being used to cut the rice, but it is still possible to find the traditional ani-ani, or hand knife, being used in various parts of Java.

RICE CYCLE AND LABOUR INPUTS, SUKAHAJI, WEST JAVA

Task	Average labour input/ha (hours/ha)
Prepare seed bed	20
Prepare main field	
repairing bunds/burning off hoeing-in stubble	170
ploughing harrowing	50
rolling	16
raking	10
Removal of seedlings	10
Transplanting and patching	150
First fertilisation	36
First weeding	120
Second (and third) fertilisation	40
Second and third weeding	240
Total	862
Days per hectare	172
Yield per hectare (tonnes)	5.5

The 100 days from transplanting to harvest is for modern varieties; traditional varieties may take another 40 to 50 days to reach maturity. Labour inputs for harvesting are not included as it is not part of the cultivation process.

Source: Hardjono, J. (1987).

Harvesting deepwater rice, a non-irrigated form of wet rice cultivation.

«««Wet rice cultivation is extremely labour-intensive, each rice plant is transplanted manually.

The Wet Rice Field Ecosystem

The flooded rice field is an artificial, almost self-contained, ecosystem. Rice is the only staple crop normally produced in semi-submerged conditions, and this results in a unique set of ecosystem characteristics which help to account for the high, and sustained yields usually produced.

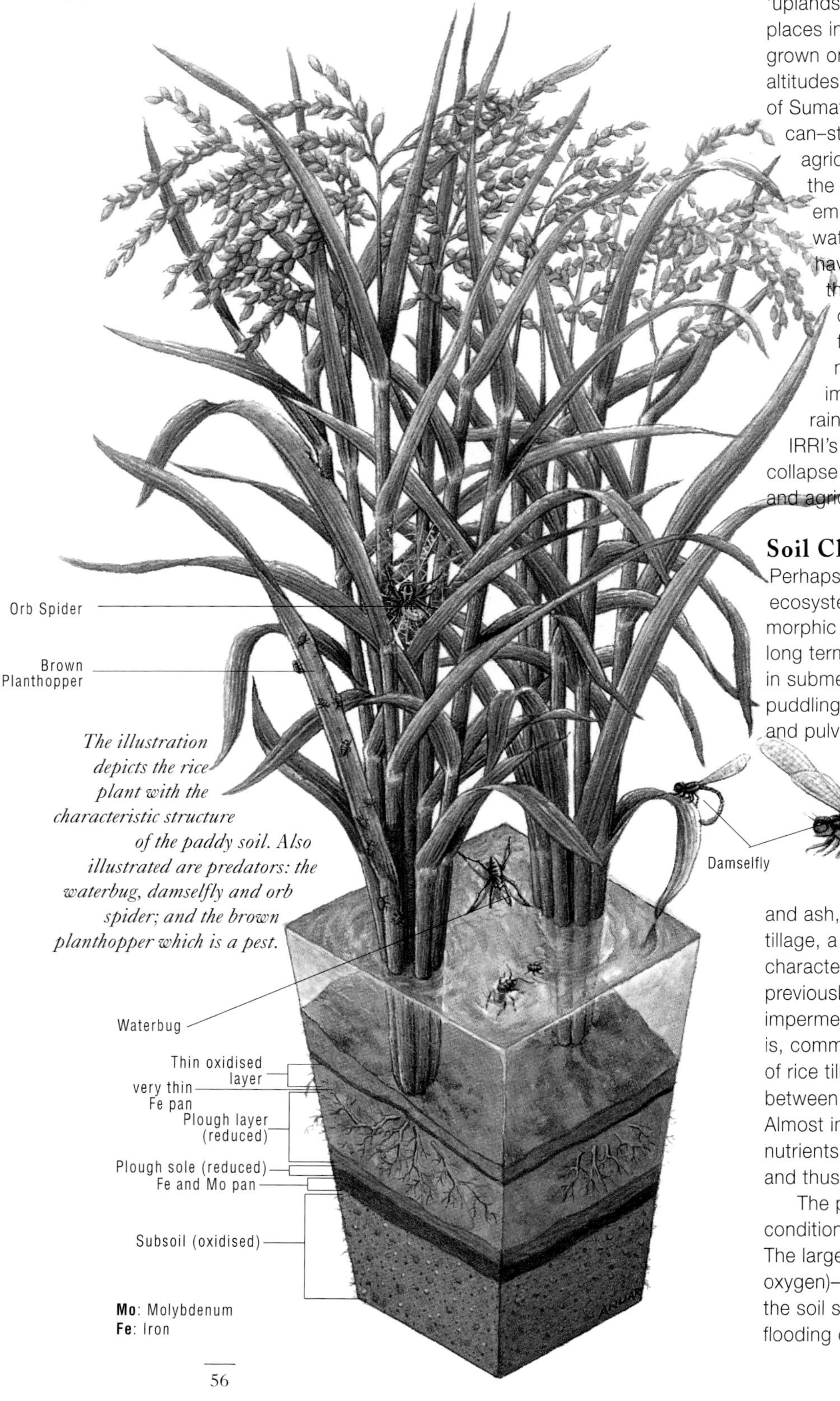

Orb Spider

Brown Planthopper

The illustration depicts the rice plant with the characteristic structure of the paddy soil. Also illustrated are predators: the waterbug, damselfly and orb spider; and the brown planthopper which is a pest.

Waterbug

Thin oxidised layer

very thin Fe pan

Plough layer (reduced)

Plough sole (reduced)

Fe and Mo pan

Subsoil (oxidised)

Damselfly

Mo: Molybdenum
Fe: Iron

Rice Classifications

Rice classification systems are useful tools to make sense of the diversity of rice cultivation in Indonesia. The most widely used classification of rice systems is that of the International Rice Research Institute (IRRI), summarised on the facing page. The classification identifies five types of rice ecosystems: upland; irrigated, rainfed lowland, deepwater and tidal wetlands rice (floodprone rice).

There are, however, some limitations to this classification system. It equates dry rice with 'uplands' and wet rice with 'lowlands'. There are places in Indonesia where rainfed 'lowland' rice is grown on terraced fields in steeply sloping areas at altitudes of up to 1,500 metres (for example in parts of Sumatra and Java). At the same time, lowland rice can–strictly speaking–include both wet and dry rice agriculture. The IRRI classification includes only the latter. In the same vein, 'irrigated' rice embraces a wide range of forms of artificial water supply ranging from places where farmers have close control of water, to areas where there is little to distinguish, in terms of water control, irrigated from rainfed fields. For many farmers the distinction between shallow, medium and deep water cultivation is more important than that between irrigated and rainfed. Although classifications such as the IRRI's are useful, it should be accepted that they collapse what are, in fact, a wide range of ecotypes and agricultural systems into a handful of categories.

Soil Chemistry

Perhaps the most distinctive element of the rice field ecosystem is the creation of an artificial, hydromorphic soil or paddy soil. This comes to exist in the long term as the result of the process of tilling the soil in submerged conditions. Intensive ploughing, puddling and harrowing destroys the original top soil, and pulverises it into a homogenous mud which, in terms of its texture, is usually heavy. The addition of organic matter such as manure, compost, and mulch, and non-organic material like chemical fertilisers and ash, helps to enrich the mud. After years of such tillage, a 10-20 centimetre plough layer evolves–the characteristic paddy soil–which can transform a previously free-draining soil into an almost impermeable artificial gley. Beneath the plough layer is, commonly, the plough pan. This is again a product of rice tillage operations, and marks the interface between the cultivated and non-cultivated soil. Almost impermeable, it prevents the leaching of nutrients out of the soil and helps to maintain fertility and thus, yields.

The process of cultivation in submerged conditions also creates unique chemical conditions. The largely anaerobic environment (absence of free oxygen)–excepting the thin brown oxidised layer at the soil surface which disappears fairly early in the flooding cycle–leads to the reduction rather than the

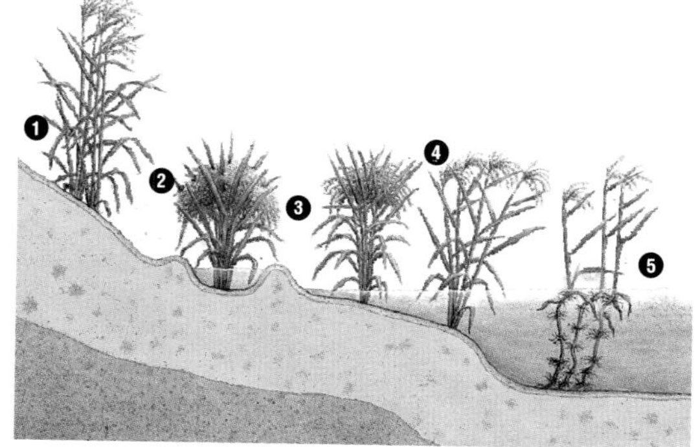

oxidisation of minerals. In addition, water-logging has an important effect on the acidity of the soil, in that it stabilises it at a pH of about 6.5. This slightly acid environment is the optimum point for ensuring the maximum availability of essential nutrients. It is important, however, that conditions do not become so anaerobic that sulphides are released, for these would kill off the rice plants. Thus some drainage and careful water management are critical components of the system. With these in place, the maintainance of soil fertility is relatively easy in wet rice fields, representing one of the great advantages of the system. Although the chemical reactions associated with flooding are largely advantageous for plant growth they do not solve the critical issue of nitrogen supply. The application of organic fertilisers and nitrogen entering the system with irrigation water are not sufficient to maintain yields over the long-term without chemical fertilisers. Also crucial in making up the deficit is the nitrogen produced by nitrogen-fixing micro-organisms such as blue-green algae and photosynthetic bacteria which proliferate in the water and the saturated upper part of the soil.

Pests and Predators

In addition to blue-green algae and bacteria, the wet rice field–in its traditional form–also supports a range of other flora and fauna which help to stabilise and sustain rice production. Traditionally, rice was grown in conjunction with fish, which were raised in the flooded field. The fish eat insects harmful to the rice plant, help to fertilise the system, and provide an important source of animal protein and income for rural people. Frogs, shellfish, crabs and other aquatic animals play a similar role, and are now recognised as important elements in both rural diets and in integrated pest management in which yields are sustained through maintaining a balance between pests (such as the brown planthopper) and the predators that prey on them (such as spiders and beetles). Plants and trees cultivated on bunds also provide an input of leaves to the system (as well as firewood and fruit for farmers), although shading may serve to reduce yields.

Ecosystem Characteristics

The process of flooding the rice field leads to an inflow of silt and clays rich in absorbed nutrients and soluble bases, organic matter and algae. The nutrient quality of the water is closely associated with the geological conditions to be found in the river catchment area–the type of parent rock, the degree and rate of weathering, and the quantity of rainfall, for example.

The artificial rice field ecosystem is a multi-strand, complex system where rice–the main product–can be grown in conjunction with fish, fruit trees, frogs, crabs, trees for firewood, and vegetables. Each element plays an important role in the functioning of the whole system and therefore in yield maintenance, and also in rural livelihoods. From a human perspective, the system is poly-cultural, not monocultural, and humans enter the rice field food 'chain' at many points.

The simplification of this system associated with the technology of the Green Revolution remains a major cause for concern, and research at the International Rice Research Institute in the Philippines and also at research centres in Indonesia is trying to revive some of the key advantages of stability and diversity inherent in the traditional system.

The upper limits of rice cultivation in the Indonesian Archipelago lie at about 1,500 metres above sea level. Rice is grown at these altitudes, and in one or two cases above 1,500 metres in Sulawesi, Java and Sumatra.

RICE ECOSYSTEMS (AFTER IRRI)

1 UPLAND RICE
Rice is directly seeded in non-flooded, well-drained soil on level to steeply sloping fields. Yields are comparatively low and crops are threatened by lack of moisture and inadequate nutrition.

2 IRRIGATED RICE
The only rice ecosystem in which the farmer has close control over the water supply. Rice is transplanted or directly seeded in puddled soil on levelled, bunded fields with water control, in both dry and wet seasons in the lowlands. Fertilisers are heavily utilised and yields are comparatively high.

3 RAINFED LOWLAND RICE
Rice is transplanted or directly seeded in puddled soil on level to slightly sloping, bunded, or diked fields of variable depth and duration of flooding, depending on rainfall. Soils may range from flooded to non-flooded.

4 DEEP WATER RICE

5 TIDAL WETLANDS RICE (FLOOD-PRONE)
Often grown in flood-prone, lowlying areas. Rice is directly seeded or transplanted during the wet season on fields characterised by medium to very deep flooding (50-300 centimetres) from rivers and tides from river mouth deltas. Flood-prone rice grows as the water level rises and is harvested after the water recedes. Yields are often low and unpredictable due to soil salinity and toxicity problems as well as the unpredictability of flood and drought cycles.

« WET RICE ECOSYSTEM

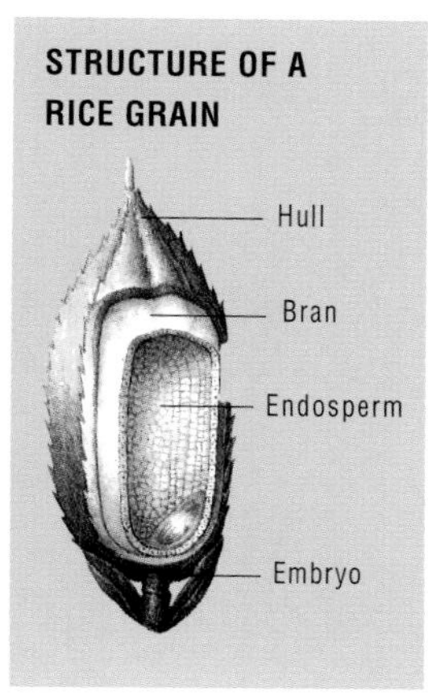

The Gift of Water: Irrigation and Agriculture

The ability of wet rice and certain horticultural systems to support high population densities in many parts of Indonesia depends largely on complex irrigation schemes. In Java these are mostly built and maintained by the state through the Department of Public Works and the Department of Agriculture. In Bali and some other islands, local-level, agrarian systems and institutions are critical.

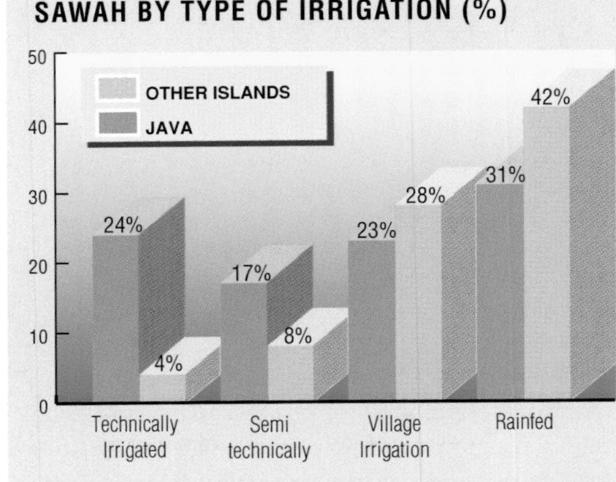

Although the division is not clear cut, 'technically irrigated' refers to centrally-controlled, large-scale, permanent irrigation schemes utilising a high level of exogenous technology and expertise. 'Semi-technically' irrigated refers to centrally-managed schemes, with partial control over village irrigation.

A stone altar to the gods, decorated with offerings, along an irrigation canal leading into the rice terraces, Bali.

Dani vegetable garden.

» Rice shaped into an image of the rice goddess.

A complex system of canals and sluices channels water to Bali's rice fields.

Water Management

Java has an average population density of over 800 people per square kilometre. In places like the area south of Tegal on the north coast, the agricultural population density may exceed 2,000 people per square kilometre. Yet despite this immense pressure of people on the land, Java is self-sufficient in rice production. The Javanese irrigation systems allow up to three crops a year to be harvested; and sustained, high yields to be achieved. Since the mid-1960s, the introduction of Green Revolution technology has led to further increases in output in many areas. However, the success of the new technology in raising yields has been predicated on the effective control of water–in other words, on irrigation.

Until the turn of this century, expansion of irrigation owed little to government investment. It was only in the early years of the 20th century, and especially during the Depression, that the Dutch administration began actively to promote 'technical irrigation'. Before then, water management was the concern of farmers and local-level groups. Almost without exception, this state-directed investment in irrigation was concentrated on Java–a pattern which remains true today. All 'technical' and 'semi-technical' irrigation systems are controlled by the Irrigation Service down to the tertiary canal heads. At this point, village coordinated systems take over the water until it enters the individual field. There are also large areas where so-called 'village' irrigation systems dominate and where the Irrigation Service plays no significant role. These are usually found near the upper reaches of river systems.

In some areas where farmers receive their water from state-run irrigation schemes, village-level committees remain important in coordination at the local level. On Bali, attempts by the government in the 1970s to take over some of the duties traditionally held by local groups led to considerable friction and–critically–to a loss of efficiency in water management and a decline in yields.

Bali-Subak

Bali is drained by over 150 rivers and streams, of which half are perennial. Because most flow within deep-cut gorges, the Balinese have had to build weirs and dig tunnels, some of which are over one kilometre long, to divert water to their rice fields. The earliest reference to irrigation in Bali is found in an inscription which records the digging of an irrigation tunnel in 944 AD. Yet despite the immensity and complexity of Bali's irrigation systems, they are now thought to have their roots in village-level management structures–not in the over-arching control of a 'despotic' state. This theory, originally put forward by Karl Wittfogel in 1957, offered the view that the construction and management of immense and complex irrigation works required the controlling hand of an all-powerful (despotic) state.

Yet, this is not to say that each village is–or was–an independent 'little republic'. The reliance of every farmer on the irrigation system for a successful harvest, means that, in a quite literal sense, a silver ribbon of water binds thousands of farmers together into a single system. At the lowest level, each farmer is a member of a *subak*. Membership is restricted to those *subak* fed from a single dam, and the members elect a head or *klian subak* from among their number. In the case of larger *subaks*, the lowest level of organisation is the *tempek*, where membership is restricted to those farmers whose lands are fed from the same canal. The *subak*, in their turn, are linked to mountain temples or *pura masceti*, which come under the sway of one of two lake temples: Pura Batu Kau which coordinates irrigation in west Bali, and Pura Ulun Danau which does the same for north, east and south Bali. Water temples hold their festivals every 105 days, a period which corresponds with the 105-day growing season of native Balinese rices. Their ritual calendars are used to time the opening and closing of canals and sluices to ensure that plantings are staggered and that water is allocated in the most efficient and equitable manner. Stephen Lansing in his book *Priests and Programmers* asked the head of Sukawati village how the system operated. The village head explained: 'The Pura Er Jeruk is the largest temple hereabouts, that is, the temple whose congregation includes all the farmers of the village of Sukawati. Now below this temple there are also smaller temples, which are special places of worship for the *subaks*–each *subak* has its own. There are fourteen of these temples, all of which meet together as one here. Every decision, every rule concerning planting seasons and so forth, is always discussed here. Then, after the meeting here, decisions are carried down to each *subak*. The *subaks* each call all their members together: In accord with the meetings we held at the Temple Er Jeruk, we must fix our planting dates, beginning on day one through day ten. For example, first *subak* Sango plants, then *subak* Somi, beginning from day ten through day twenty. Thus it is arranged, in accordance with water and *Padewasan* –that is, the best times to plant.'

The Baliem Valley Irrigation System

On the morning of June 23rd 1938, the American explorer Richard Archbold 'found' the fertile Baliem Valley in Irian Jaya. This valley lies at an altitude of 1,500 metres, encircled by towering peaks and stretching 60 kilometres from north-west to south-east. In places it is as much as 15 kilometres wide. The Dani of the Baliem number approximately 50,000. The explorers found the Dani people maintaining a complex system of drainage and irrigation works capable of supporting a population density of over 200 people per square kilometre, thereby making this the most densely settled agricultural area in New Guinea. The agricultural achievement of the Dani people is a result of their highly productive system of sweet potato cultivation.

« *Dani woman tending to her sweet potato garden.*

Along with pigs, sweet potatoes are the Dani's most important food source, representing about 90 per cent of their diet. Most of their sweet potato are grown in an elaborate ditch system which dissects the valley floor into a curvilinear chequerboard of raised 'fields'. The ditches serve a three-fold purpose: during periods of heavy rain, they drain water from the land; during drought they provide irrigation water; and throughout the year they are used for mulching–the rich mud being ladled onto the crops to promote growth and raise yields. Not only are population densities exceptionally high for the area, but the anthropologist Karl Heider maintains there is no evidence of over-population. The Dani people's system of horticulture is at once sophisticated, sustainable, and highly productive.

BALI SUBAK

An idealised subak system (not to scale).
1 The subak temple Pura Ulan Batur where farmers from all the subak in the region make offerings.
2 Weir along ridge line, and where water channel divides.
3 Irrigation channel.
4 Field shrine where farmers from a single subak will make offerings.

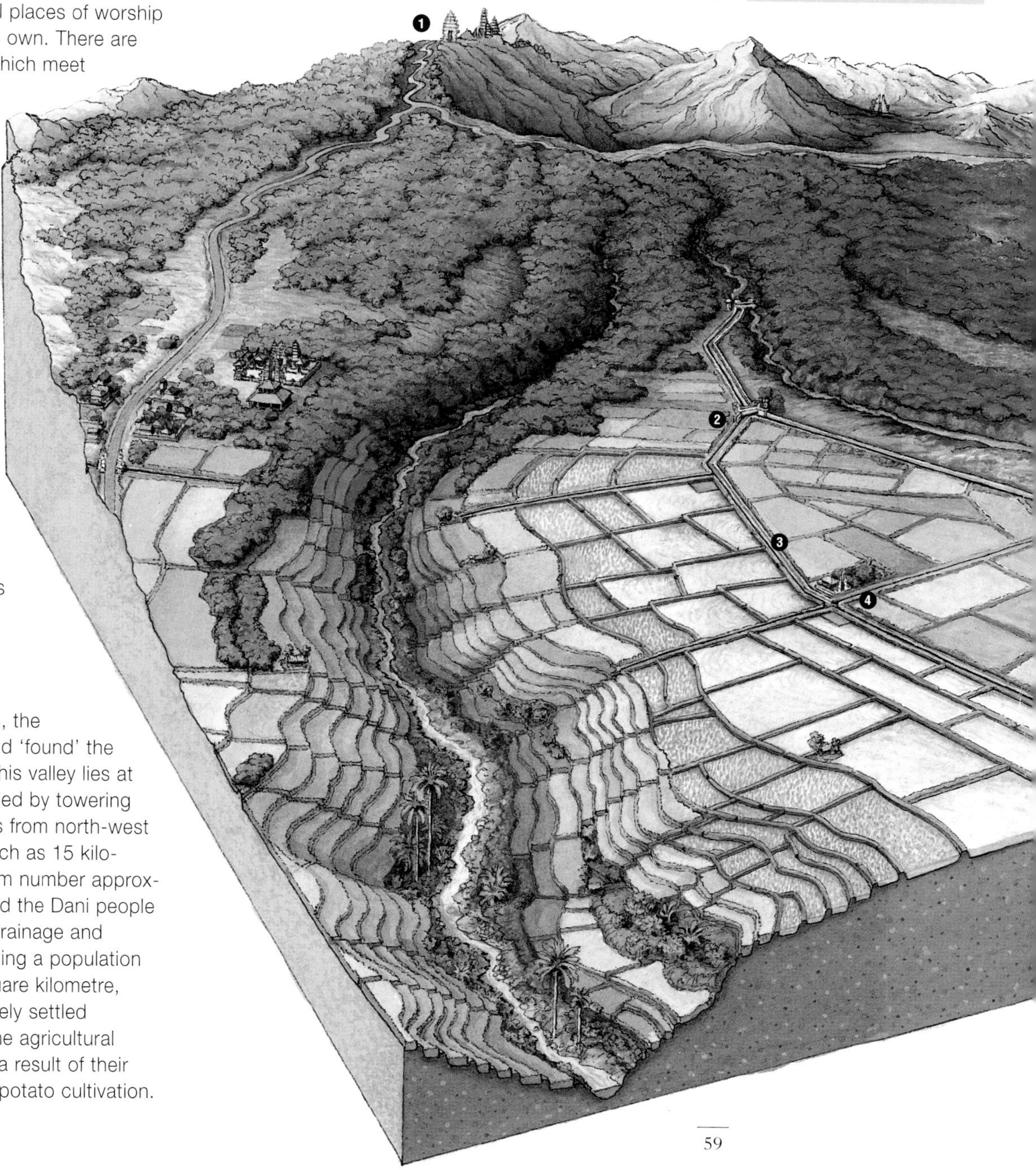

Local Knowledge, Expert Knowledge

In recent years, researchers have come to realise that farmers have built up a vast store of experience and knowledge based on long-term and intimate interaction with land and crops. Researchers who have studied this indigenous knowledge, or indigenous technical knowledge, argue that scientists must also learn from farmers, and that agricultural development programmes must be designed with farmer's direct input.

Harvest offering dedicated to Dewi Sri, and placed in the fields during harvest time, and in the rice granaries. Dewi Sri is the rice goddess.

Traditional bird scarer. These platforms and their occupants (usually small boys), were once common sights in parts of Indonesia.

Indigenous Knowledge

The advance of indigenous knowledge is associated with a wider shift in development planning towards people-centred, participatory methods. These systems allow local people to become subjects of development, and not just the objects. Although traditional systems of production tend to be lower yielding than modern systems, they are also more sustainable. As agricultural problems have emerged, so increasingly researchers and officials have turned to farmers for alternatives.

The various traditional agro-forestry systems such as the diverse, multi-storied home gardens (*pekarangan*), mixed gardens (*kebun campuran*), and forest gardens (*kebun talun*) of Java have been identified as an effective means of controlling erosion on steep slopes and of improving nutrition.

Modern systems which often encourage the excessive use of insecticides can lead to the development of resistance in pest species. Resistance spreads through populations because the individuals that are able to survive the effects of the insecticide using behavioural, biochemical or physiological means, pass on these genetic adaptations to the succeeding generation. Another negative side effect is that chemical pesticides often kill off the natural predators of insect pests indiscriminately. In places the government has turned to traditional forms of pest management as a cheaper, more stable and an environmentally-friendly method of limiting crop losses from pest attack.

These traditional methods are based, not on the use of chemical pesticides but rather on maintaining a balance between predators and prey. Insect pests, unfortunately, often have high reproductive capabilities, an adaptation developed in order to offset the naturally high mortality rates that they face in nature. For example, a female brown planthopper, a particularly threatening pest, is capable of producing large numbers of offspring. However, through the action of predators and diseases, only one or two offspring will survive after one generation. In fact, it is not uncommon for 98-99 per cent mortality to occur.

The traditional diverse rice field which combined rice, fish, frogs, insects, ducks, and fruit and vegetables in a productive, multi-strand and stable agro-ecosystem, is now beginning to reappear in Indonesia. Farmers have discovered that it is a more effective system of pest control. The agricultural methods of shifting cultivators have been built into systems designed for transmigration settlements in the Outer Islands. In some areas, transmigrants themselves have abandoned officially 'approved' agricultural systems in favour of those used by local agriculturalists, finding them more appropriate to local conditions. In Bali traditional irrigation systems and rituals are once again determining the pattern and timing of cultivation after the confusion and production losses of the 1970s and 1980s.

These examples and numerous others are proof that sometimes traditional agricultural systems are more productive, sustainable and appropriate in the long term than modern systems.

HARVESTING IN JAVA

Just as modern technologies have displaced indigenous ones, so too have the processes of agrarian change altered or eclipsed traditional systems of agricultural management. In Java, the best such example is the displacement of the *bawon* system of rice harvesting with the *tebasan* system. Under the traditional 'open' *bawon* system, every member of a village has the right to help in the harvest of any piece of land, and up to 500 harvesters have been recorded working on fields as small as 0.25 hectares. The rice is harvested with a finger knife or *ani-ani*, the panicles being cut one by one. For their work the harvesters receive a share–or *bawon*–of the rice they harvest, usually between one seventh and one ninth, depending on their relationship to the land owner. There are two sorts of *bawon*, an open system (as above), and a closed system. In the closed system, only friends and relatives invited by the owner can join in. In some cases, small farmers have been forced to 'close' or restrict the harvest because they lose too much of the crop. One way of doing this is to sell the crop before the harvest to a trader (*penebas*), who selects his own harvesters and pays them either in cash or rice, in proportion to what they cut. The trader under this *tebesan* system is not constrained by community obligations and is sometimes free to exclude villagers who enjoyed community rights to the harvest under the open *bawon* system. Java's harvesting systems were traditionally varied; economic and social change has made them more varied and complex still. Short-stemmed, modern rice varieties are hard to cut with a finger knife and sickles are used instead, often, but not always, using a form of the *tebasan* system. Traditional rice varieties tend still to be harvested using the *ani-ani*, but participation in the harvest is now rarely 'open' and restrictions on the harvest are the norm. The role which the new rice technology has played in these changes is still, however, hotly disputed.

The Wereng Challenge

In 1974, the brown planthopper (*Nilaparvata lugens*), or *wereng*, devastated rice across Java and Bali. This pest damages rice plants by sucking the sap, leaving the rice plant open to fungal and bacterial infection. Hoppers also transmit grassy stunt, and wilted stunt virus diseases. Critics of the Green Revolution pointed out that the spread of modern varieties had narrowed the genetic base, with almost half the rice land being planted with four closely related varieties. In combination with the spread of double and triple cropping and the use of chemical inputs, this made rice agriculture highly vulnerable to pest attack on a massive scale. The highly mobile *wereng* breeds extremely quickly. Furthermore, it has the ability to produce new bio-types in response to the introduction of resistant rice cultivars.

Chemical pesticides used against the *wereng* also killed its natural predators, like spiders which would normally help to control *wereng* populations. For example, the wolf spider (*Lycosa pseudoannulata*) is a highly mobile predator that readily colonises newly prepared wetland or dryland ricefields. As they colonise fields early, they are able to prey on pests before the latter increase to damaging population levels. Wolf spiders can consume 5-15 prey a day. Over three years, between 1974 and 1977, *wereng* caused the loss of 3 million tonnes of rice production. The International Rice Research Institute (IRRI) in the Philippines reacted quickly, breeding *wereng*-resistant rice varieties such as IR-26, 30, 24, 28, 32 and 34 to counter the threat posed by the insect. But, in turn, resistant *wereng* bio-types appeared that were able to feed off the new varieties and it was not until the release of IR-36 and 38 in 1977 that the outbreak was controlled.

For those people who support the new rice technology the continuous development of *wereng*-resistant rice strains has demonstrated the ability of rice breeders to deal with different problems successfully. In contrast, for its critics, it has illustrated the dangers inherent in narrowing the genetic base to such a degree, and the risks that the future holds.

In 1987 the government accepted that due to overuse some pesticides were becoming counter-productive in terms of pest management, and 57 varieties of broad spectrum insecticides on rice were banned, including those specifically linked to the *wereng* outbreaks of the 1970s and 1980s.

The Indonesian government embraced Integrated Pest Management (IPM) as the best way forward, a low-input system which builds on traditional strategies of pest management. IPM aims to integrate both biological and chemical pest control. Chemicals, while still being used as necessary, are only used in a way which is least disruptive to biological pest control.

Many experts have also expressed the view that the problem had its origins in the heavy subsidies on agro-chemicals that encouraged overuse. Since 1987, insecticide use has dropped by about 50 per cent while rice output has increased by 12 per cent. From the original 200,000 hectares, only about 20,000 hectares of rice land are now infested by the *wereng* pest.

Traditional Rice Pest Control in Bali

Control Type	Pest Control Method And Example
BIOLOGICAL — Natural	• Conservation of indigenous natural enemies like parasites, predators and pathogens
BIOLOGICAL — Applied	• Artificially increasing the numbers and effectiveness of indigenous natural enemies– herding ducks through rice padi, planting obnoxious smelling plants
AGRICULTURAL	• Timing of planting and harvesting • Crop rotation • Good husbandry–weeding, water control, ploughing, burning of rice stalks • Planting resistant varieties
PHYSICAL	• Physical removal of pests– handpicking pests off infected plants, trapping or catching of pests
TRADITIONAL	• Religious offerings • Scarecrows (*lelakut*) and flags • Bamboo drums, noise makers and wind chimes • Shouting

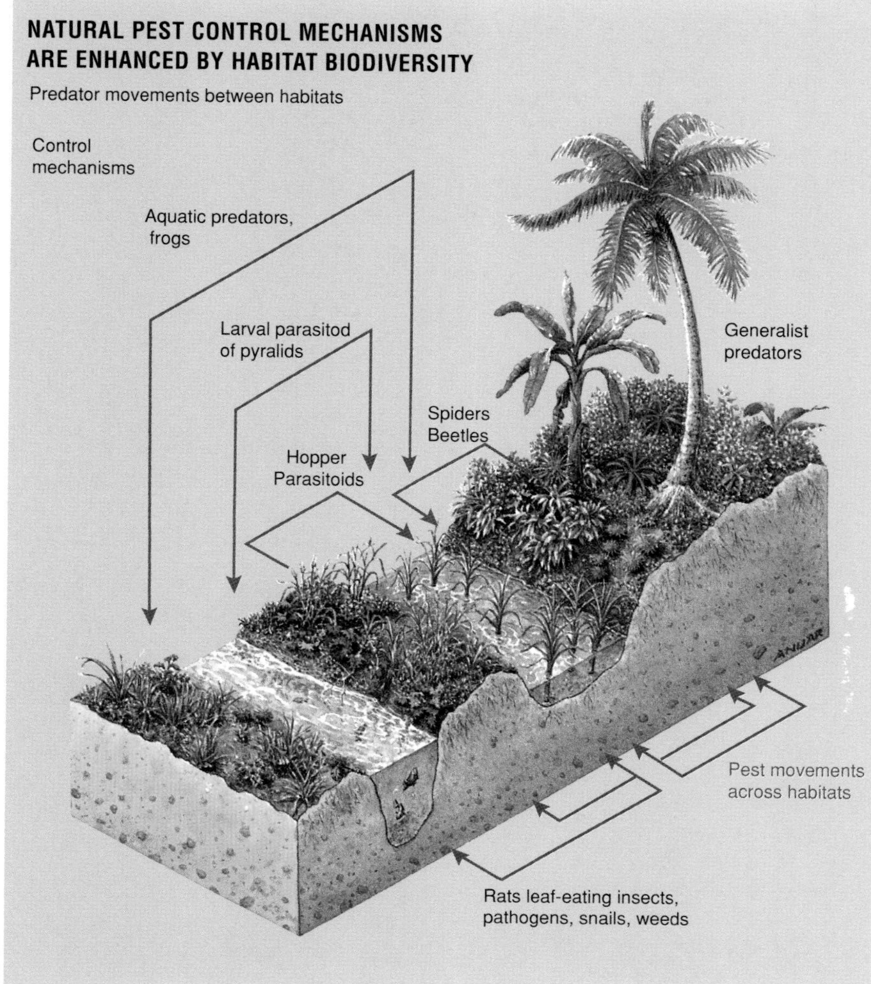

Both the adult wolf spider and spiderlings will prey on insect pests.

The brown planthopper (Nilaparvata lugens)

The brown planthopper can, in large numbers, attack susceptible rice varieties, causing hopperburn.

The Green Revolution in Rice Production

In 1980 Indonesia was the world's largest rice importer. Just five years later the country had become self-sufficient in rice production. This singular accomplishment was based on the dissemination, with massive government support, of the technology of the Green Revolution.

IRRI scientists study the effect of increased ultra-violet-B radiation on the structure and function of the rice plant. Here, they are measuring the level of ultraviolet-B radiation in a glasshouse experiment to study the impact of global climate change on rice growth and production.

The Role of the Government

The Green Revolution embraces the cultivation of new, quick-maturing, high-yielding rice varieties with large inputs of chemical fertilisers and pesticides and also with the benefits of improved irrigation.

An underlying characteristic of rice policy in Indonesia has been the assumption that rice is far too important a crop to be left to the vagaries of the market, and hence, direct government intervention in its production and marketing is essential. Regular shortfalls in production during the 1960s and 1970s, and the difficulties of procuring supplies from abroad made the achievement of domestic food security a national policy objective.

The Indonesian government has stimulated greater production by supporting prices on the one hand (by setting a floor price), and by subsidising inputs on the other. In the eight years prior to 1985, when self-sufficiency in rice was finally achieved, the government successively increased the support price for rice annually in an effort to raise output. For much of the last 15 years, Indonesian rice prices have been held at 20 per cent to 40 per cent above world prices. Fertiliser and pesticide subsidies have also been substantial, exceeding Rp.1,000 billion in 1987/88 (about US$500 million).

Seeds of Change

In 1966, the International Rice Research Institute (IRRI) in the Philippines released a new 'high yielding' variety of rice: IR-8. In Indonesia this 'miracle' rice was designated Peta Baru-8 (PB-8). Although rice breeding programmes in Indonesia dating from the early years of the century had produced intermediate or improved varieties, the release of IR-8 marks the beginning of the modern Green Revolution. In a number of respects it was a remarkable rice: it responded extremely well to applications of chemical fertilisers, was non-photoperiod sensitive and so could be grown (in theory) at any latitude, and yielded nearly 10 tonnes per hectare in trials. Indonesia's rice intensification programme was based on the dissemination of IR-8 and the varieties that were to follow it. By 1971, nearly a third of main season rice land was planted with modern varieties. Today, there are few farmers who continue to cultivate traditional varieties. Alongside this 'bio-chemical' component, there is also a 'mechanical' (tractors, hullers) and an 'institutional' (extension advice, credit) component.

Rice Intensification

Rice production can be increased either through extensification–by increasing the land area under cultivation–or through intensification, the raising of output per unit area. The former has been one of the objectives of the transmigration programme. But rice policy has been based primarily on the raising of production from existing riceland. This can be achieved either by raising yields or increasing the cropping ratio (the number of crops harvested each year from a piece of land), or both. To this end, since 1963, the government has introduced a plethora of programmes such as BIMAS (*Bimbingan Massal* or Mass Guidance). These have been designed to assist in the adoption of the New Rice Technology by giving farmers access to cheap credit, providing them with the advantages of cooperative organisation, and giving the procurement agency BULOG (*Badan Urusan Logistik* or the National Logistics Board) the means to buy rice at support prices. In 1968 the *rumus tani* or farmer's formula was introduced, explicitly linking the price of rice with the cost of fertilisers–with the aim of maintaining 'incentive parity'. Considerable sums were also invested in agricultural research and in improving the physical infrastructure, including irrigation and roads.

Since 1963, average yields have risen sharply. In Java, average yields in 1992 were 5.3 tonnes per hectare. However, the intensification programme has been accompanied by a transformation in village life. Farmers have been firmly incorporated into the money economy and the widening of inequalities and the dismantling of village institutions have become features of rural life. The role of new technology in this process is still disputed.

The production successes of the rice intensification programme are hard to refute. However, when the impacts of the new rice technology are examined at village level, clear interpretation of the situation is more difficult. Critics of the Green Revolution have focused on two issues. First, that it has been ecologically damaging, for example, when chemical pesticides are overused. Second, that the benefits of the technology have accrued to a small minority of wealthy farmers who have the resources and the power to

The mechanical component of the Green Revolution–a farmer uses his diesel tractor in the rice fields of Bondowoso, East Java

RICE PRODUCTION IN INDONESIA 1989-1994

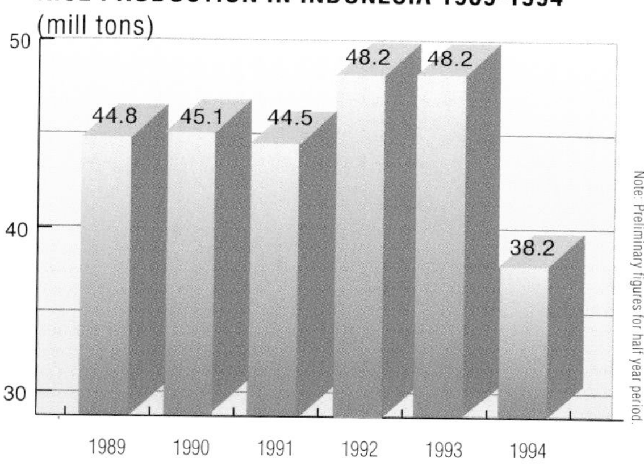

YIELD RATES OF RICE (kg/ha)

HIGH-YIELDING RICE VARIETIES (MODERN)

CropYear	Proportion of Total Area (%)
1968-69	6.1
1969-70	9.5
1970-71	12.9
1971-72	31.0
1972-73	34.7
1973-74	47.7
1974-75	NA
1975-76	53.2
1976-77	57.7
1977-78	59.5
1978-79	63.3
1979-80	68.3
1980-81	68.0
1981-82	74.5
1982-83	82.9
1983-84	81.8
1990	77.0

Note: Figures refer to area of main season rice land

use the technology to its full advantage and have then proceeded to accumulate land and further wealth and power. Therefore, although production may have increased, it has been at the expense of small, poor farmers who have been 'left out' of the process and been further impoverished as a result of these new developments. A key issue is whether technology *per se* is the culprit in this process of 'pauperisation'. Some experts maintain that since the release of IR-8 in the mid-1960s, the new rice technology has become increasingly 'smallholder friendly'. It has also benefited small farmers by enabling them to grow three rice crops a year and thus meet their own household rice needs while landless farm labourers have also benefitted by raising the demand for farm labour.

Farmers can now have their rice milled at small local hullers, which is cheaper than paying women to hand-pound the rice. Problems occur when the technology is disseminated in areas with rapidly growing populations, highly unequal patterns of land ownership, and where power is skewed in favour of a minority. But importantly, the latter two problems are institutional, not technical. Other experts widen the discussion and argue that a 'mechanical' revolution is also part and parcel of the seed-fertiliser complex. Thus, although farm machinery like tractors are uncommon, they will increasingly make inroads into rural Indonesia, displacing labour and side-lining poorer farmers unable to afford the large cash outlay required to acquire the machines for themselves. These changes may also affect men and women in different ways. Perhaps the most common mechanical innovation is the introduction of the power tiller. As land preparation is nearly always a task undertaken by men, this has led some scholars to argue that a 'feminisation' of agriculture is underway, in which men's work is displaced by machines, giving them the opportunity to work in non-farm activities and leaving the women in control of agriculture. Other mechanical innovations–such as the huller, for example–selectively displaced women. Where the source of the problem lies is still disputed. Some commentators would favour a technical interpretation, others a historical one, and still others one based on an understanding of the processes of agrarian change. With such varied physical, economic and social environments in Indonesia, it might well be that all three apply simultaneously.

Rice being threshed, West Java

The newly-developed IRRI stripper-gatherer system–which combines a stripper harvester and a thresher/cleaner into one machine–was first introduced in Bogor, Indonesia, in 1993. It is designed as an alternative to manual harvesting and threshing.

Rice being gathered after harvesting.

The Future

With the achievement of rice self-sufficiency, agriculture is unlikely to continue to receive the level of development funds and political attention it has previously enjoyed. The single, driving objective of rice self-sufficiency has been replaced by diffuse and multiple objectives. Agriculture will become even more commercialised and diversified, farmers will become more sophisticated and integrated, and the highly protected and inward-looking environment created by successive rice intensification programmes will gradually break down.

The government's aim to encourage diversification out of rice production has been pre-empted by some farmers. Studies from the mid-1980s show that for all the regions of Java, more than 50 per cent of rural household income comes from non-farm sources. In response to declining land resources and burgeoning needs, farmers are pursuing multiple livelihood strategies in which the Green Revolution is just one element in a diversified portfolio of activities encompassing both farm and non-farm endeavours.

Rice being winnowed in East Java.

Life in a Modern Rice Village

Case studies have revealed that Balinese and Javanese cultivators of irrigated rice often supplement this with an array of other strategies. The growing of vegetable crops, and activities such as food selling and home based retailing often provide additional sources of income for the rice farmer.

A Rice Village

Typically, in a rice growing village in West Java, all the land surrounding the houses will be under intensive cultivation. Such villages are generally made up of several hamlets, and the farmers' rice fields are dependent on a semi-technical irrigation system drawing water from a nearby river, for example. Those who use this water source are obliged to provide a couple of days' labour every year to keep the canal system operating, and they will pay a small fee to the community official responsible for water management.

An alternative source of employment–a farmer has set up a food stall outside his house.

Aerial view of a village in West Java , rice fields surround the settlement.

Fields being ploughed using oxen, ready for planting rice.

Land Tenure and Crops Grown

Many of the farmers in these villages own very little land, sometimes as little as 0.25 hectares. These small plots are frequently the result of land being divided up between children on their parents death. Sometimes one child will buy his siblings' shares of land from them. In many villages, few families will own more than one hectare. Individuals may find that they have to sell plots of their land to meet medical expenses or school fees, for example.

Farmers with very small holdings are pleased to sharecrop the land of other people. Today, however, with the average size of holdings decreasing, tenancy is not common. Farmers with relatively large holdings prefer to cultivate them with hired labour, and smallholders often find themselves working as agricultural labourers on the land of neighbours. Among this group of small farmers there are reciprocal relations by which they employ each other when they need additional labour during the weeks when rice fields are being prepared for the next season. Within this same group, the wives invite each other to plant, apply fertiliser, weed and harvest. Landless families are now finding it increasingly hard to obtain agricultural work of any kind.

It is possible to grow two crops of high yielding rice a year. In many villages, in the dry season from June to September, vegetable crops are planted, not because water is in short supply but because the government has begun encouraging diversification. In the 1970s, when Indonesia was still far from self-sufficient in rice production, farmers were expected to cultivate rice three times a year. These farmers are pleased about the change in policy because they know that they can get better results from the soil with crop rotation; also, they can obtain better prices for non-rice crops. Rice prices are closely regulated, and although the floor price is raised every year, the cost of chemical inputs like fertiliser and insecticide goes up too.

It is still possible to find *sawah* being prepared in the traditional way. If a farmer does not own one, he employs a neighbour who owns a water-buffalo to plough the land, while he himself repairs the bunds

around the fields with the help of hired labourers. Many villages have no tractors because fields have been dug out from undulating land and it is difficult to lift tractors up and down the terraces. In places where there is no terracing and fields are much larger, the rental of a tractor can reduce ploughing expenses to a quarter of the cost of manual labour. Rice production often involves no form of mechanisation apart from the small, diesel-powered huller where local farmers have their rice milled.

Ducks may be raised during the weeks after the rice harvest when the fields are being prepared for the new crop, and fish cultivated in small ponds. Fish and duck eggs are often important supplements to family diet and income. Small children may be used to take the ducks out every day, keeping them off fields recently treated with insecticide.

Limited Employment Options

With a growing population, only a small percentage of the people in villages still depend on agriculture for their whole income. Many must search for additional sources of income. Some individuals find employment as agricultural labourers when farm work is available, or they may act as traders, taking small quantities of village produce to the sub-district town to sell to wholesale merchants from urban areas. Women may run a *warung* in the front room of their house, selling cooked food and household necessities like soap powder to local people.

Unfortunately, there is very little scope for non-agricultural employment in the village. For many people, daily, weekly and seasonal commuting to places outside the village, for example, the city, is the only way to obtain employment. There are some jobs, like driving a minibus, that enable young men to work locally, but more typically they must seek work as unskilled labourers on construction sites in cities like Jakarta, returning to their villages only periodically.

The farmers in the village take their vegetables to the local market, Dieng, Central Java

HOME GARDENS

Home gardens are a feature of villages throughout Indonesia. They are important for two reasons: first, the vegetables, fruit and other commodities that they produce provide much of the supplementary food needed by the family; and second, they represent a source of household income, for products can be easily marketed at any time.

The typical home garden gives an impression of disorder and even neglect at first glance but a closer inspection shows that it is really a stratified and complex artificial ecosystem. Close to the ground there are cooking herbs, together with sweet potatoes and vegetables like tomatoes and chilli.

There are also likely to be several cassava plants, whose roots and leaves can both be eaten. Vines that produce beans, squash or edible berries are often cultivated on bamboo trellises around the edge of the garden, along with bananas, while one or two tall fruit trees and sometimes coconut palms provide protection or shade for the smaller plants growing beneath them.

1. Banana
2. Papaya
3. Coconut
4. Cassava
5. Sweet potato
6. Cabbage
7. Tomato
8. Chilli

The Asmat of Irian Jaya have an intimate relationship with the forest, expressed in rituals like this sago ceremony

Many people still rely on the gathering of forest products for their livlihood. This Dayak from West Kalimantan is cleaning dammar.

Pesticides being sprayed at an apple plantation at Batu, East Java.

Communal planting by swidden cultivators, Lampung.

FIELD AND FOREST

Statistics show that less than one fifth of Indonesia's agricultural land is classified as *sawah*–land for wet rice cultivation. In other words, more than 80 per cent is being used in other ways, to grow dryland crops (which includes dry rice), graze livestock, cultivate plantation crops, or lies temporarily fallow. Although rice may be the dominant single crop of the Archipelago, its cultivation still accounts for only a small proportion of agricultural land. This chapter describes that 'residual' part of the Indonesian agricultural economy which is not wet rice.

'Rice', to many, means wet rice. Yet rice grown on dry land is also highly important in the Indonesian context. It tends to embrace differing environmental and cultural worlds, being concentrated in more remote, forested areas and is often associated with tribal groups–although pressure on land in established wet rice areas is forcing sedentary agriculturalists to move into the forest and become incipient shifting cultivators.

As the chapter will show, the environmental and economic cannot be divorced from the cultural. The rituals of swidden cultivation are an integral part of the cultivation process and have persisted in some places even though many traditional shifting cultivators may have embraced Christianity. The same inter-linkages between economy and society are evident in hunting-gathering societies. Nor is hunting and gathering unproductive; in terms of returns to time expended, it is more efficient and productive than most agricultural systems. The tendency to view agricultural systems as a hierarchy from 'advanced' wet rice culture 'down' to 'primitive' swiddening and hunting and gathering, makes little sense in these terms. In the drier parts of Indonesia, non-rice food crops, known as *palawijia*, play an important role. These include maize, cassava, soybean, groundnuts and sweet potato. Sometimes such crops are grown–during the dry season-on *sawah*, but mostly they are cultivated on land which is unsuited to wet rice. Today, attention is being re-directed towards this important sector, long ignored while the emphasis of research and development was squarely on rice. On some islands in eastern Indonesia a highly distinctive and traditional form of agriculture is the management of the *Borassus* or *lontar* palm. Many dryland crops are also grown for sale either domestically or for foreign markets. Tree crops like oil palm, coconut and rubber are important exports while vegetables, fruits and poultry are in demand by the expanding urban population.

Shifting Cultivation

Shifting cultivation or 'slash and burn' agriculture is of considerable importance in parts of Indonesia. Estimates suggest that about 11 million hectares and six million people are involved, although these figures vary depending on different definitions of shifting or swidden (an old English word meaning 'burnt' field) cultivation. A piece of land is normally cultivated from between one and three years and then left fallow when the soil's fertility is depleted. Cultivators may return to the field after its nutrients have been restored.

Dayak woman planting rice in East Kalimantan.

Definition and Types

Over 25 years ago, Spencer defined shifting cultivation as 'a long-range rotation of land-use, ecologically in balance with tropical environments.' Such a definition draws attention to the alternation of cultivation and fallow on a piece of land and the fact that such a system is often sustainable, as long as land and population density remain in balance. Most shifting cultivators move over limited areas, using lands to which they have traditional rights, and return to the original plot after some years. They are not 'nomads', although in the past some were active colonisers, frequently opening new forests to cultivation. In some remote areas, long-fallow shifting cultivation is still practised, one or two years of cropping being followed by 20 years of fallow. Far more common in Indonesia today, though, are shorter fallows–ten years or even five–where some fields may be under permanent farming of tree or food crops. A fallow period of about ten years is necessary for the natural restoration of soil fertility following cropping. A change to shorter fallows may lead to invasion of light-loving weeds, especially grasses, although grasses are sometimes deliberately encouraged for hunting or cattle grazing.

The chief areas of shifting cultivation lie mainly in those areas with a relatively sparse population. Kalimantan has the most land under shifting cultivation, followed by Sumatra, Maluku and Irian Jaya, but in terms of numbers of people involved, Sumatra, Sulawesi and East Nusa Tenggara are ahead of Kalimantan. The impact of growing numbers and increasing needs for cash income have everywhere generated a variety of spontaneous adjustments to traditional techniques, while external pressures from government agencies have sometimes forced other changes.

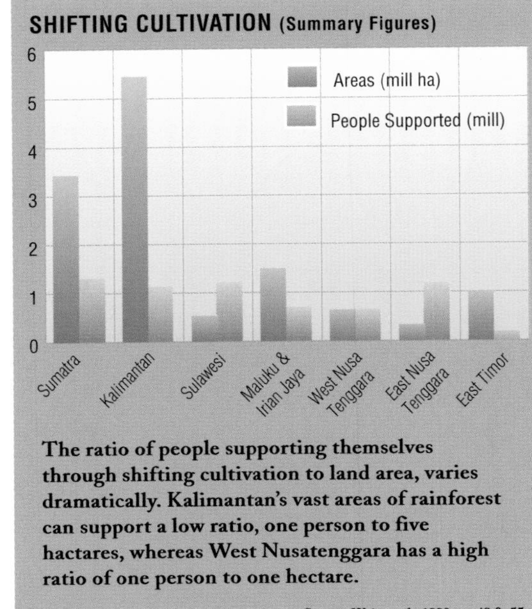

The ratio of people supporting themselves through shifting cultivation to land area, varies dramatically. Kalimantan's vast areas of rainforest can support a low ratio, one person to five hactares, whereas West Nusatenggara has a high ratio of one person to one hectare.

Source: Weinstock, 1990, pp 48 & 55

A forested area on Pulau Rempang, Riau, is cleared for shifting cultivation. Note the farmer's temporary field house and the secondary forest in the background.

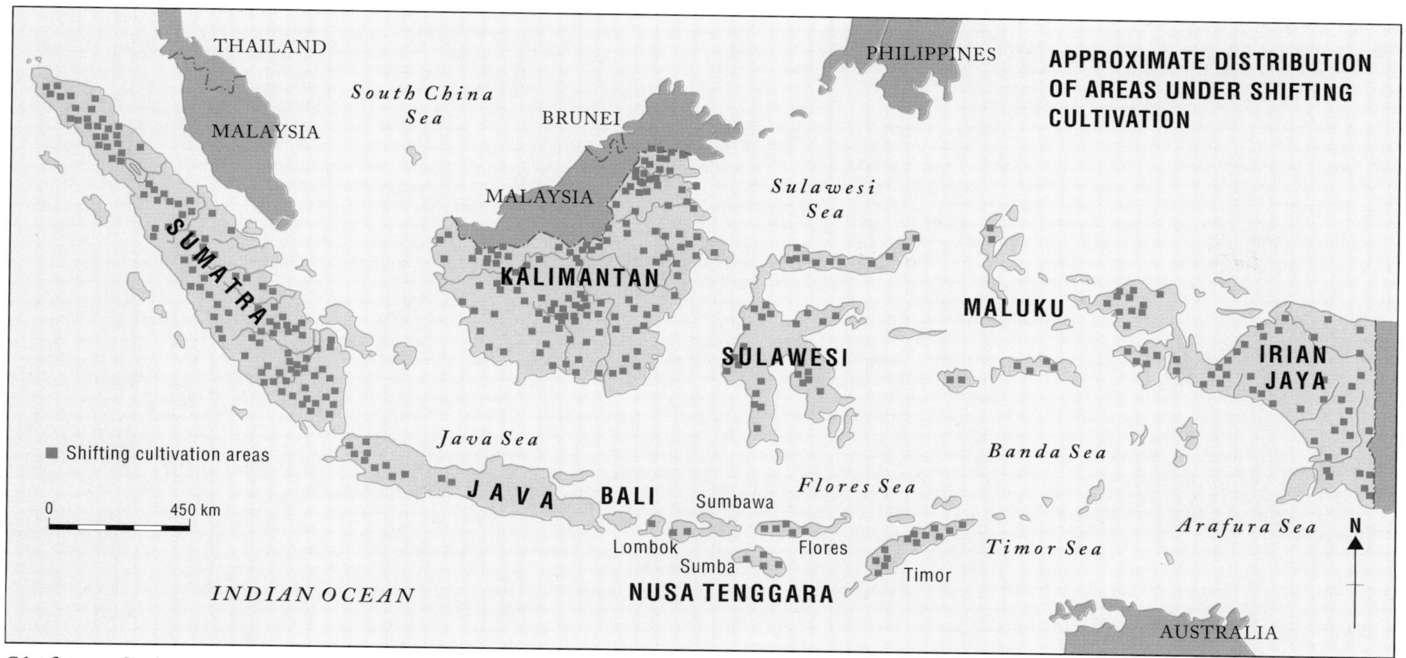

Shifting Cultivation Cycle

Typically, shifting cultivation is practised in forested areas. The forest may be 'primary', uncut for many years, or 'secondary' re-growth. The latter is often preferred by farmers. The modern logging industry has penetrated even remote areas of Indonesia, so that much of the remaining forest is in various stages of regrowth. Such logged-over sites are easier for shifting cultivators to work. After burning the site, crops such as rice or corn will be sown using digging sticks, which barely disturbs the soil. Protection of crops from deer, wild pigs, monkeys and birds often requires the construction of small shelters, which people inhabit for some months. If burning has been successful (more ash means more soil nutrients) and the rains are adequate, reasonable yields can be obtained, at least for a year or two. To obtain cash incomes, shifting cultivators in forest areas may seek seasonal employment with logging companies. They also collect saleable forest products, such as rattans, timber or *gaharu* (aloe wood), or plant useful species in their fallows, which in a few years become available for harvesting. Rubber, rattans, sugar palms and fruits are common crops of 'enriched' fallows, while permanent agro-forests may develop near villages, yielding a steady income from the sale of fruits, vegetables, resins and fibres. Those with access to markets may use chain-saws to clear much larger areas than in the past, and then grow rice for sale. This behaviour is more destructive of forests than traditional systems. Sometimes the pre-existing vegetation may not be forest, but only a light scrub or even grass. A different tool, such as a hoe or plough, is used to prepare the soil. Crop yields tend to be poorer than on formerly forested sites; shifting cultivators will usually avoid such areas unless they have the capital to purchase fertiliser and buy or hire cattle for ploughing. Such semi-permanent systems lie midway between traditional shifting cultivation, with long fallow periods, and permanent field agriculture.

In parts of east Indonesia where the dry season is long, open forest or grassland is the natural vegetation. Here, competition exists between free-ranging cattle and shifting cultivators, and farmers have to spend time and effort constructing and maintaining fences to prevent damage to their crops. A solution is to plant leguminous trees in the fields, the branches of which are lopped and fed to tethered cattle. The trees also increase soil fertility by fixing nitrogen, thus improving both crop yields and cattle quality.

Yet another type is the 'wet shifting cultivation' or *paya* system, of West Kalimantan. The fields are not levelled or bunded but more productive wet rice varieties are planted in place of dry rice as the land floods in the rains. Some of the area will be left fallow and the crop rotated. *Paya* cultivation may eventually give way to wet rice cultivation. These different cultivation systems may occur next to each other with a patch of *paya* or *sawah* at the bottom of a hill and a dry swidden on the slope above it.

Local people have an immense knowledge of the forest and its products, a knowledge rarely appreciated by government officers, who see only large areas of 'unproductive' fallow land and small burnt patches.

Dry rice growing on deforested land, Riau, Sumatra.

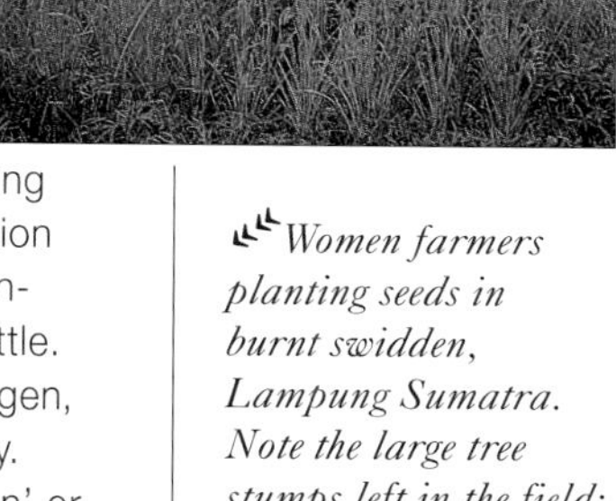

Women farmers planting seeds in burnt swidden, Lampung Sumatra. Note the large tree stumps left in the field: they are too big to remove without heavy machinery.

Temporary field house, Lampung Sumatra.

The Swidden Ecosystem

In forest-based shifting cultivation systems, the swidden plot may be viewed as a temporary gap in the canopy. After a brief period of cultivation, normal processes of vegetation colonisation and re-growth will take their course. While it is a larger gap than results from natural tree fall, the average size of isolated clearings–between one and two hectares–is considerably smaller than timber camps and log ponds.

A forest clearing after it has been burned, East Kalimantan

The Swidden Cycle and The Forest Ecosystem

The location of the swidden plot, may dictate its ecology. Factors involved in the farmer's choice might include a preference for either secondary or old growth forest, existing rights over certain lands, or a desire to farm near kin. There are Indonesian localities where cycles of shifting cultivation have long persisted. The character of the forest has gradually changed as a result of human activity, to support a different mix of species. Examples also exist of shortened fallow cycles or lengthened cropping periods, where the ability of the forest to regenerate becomes impeded. Population pressure may be responsible, but equally important is expanded cash crop production or perhaps a decision to raise cattle, promoting grassland at the expense of forest. Where numbers are increasing, people will often make adjustments to their agricultural systems.

❶ Cutting and Drying the Vegetation

Old growth forest is felled before secondary forest, with valuable honey trees (*Koompassia excelsa*) and fruit trees left standing. The heavy work of clearing the forest is a male task. The stumps of larger trees are usually left in the ground as suckers from them, and the shallow nature of cultivation, assists later re-growth. During the drying period, insects, fungi and bacteria are active, initiating the process of decay. Many seeds are destroyed at this time.

❷ Burning the Cut Growth

Burning occurs just before the main rainy season and usually takes place from the edge of the clearing toward the centre, avoiding the risk of fires escaping into the surrounding forest. The main purpose of the burn is to clear a space for planting, while at the same time releasing nutrients from the forest vegetation. While some elements, especially nitrogen, are lost during the burn, the ash provides potassium and improves the availability of calcium and magnesium, as soil acidity decreases. Levels of organic matter are high because partially burned material gradually decays as the crops grow. Depending on soil quality, between one and three years of cropping are possible before significant fertility decline occurs.

THE SWIDDEN CYCLE

❸ Planting and Weeding

Planting should begin quickly after the burn, before the resulting ash bed, with its important nutrients, is blown or leached away. Furthermore, heavy rains may cause the bare soil to erode, especially on sloping sites. Planting is usually done in communal groups, each field being completed in a day. Ceremony and ritual surrounds the first sowing of the main staple, usually rice, but is absent with lower-status crops. Often a number of different rice varieties will be planted, some better able to tolerate problem conditions, others for their flavour or yield. In two Apo Kayan villages in Kalimantan, 45 varieties of hill rice and 13 of glutinous rice were found, although not all on the one plot. Shallow holes are made with digging sticks into which the seeds are dropped. Regular rains encourage rapid growth.

Weed seeds are blown or carried to the site, or are already present below the surface. They flourish in the open conditions, taking nutrients, and must be frequently removed for good yields to be achieved. More weeds are present in a swidden cut from secondary forest and more work is needed to control them. Tenacious grasses such as *alang-alang* (*Imperata cylindrica*), appear especially after the first year. They become more of a problem if cultivation continues for longer periods or fallows are shortened, inhibiting the growth of other plants and tree seedlings and impeding forest regeneration.

❹ Harvesting

Harvests of upland rice are reasonable in good years but vary with weather conditions, and especially rainfall. The best seed is preserved for next year's planting. Farmers usually live on their fields in the weeks prior to the harvest, protecting them from wild pigs, deer and birds. Harvesting is done with a finger knife as local rice varieties tend to be tall and bend under the weight of the grain. Many subsidiary crops are also cultivated, either simultaneously with the rice or immediately following it. After the main crop is reaped, fruit trees, rattans or rubber may be planted in the fallow.

A swidden farmer has built his hut next to his swidden fields.

❺ Fallowing

After one or two harvests the swidden will be allowed to revert to forest. Large-leaved pioneer tree species–such as Macaranga in Kalimantan–quickly become dominant, together with climbers and thorny shrubs. Grasses and herbs, initially prevalent, will be shaded out after three or four years, unless the cropping period has been extended. A closed canopy secondary forest will be established in about ten years, after which the level of nutrients in the vegetation will have been restored sufficiently for the cycle to be repeated.

Social Aspects of Swidden Cultivation

Shifting cultivation is not a primitive farming system practised by ignorant people, but the core of a well-developed complex of economic and cultural activities. Its yearly cycle is the backdrop for all village labour, both within and away from the swidden fields. Although several ethnic groups in Indonesia practise shifting cultivation, much of our detailed knowledge comes from studies in Kalimantan.

Ritual offering placed in new rice field at the time of planting by the Limbai Dayak, Melawi River, West Kalimantan. It contains a chicken, vegetables, fruit and cooked rice for the spirits of the field.

» Houses for sawmill employees and their families.

Collecting rattan in the forest, West Kalimantan

The Centrality of the Swidden

The main feature distinguishing the Dayak people in the Meratus Mountains of South Kalimantan from other ethnic groups, and in particular the Malay Banjaraese, is that their rituals are aimed at beautifying swidden rice farming. The rice-growing unit, which in most cases comprises an extended family, is the most important social group. The range of individual crops and the many cultivars of rice, vegetables and fruit produced on the swidden fill a variety of food needs. After the birth of a child the mother faces a number of taboos on the types of foods that she is allowed to consume. These are identified as particular varieties of fruit and vegetables, so that a wide range of cultivars becomes essential. The growing child and the growing swidden are compared in this society, highlighting what has been described as an 'aesthetic of diversity'. Such diversity is encouraged by planting patterns on the swidden itself. Ritually important plants such as turmeric, ginger and bright-leaved coleus are placed in the centre of the field; sweet potatoes, green beans or squash are grown in patches around stumps where they will not compete with the rice; cucumber and millet which ripen at the same time as the rice are sown together with the rice seed. Other crops are planted to mark field boundaries, while patches of herbs among the rice 'beautify' the plot as well as having particular uses. Between five and 25 varieties of glutinous and non-glutinous rices are grown, sometimes subdivided into early and late maturing types.

Like many others, the farmers of Gerai, in southwest Kalimantan, believe that rice has human ancestry: it provides the gift of its grain and must feel 'needed' or it might withdraw from the relationship. It must therefore receive offerings at planting and be surrounded by ritual plants to protect and nurture it. While the rice is ripening, large red flowers bloom throughout the field, providing 'lights' showing it to be among friends. The ability to produce a good harvest indicates the spiritual worth of the farmer. Rice is the supreme food, which its cultivators believe must be eaten daily to maintain health.

Omens and Rituals

When selecting a plot, farmers particularly note the size and type of regrowth vegetation. Indicator plants such as wild banana reveal a good quality soil, but soil colour and taste may also be checked. Omens are also highly influential. Among the Meratus Dayak, the farmer examines a likely plot, then analyses his nightly dreams before making a decision. The Kantu' of West Kalimantan pay great attention to the flight and calls of seven 'spirit birds' which the farmer tries to contact while seated on the potential site. The white-rumped shama is a 'cool bird', protecting upland sites from drought, while the scarlet-rumped trogon is a 'hot bird', preventing flooding in low-lying areas. The position of constellations such as the Pleiades or Orion indicate the time for clearing. Once the field has been planted, work may be prohibited on the day of the full moon, if a rainbow is seen, or if snakes or deer are encountered while people are travelling to the field. The Limbai of the Melawi River in West Kalimantan do not farm forest in which a death or injury once occurred; as much of their land is now scrub and grassland, these patches of untouched forest stand out clearly. Other intact forest includes *kramat*, or sacred groves.

Events in the rice-growing calendar are accompanied by appropriate rituals which are almost always conducted by *adat* leaders. On the occasion of forest clearing, offerings are made. These invariably include rice, betel nut, salt and eggs, and prayers are delivered to the different spirits of trees and rice deities. The day of communal rice-planting necessitates further offerings to the rice spirits, and these may be placed in the centre of the field. The Limbai include sacred fertility stones among the offerings, daubed with chicken blood inside a basket, together with rice and *keladi* (*Colocasia esculenta*). The Meratus Dayak construct a platform in the centre of the field, on which are placed ritual offerings and decorations; special herbs are planted underneath. Even Moslem Banjarese shifting cultivators in the Meratus Mountains, use the Dayak-made *kurung-kurung*. This is a long bamboo pole with a rattle at one end, designed to provide joyful music during communal rice planting. Some Maloh and Iban households possess 'sacred rice', which is sown in specially demarcated sections of the field, presented with offerings and harvested separately. The completion of the rice cycle is followed everywhere by communal harvest feasting.

The Division of Labour

As in many Indonesian societies, growing crops entails a division of labour between men and women. The initial selection, clearing of large trees and burning of a plot are regarded as men's work, both men and women participate in the communal activity of sowing. Once that is completed, the nurturing of the plants, especially weeding, becomes the responsibility of the women. Women are also the main harvesters, using the finger knife to remove only the ripe heads, and leaving the 'body' of the rice undamaged. Men take over again in transporting the grain in baskets while both sexes may be involved in threshing. Women previously used to pound the unhusked grain by hand, but mechanical mills are now available in some districts. During the crop growing period, men are free to engage in other pursuits, which include collecting forest products such as rattan and ironwood (*Eusideroxylon zwagerei*), hunting and fishing or perhaps working for timber companies. After the rice harvest, the dry season is best for panning for gold, as stream levels drop or tapping rubber from trees grown in fallows. Meanwhile, other crops are harvested on the swidden and the search for a new plot must begin.

The Case of the Schwaner Mountains

The Schwaner Mountains, on the borders of West and Central Kalimantan, form one of the more remote regions of the provinces. Part of the mountain range was declared a National Park, but there are timber concessions on the lower slopes. When one of the concessionaires arrived in 1982, Dayak villagers living in the forest on the Central Kalimantan side could not communicate in Bahasa Indonesia and had no access to government services such as schools and health posts. Their farming system was based on shifting cultivation, with rattan being planted in the fallows and sold as a cash crop. Many animals and birds were hunted and forest products collected, such as aloe wood (*gaharu*), or the irregularly fruiting but oil-rich illipe nut (*tengkawang*, *Shorea sp.*).

Eleven years later there are schools (the teachers paid by the concessionaire) and even a generator-operated television 'dish' for each village, one of the few government initiatives in the district. People are now familiar with the national language and communicate easily with outsiders. Many young men are working for the concession while women grow vegetables for sale at the timber camps. Local livelihood systems basically remain intact, though the loggers help themselves to forest resources, such as honey, wild rattans or fruit, which the villagers believe belong to them. Some pressure is being applied by the company for adoption of wet rice cultivation and one village has begun to lay out *sawah*, although all retain their dry fields. While their isolation has been reduced, these villages have become quite dependent on the timber company, which has provided them with services that are otherwise unavailable.

This dependency is even more acute for their Dayak counterparts on the West Kalimantan side, who are largely surrounded by *alang-alang* and fast running out of accessible forested lands for making dry fields. Perceiving their situation to be 'critical', the company has promoted rapid agricultural change. The company's aim is to encourage villagers to adopt wet rice cultivation where possible, but otherwise to change to permanent dry rice by working the grassland with company-supplied hoes, free fertiliser and pesticide.

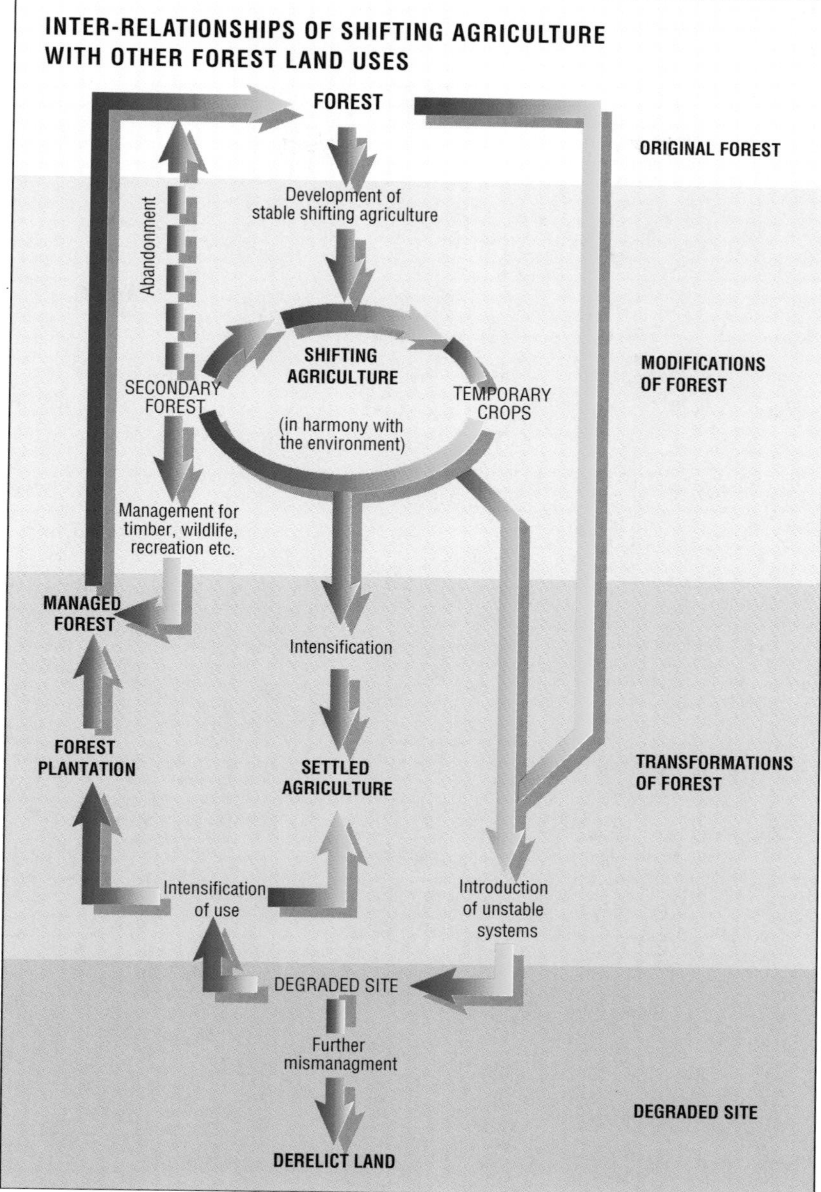

Banjarese Muslim shifting cultivators from the Meratus Mountains, South Kalimantan, have adopted the musical instrument, kurung-kurung, from local Dayak for use in their rice planting ceremonies. The long bamboo poles with a rattle provide pleasant music to accompany rice planting. The bearers of the pole precede the line of male planters down the hillside. It is possible that the ancestors of these farmers were themselves Dayak.

Hunter-Gatherers

The mobility of hunting-gathering groups in Indonesia is an adaptation to the tropical rainforest environment they inhabit. Instead of being isolated groups of 'primitive' peoples, historically, they have had contact with settled agriculturalists and were participants in the international trade of rainforest products. However, as these habitats disappear with modernisation, their way of life is becoming increasingly untenable.

Due to their need for mobility, the dwellings of this Kubu group are simple structures made from forest materials.

A beauty of the Musang tribe, on a tributary of the Iwan-a left hand tributary of the Kayan River, Kalimantan. Her beads and other ornaments were bartered from Dayak in exchange for baskets, mats and rhinoceros horn.

These Punan baskets are made of woven rattan.

Forest Nomadic People

Perhaps the two best known hunting-gathering groups in Indonesia today are the Kubu of Sumatra and the Punan of Kalimantan ;. There is no reliable demographic information but in total they probably do not exceed 10,000 people. Smaller groups like the Toala of Sulawesi have already been absorbed by surrounding populations. However, the terms 'Kubu' and 'Punan' do not refer to homogeneous tribal groups. Instead, they are cover terms, used by coastal and lowland populations, to denote small, mobile groups which broadly share the same ecological niche in interior forests and are perceived as 'primitive' and 'backward'.

These various nomad societies who live in Indonesia's forests comprise a culturally and linguistically diverse collection of differently named groups, representing a sophisticated adaptation to rainforest environments. A traditional, popular view of hunter-gatherers is that they are the remnant populations of an early, technologically simple stage of evolution from which the more complex economic and cultural systems of settled agriculturalists have developed. Recent research suggests that this view is misleading, and that while hunting and foraging economies were certainly more common in the distant past, some previously settled cultivators also adopted a more mobile forest-based existence to take advantage of the opportunities offered by the abundance of the rainforests.

Indeed, hunter-gatherers in Indonesia do not form distinct and separate societies from the surrounding farming communities. Like the Malays, Batak, Minangkabau and Dayak, they are Austronesian language speakers and share many of the cultural attributes of their neighbours. Furthermore, historically, forest nomads have had close social, economic and commercial relations with agriculturalists, and for a considerable time have been linked into the international trade in rainforest products.

The major subgroups of the Kubu are found scattered throughout the east coast lowlands of Sumatra and into the foothills of the Barisan range. Those usually referred to as Kubu are located in the Palembang and Jambi area of southern Sumatra. However, to the north-west there are several named groups such as the Mamak (Mamaq), Sakai, Akit, Talang, Tapung and Lubu. The main groups of Punan usually dwell in the headwater regions of Bornean rivers, although small numbers are found nearer the coast in East Kalimantan. Among the main subgroups are the Bukat-Ukit, the Aput-Busang, Merah, Basap, Kelai-Segah and Murung.

Trade in Forest Products

Archaeological evidence indicates that, about 4,000 years ago, the ancestors of present-day Indonesians lived in forest caves, used stone tools and survived by hunting, collecting and fishing. By the early centuries of the first millennium AD, Southeast Asian forest products were being traded to India and China in an emerging pattern of world trade. Interior forest hunters and collectors were vital in supplying these commodities to the settled coastal traders in return for metal tools, beads, brassware, ceramics, textiles, salt and tobacco, products they could not produce themselves.

The forest product trade continued to be important during the European colonial period, and prior to the rapid increase in earnings from raw timber, estate crops, and minerals during the early 20th century, forest products were a vital source of revenue for the local populations and for the colonial administration. Even today, forest products are still important in trade and are significant elements in local economies.

Lifestyle Patterns

Nevertheless, the forest dwellers also had to meet their local subsistence needs. As populations expanded up the major rivers into the interior, so it is likely that the collection of wild sago (*Eugeissona utilis*) and other foods and materials from the forest, along with hunting, became increasingly important. In some areas sago flour is still eaten by forest nomads, as well as tender sago shoots. Hunting ground animals like wild pig and deer was an important undertaking. They used spears and packs of dogs. Arboreal creatures like civet cats, squirrels and macaques as well as different kinds of birds were hunted with blowpipes and poisoned darts. Some nomads fished with hook-and-line, cast-nets and floating-nets, harpoons and poisoned derris root (tuber). They would also have collected shellfish and forest fruits and vegetables.

WEALTH FROM THE FOREST

The rainforests are abundant in resiniferous trees, and the great variety of resins or 'plant fluids', generally called damar in Indonesia, were historically sought after in Asian markets as illuminants, sealants, glues, glazes, colourants, paints and medicines; and as food sources. Some are still used in incense, perfumes and cosmetics. An early trade item collected from interior Sumatra is benzoin, used as incense and for medicinal purposes. An aromatic medicinal wood was *gaharu* bark or lignum aloes (*Aquilaria microcarpa*). 'Dragon's blood' was a general term applied to a number of red resins from a variety of Southeast Asian plants; one such was the *rotan jaranang* (*Daemonorops didymophyllus*), used as an aromatic drug and a dye. Another widely-known early trade item collected from interior northern Sumatra and Borneo was camphor, especially popular in Chinese markets. Camphor, which forms in the crevices and the decayed heart of old trees of the species *Dryobanalops aromatica*, was used in medicines and as a fumigant and incense. Of the fauna of commercial significance were species of cave-dwelling swift, such as *Collocalia fuciphaga*, whose nests–constructed from strands of glutinous saliva–are a Chinese delicacy and prized as an aphrodisiac. Bezoar stones, used as a medicine, are found in the gall bladders and intestines of certain monkeys (*Semnopithecus hosei* and *S. rubicundus*). Rhinoceros 'horn' was sought for its curative properties and as an aphrodisiac; anteater scales for magical charms; feathers of tropical birds (right) for decoration; carved 'ivory' from the hardened casque of the helmeted hornbill (left), for containers and jewellery; and deer antlers for carving and decoration.

There was traditionally no single dwelling. Presumably in the distant past convenient caves were used. Some shelters were simple lean-tos made of saplings, bamboo, palm-leaves and tree-bark, or low raised platforms; others were huts either on the ground or on stilts. Some groups such as the Sakai of Sumatra built multi-family houses in the Malay style, while various Borneo groups erected longhouses like the neighbouring Dayak.

Some nomadic bands were more mobile than others, moving in small groups from one base to another over long distances, and usually on foot. Others organised themselves by establishing base-camps and dividing themselves up into smaller groups consisting of a few families each, to exploit different sections of forest, returning periodically to the main camp. This mobile way of life required a flexible form of social organisation: relative age was an important social principle, and bands were commonly led by older respected men. Social classes did not exist, and small families of husband, wife and children were the basic units of social and economic organisation.

A Disappearing Society

Given growing contacts with settled groups, many hunter-gatherers have recently settled down, adopted agricultural lifestyles to cultivate both subsistence and cash crops, and embraced Islam or Christianity. Some have even been absorbed by such groups as the Malays and Minangkabau. As forests are exploited and cleared for roads, plantations and mines, the resources on which nomads depend have decreased and in some regions disappeared altogether.

Governments, from the colonial period onwards, have had policies to resettle these groups into permanent communities. Basic facilities such as schools and clinics have been provided for that purpose. There would seem to be no place for a hunting-gathering society in the modern world, unless it is preserved in restricted areas of national parks and forest reservations where it can continue, while nomads also serve as guides, park-rangers and as objects of tourist fascination.

An Asmat hunter from Irian Jaya returns from an expedition in the forest with a wild pig he has killed.

FISHING EQUIPMENT

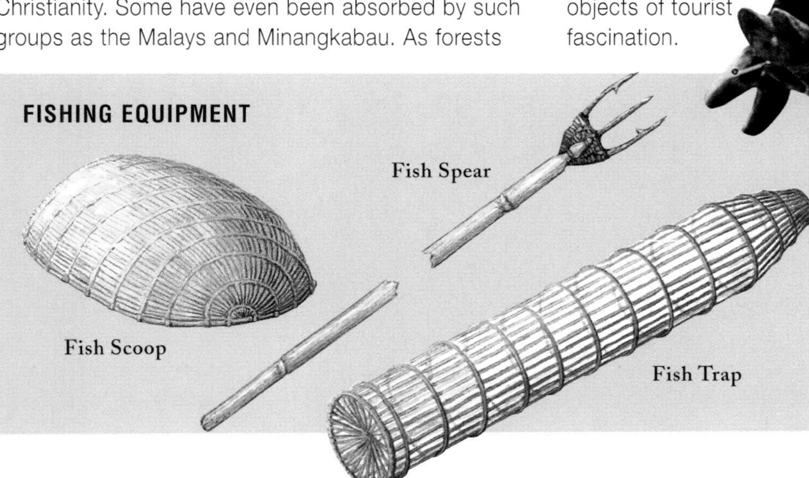

Dryland Farming and Livestock Systems

Dryland farming is either rainfed or dependent on the residual water which remains in irrigated fields following the harvest of the main crop. Such farming systems usually embody a complex association of plants and animals, including at least 50 species of annual vegetable and fruit crops, and over 100 perennial species of trees and shrubs.

❶ *Cloves*

❷ *Coconuts*

❸ *Bee hives*

❹ *Bamboo*

Features of Dryland Systems

Dryland farming in Indonesia basically occurs in areas where wet rice is not farmed. This type of farming system can take many forms. Dryland systems vary according to location, access to capital and labour, the suitability of the land for cultivation and the extent of risk associated with the degree of uncertainty relating to rainfall, water supplies and markets. The guiding philosophy of farmers engaged in these kinds of subsistence systems tends to be risk minimisation rather than profit maximisation.

There are also, however, constraints to developing dryland areas which include low soil fertility, acidity combined with sometimes toxic levels of manganese and aluminium, and erosion. Development therefore requires careful management and attention to conservation.

In areas of Indonesia with a long wet season, it is estimated that around 20 million hectares of dryland has agricultural potential. In addition there are also millions of hectares more of dryland in areas with a short wet season, particularly in eastern Indonesia which are also suitable for improved systems of farming.

Dryland Crops

Upland or dry rice is grown in the wetter regions of West Java, Sumatra and Kalimantan. It may either be seasonally irrigated or rainfed. Early maturing maize is planted at the beginning of the wet season in September and then intercropped with upland rice after the maize has emerged. It is then either relaid about a month later with cassava or a second crop of maize after the rice is harvested. Cassava can be harvested as required from four to eight months after planting or 14-24 months.

Cassava, which is grown from selected cuttings, is the third most important starch crop in Indonesia, producing about eight per cent of the nations' carbohydrate from crops. It can be grown in the drier regions of eastern Indonesia, where it is used as a living starch store to be harvested at critical periods when food supplies are threatened. The leaves can also be eaten as a vegetable, and together with the roots provide an valuable source of food for livestock, particularly pigs which are important in Bali and East Nusa Tenggara where Islam is not the predominant religion.

Maize is grown in dryland areas throughout Indonesia. It is the most important cereal crop in the eastern Islands, although only one crop can be harvested from the short three to four month growing season. It is often intercropped with legumes such as groundnut, soybean, mung bean, cassava or sweet potato, which mature after the maize is harvested.

Dryland soybean hectarage is increasing steadily. The legumes provide an important source of protein and are widely used in indigenous processed foods such as bean curd (*tahu*), *tempe* and soysauce (*kecap*). The waste from soybean processing, like that from cassava, can be used as an animal feed. After harvest the dried plant can also be used as fodder or fertiliser.

Trees and shrubs, mostly leguminous, are grown in hedgerows along contours with food crops planted in the alleys between the rows. These trees and shrubs provide fodder for livestock, fuel for cooking and green manure for crops while also helping to stabilise the soil against erosion.

Livestock

Although cattle, pigs, sheep, goats and poultry are all integral part of dryland farming, as are horses for transport and dogs (a delicacy in places), Indonesia has the lowest per capita protein intake of any ASEAN country. The Government, however, is committed to improving this situation. Over the last 15 years, there has been a steady increase in wealth

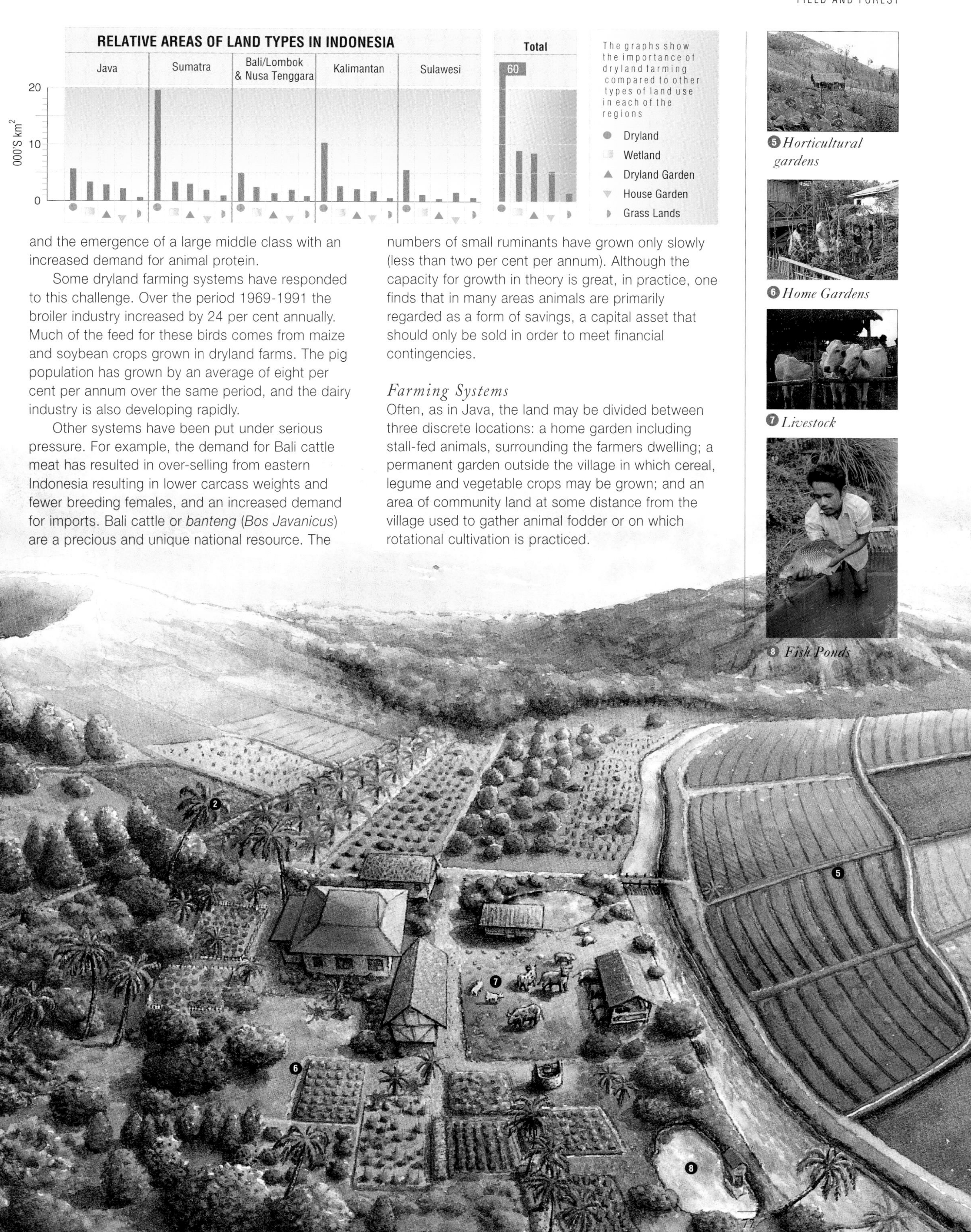

5 *Horticultural gardens*

6 *Home Gardens*

7 *Livestock*

8 *Fish Ponds*

and the emergence of a large middle class with an increased demand for animal protein.

Some dryland farming systems have responded to this challenge. Over the period 1969-1991 the broiler industry increased by 24 per cent annually. Much of the feed for these birds comes from maize and soybean crops grown in dryland farms. The pig population has grown by an average of eight per cent per annum over the same period, and the dairy industry is also developing rapidly.

Other systems have been put under serious pressure. For example, the demand for Bali cattle meat has resulted in over-selling from eastern Indonesia resulting in lower carcass weights and fewer breeding females, and an increased demand for imports. Bali cattle or *banteng* (*Bos Javanicus*) are a precious and unique national resource. The numbers of small ruminants have grown only slowly (less than two per cent per annum). Although the capacity for growth in theory is great, in practice, one finds that in many areas animals are primarily regarded as a form of savings, a capital asset that should only be sold in order to meet financial contingencies.

Farming Systems

Often, as in Java, the land may be divided between three discrete locations: a home garden including stall-fed animals, surrounding the farmers dwelling; a permanent garden outside the village in which cereal, legume and vegetable crops may be grown; and an area of community land at some distance from the village used to gather animal fodder or on which rotational cultivation is practiced.

Palm Economies of East Nusa Tenggara

On Rote, Ndao and Savu, the utilisation of the lontar and gewang palms has enabled relatively large populations to be supported on these dry islands. In addition, various parts of the lontar palm are used for a wide variety of purposes from construction materials to clothing.

This man in the crown of a lontar is pouring harvested lontar juice into a lontar leaf basket.

Lontar syrup can also be distilled into an alcoholic drink. This Rotenese man in a hut is tending to his gin still.

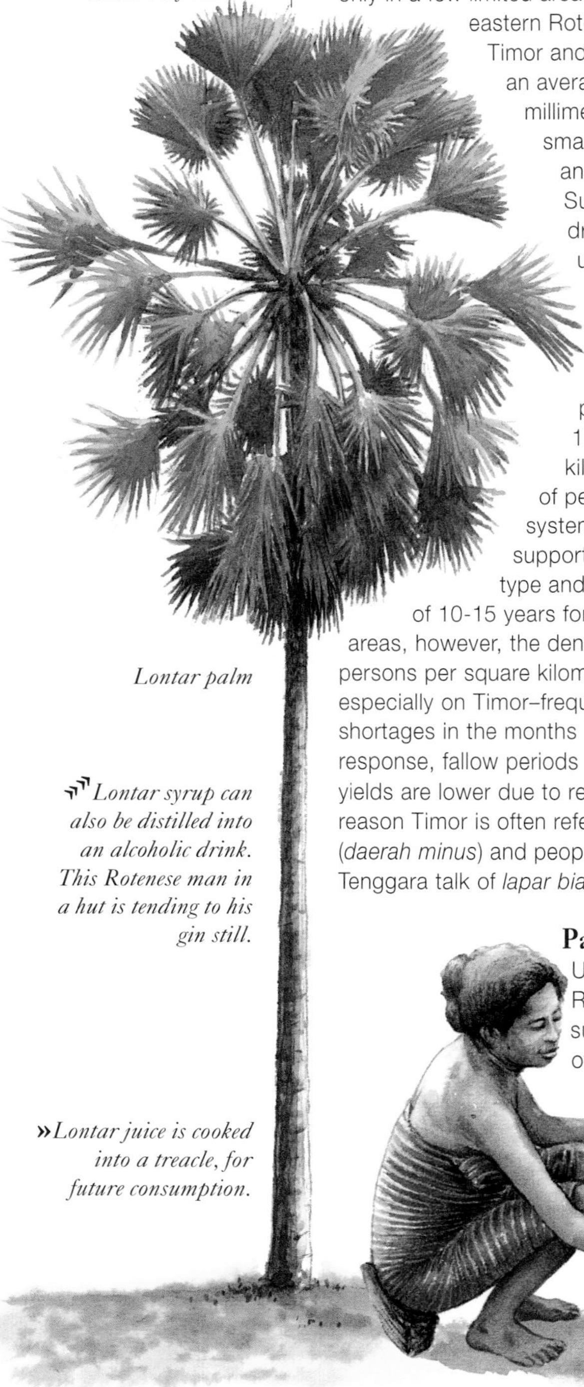

Lontar palm

Lontar juice is cooked into a treacle, for future consumption.

Subsistence Systems

The subsistence economy of much of East Nusa Tenggara is based on diverse multi-crop, dryfield cultivation systems. Wet rice cultivation is possible only in a few limited areas, for example, parts of eastern Rote and western Sumba. Timor and Sumba are arid islands with an average annual rainfall of 775 millimetres, while the much smaller islands of Rote, Savu and Ndao, lying between Sumba and Timor, are even drier. The extensive agricultural systems of Timor and Sumba, incorporating rice, sorghum, maize and millet cultivation, can support an 'ideal' population density of only 19-26 persons per square kilometre. This is the amount of people that the cultivation system on these islands can support given the soil fertility and type and allowing for a fallow period of 10-15 years for the soil to recover. In many areas, however, the density already exceeds 50 persons per square kilometre, and rural populations–especially on Timor–frequently experience food shortages in the months before the harvest. In response, fallow periods are shortened but resulting yields are lower due to reduced soil fertility. For this reason Timor is often referred to as a 'deprived area' (*daerah minus*) and people across East Nusa Tenggara talk of *lapar biasa* or 'normal hunger'.

Palm Juice Production

Unlike Sumba and Timor, Rote, Savu and Ndao easily support population densities of up to 100 persons per square kilometre. The islanders rely on the *lontar* palm (*Borassus sundaicus*) and in the case of Rote the *gewang* palm (*Corypha elata*) as well, for their subsistence. The lontar palm is one of the world's most efficient sugar-producing plants. The lontar palm produces about five, very large inflorescences and the juice is extracted from both the male and female lontar. From the inflorescences produced by the palms, a sweet juice is extracted which may be drunk fresh. The male produces 50 centimetre long green anthers while the female palm produces a spherical brown fruit. These structures would, if they were not tapped, normally ripen, produce pollen and ova respectively, then fall off the tree. Cuts are made in the structures while they are still young and fleshy. A good palm with five inflorescences will yield over 6.7 litres of juice a day or 47 litres of juice a week. A palm at the end of its tapping period with only one productive inflorescence will rarely produce less than 2.5 litres a week. The skill with which the lontar palm is tapped and slivered, to a large extent, determines the length of time a palm will be productive. The lontar's juice is collected in leaf buckets, but because it sours quickly, the juice is cooked to a thick dark treacle, or a lighter brown syrup which may be stored in vats. Mixed with water this syrup makes a substantial food substitute. The Savunese cook the juice longer than the Rotenese, consequently, they produce a thicker, darker syrup. A beer may also be fermented from the syrup. Two palms yield sufficient juice to support a family throughout the period during which the lontar is producing juice. This more or less coincides with the dry season. An excess of juice is usually collected and the surplus is converted to syrup or treacle which is consumed during the wet season. Some of the juice is also sold. The Butonese of Sulawesi may travel for days to purchase it. Although most palms grow wild, in parts of Savu where palms have become less available for tapping, people have started to plant lontars in walled enclosures, thus ensuring ownership and permitting greater efficiency in tapping. Captain Cook and Joseph Banks visited Savu in 1770 and recorded its lontar tapping economy. Bees also thrive in the region, and the honey they produce is collected and exported.

Other Economic Activities

Lontar juice also feeds a pig population that is an important source of protein for the people of these islands. Increased palm utilisation has led to intensification in the rearing of pigs. Old gewang palms are felled and cut into blocks which are soaked in water to produce a sago mash used for pig feed, and most families own seven to eight pigs. The wood, bark and fronds of the lontar also yield a wide range of articles including construction materials (timber, fencing, thatch), household utensils (baskets, buckets, mats) and clothing (hats, belts, work clothes and sandals).

The main period for collecting palm juice is between April and November, with two particularly busy periods in April and May, and then again at the end of September and beginning of October. This flexible system allows the islanders to pursue other economic activities for the rest of the year.

Field rotation has almost entirely ceased, and permanent garden plots fertilised with fired palm debris often produce higher yields of millet, maize and sorghum, than do the swidden fields of neighbouring Timor and Sumba. Animal manure is used on tobacco gardens. Goats which are allowed to wander, and sheep, are also raised for consumption. The sheep are not allowed to wander freely as on Timor and Sumba, but are penned and corralled to prevent them damaging gardens.

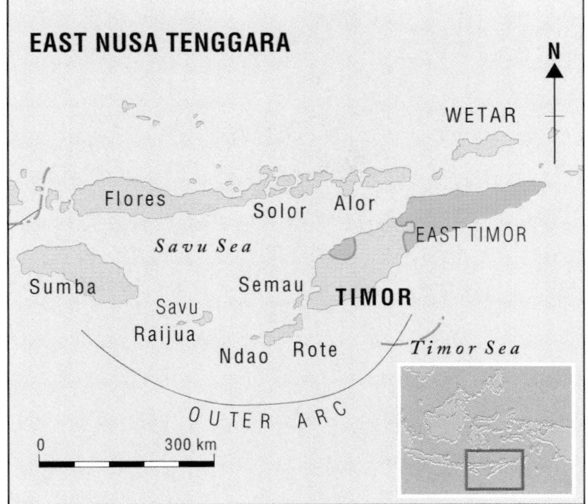

Offshore fishing is also a popular pursuit among the people of these islands during the dry season. Stone fish walls are built along the shoreline which act as weirs, trapping the fish in the ebb tide. The Rotenese also fish at night by torch, and less regularly using net, line and trap. The Ndaoese people supplement the income from their agricultural economy with employment as gold and silver smiths, producing jewellery for the Timorese who pay them in foodstuffs and small livestock.

As a result of the hardy nature of these two species of palm, lontar and gewang palm savannas have developed in parts of other islands in Nusa Tenggara such as Sumba and Timor. On these islands the traditional cultivation system, swidden agriculture, deteriorated to the point of collapse after frequent burning of the land. Along the alluvial plains and dry coastal regions where this has occurred on a wide scale, migrants from Savu and Rote have moved to Sumba and Timor respectively to exploit these new palm groves.

The inflourescences at the crown of a male lontar palm is squeezed prior to tapping.

««Lontar leaf baskets

Sago Club

Sago Oven

SAGO MANUFACTURE IN MALUKU

The staple food in the Maluku islands has long been sago; a starch obtained from the *Metroxylon sagu* palm. The sago resources of eastern Indonesia consist of several thousand square kilometres of sago palm swamp spread over Seram, Halmahera, Buru, Aru and parts of Irian Jaya. In addition to its use as a staple food, the sago palm–like the lontar palm–is a multi-purpose tree producing liquor, firewood, utensils, construction material and medicine among other things. Many of the main sago producing islands are able to export sago to those islands with scarce food resources.

The first Western reference to sago appears in Antonio Pigafetta's 16th century account when he wrote of 'saghu'. In 1869 Alfred Russel Wallace described the traditional method of producing sago in Seram in *The Malay Archipelago*. A mature tree was felled, and the pithy interior exposed by stripping back the outer bark. A heavy wooden club with a quartz end was used to beat the pith and break it down into a coarse powder. This was placed in sago leaf troughs, and water then poured over the powdery pith. Then, the pith was kneaded and pressed against a strainer until the starch dissolved and formed a sediment at the bottom of the trough. After the surplus water was discarded, the raw sago was then made into 15 kilogramme cylinders ready for sale. The raw sago could then be made into 'bread' by breaking it down into a fine powder and baking it in a clay oven. This 'bread' could be eaten fresh, or stored for several years. The method of extracting sago flour from the palm has hardly changed since Wallace's day, though today the flour is eaten in different ways. A good palm can yield up to 300 kilograms of sago flour, enough to feed a person for up to a year.

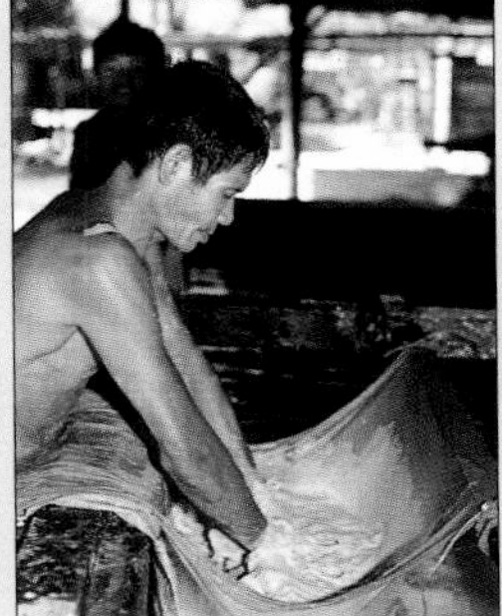

Plantation Agriculture

Plantation agriculture usually involves the systematic cultivation of mainly tree crops for commercial purposes. Apart from coconut, most Indonesian plantation crops began to be grown on a large scale only after the mid-19th century for the expanding cash economy. Today they provide a livelihood for some 20 milliojn Indonesian farmers and their dependants and generate important export revenues.

Sugar cane is largely grown in Java.

Picking coffee berries, Jember, East Java.

The native rubber tree (ficus elastica) was tried as a plantation crop in West Java and on the east coast of Sumatra from 1864. Before the rubber tapper makes his cut, the congealed latex from the previous cut is pulled from the old cut. Fresh rubber is tapped by drawing a knife down the cut, excising a thin sliver of bark. Latex then runs down from the cut and is collected.

Plantation Agriculture

Major Indonesian plantation crops include tree crops like coconut, rubber, oil palm, coffee, and cloves, and also non-tree crops like sugarcane and tobacco. While sugarcane and tobacco are largely grown in Java, most other plantations are in the Outer Islands. There are large concentrations of coconut in Sulawesi, and of other tree crops in Sumatra and Kalimantan. Tree crops are most appropriate when land is relatively abundant. Although their cultivation first entails clearing jungle or scrub, after they have become established, they then provide good cover and help to prevent further land degradation.

While sugarcane, rubber, oil palm and tea are often cultivated on big commercial estates running to hundreds or even thousands of hectares, other plantation crops are grown on family-operated smallholdings of a few hectares, frequently in combination with other husbandry activities. Estates first appeared on a major scale in the 19th century, when Dutch and other European interests established them for sugarcane and tobacco production. Later, however, they came to include rubber and other crops. Their remote location in areas of low population density necessitated importing large numbers of labourers from Java, frequently to work in insanitary and disease-ridden conditions for very low wages. Yet these people commonly settled in their new abodes, and their descendants still work on the same estates today. Despite their colonial origins, estates have proved a flexible and viable method of producing certain tree crops, and most continue to operate profitably. Yet parallel to the estate developments–which were frequently on the best land–there was a great burgeoning of smallholder plantations farmed mainly by local people. In recent years, these have expanded even more dynamically than the estates.

Production and Processing

All tree crops involve similar sequences of operations in their production. Land is cleared by cutting and burning. Young trees are established in 'nurseries', and then transplanted to regimented blocks and rows. The new trees take some years to reach 'maturity', and are then harvested regularly for up to 25 years or more before they too become old and exhausted, and need to be cleared and replaced. The harvested crop from plantations is processed at central factories into an 'intermediate product', and then consigned through dealers to central markets, final processing facilities, and points of export.

There is of course considerable variation between crops. While rubber is tapped every other day through most of the year, oil palm, coconut and tea are gathered every 1 to 2 weeks and coffee, cloves and cocoa are only collected during definite harvesting seasons. In contrast to tree crops, sugarcane has a far shorter life cycle, and is usually harvested only once, 14 months after planting. Tobacco is grown and harvested over a four month period, often as a dry season crop after rice.

Coconut is grown and consumed by producing households as well as sold as copra, but coffee, cloves, sugar, tobacco and cocoa are chiefly taken up by consumers elsewhere in Indonesia. Much palm oil, and the bulk of rubber and tea, are exported to overseas destinations. New technologies have had huge impacts on the cultivation, production, processing, and marketing of all these crops in the 20th century, and helped Indonesia to remain competitive in both local and world markets.

Improved techniques of processing and making end-products have considerably stimulated plantation agriculture in recent years. They have enabled the production of better-quality outputs and also led to the expansion of Indonesian factories making the end-products concerned. Both outcomes have acted to improve the incomes of those employed in the industries.

Technology–Key to Viability and Success

New technologies have had a major impact on plantation agriculture throughout the 20th century. Thus in the 1920s and 1930s the increasing use of bulldozers and other heavy machines hugely facilitated the quick clearing land for planting, and making

PLANTATION CROP PLANTED AREAS, 1993
('000 HECTARES)

ESTATES		SMALL HOLDINGS	
Rubber	490.8	Rubber	2, 698.2
Coconut	118.2	Coconut	3, 474.5
Oil Palm	903.2	Oil Palm	539.4
Coffee	48	Coffee	1, 104.9
Cocoa	126.7	Cocoa	257.7
Tea	69.0	Tea	51.7
Clove	15.9	Clove	555.2
Tobacco	7.3	Tobacco	203.6
Sugarcane	376.4	Sugarcane	0
Cashewnut	0	Cashewnut	376.9

Source: BPS 1994

new roads providing access to outside markets.

From the 1930s, improved high yielding varieties based on selecting the best seedlings and subsequently bud-grafting them, meant that yields have continually risen. Today yields are two to three times greater than those achieved in the 1910s. The performances and yields of new varieties have been further enhanced by parallel developments of fertilisers, pesticides and weed-killers. In contrast, the labour-intensive harvesting of plantation crops has been barely amenable to improvement, and excepting sugar cane to some extent, has changed little during the century. Markets have been revolutionised by modern communications, meaning both that 'signals' concerning consumers' requirements are passed back more effectively to producers, and that transportation methods are more efficient. For tree crop producers in northern Sumatra, for example, the 1980s saw major increases in the information available to farmers, substantial road improvements, and the upgrading of Belawan port near Medan to a modern container terminal connected by fast ocean freighters to destinations around the world.

A key challenge for the Indonesian plantation sector is how to encourage smallholders to adopt new technologies and methods so that they too might benefit from these production, processing and marketing advances. Partly, the problem relates to a simple scarcity of cash. It is also true, however, that small farmers also lack access to sources of information about external markets and credit facilities, lack the training to adopt some technical innovations, and are often unable to 'risk' innovating where the appropriateness of an advance has not been locally demonstrated. It is for these reasons, and notwithstanding attempts by the Indonesian government to improve the productivity of smallholder plantation agriculture, that the dualism noted by J. Boeke in the early 1930s still persists.

Frying coffee beans.

Grinding coffee beans.

Making coffee.

Harvesting oil palm fruit bunches, using a sickle attached to the end of a pole. An arduous and back-breaking job, although new South American pole designs promise much improvement.

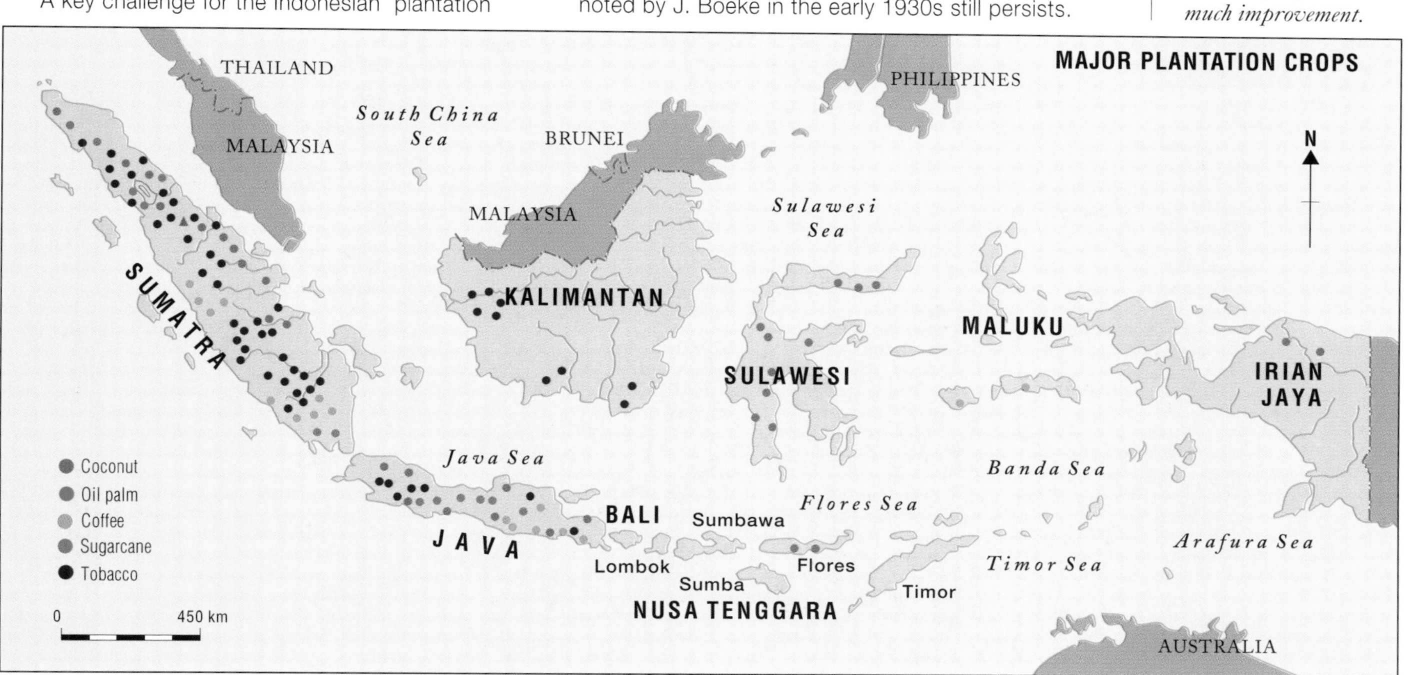

Plantation Crops: Estates and Smallholdings

Plantation crops are grown both on estates and smallholdings. The comparatively large ouput of estates has allowed them to reap economies of scale. However, by supplementing the cultivation of plantation crops with a range of other activities, smallholdings have, to an extent, shielded themselves against price fluctuations for specific plantation crops, an option that is not open to most estates.

Two smallholders in Jambi, having just cleared their swidden plot. The area has also been burned over. The crops that are already growing on the plot include cassava and banana.

A smallholder from West Java, carries his harvest of raw rubber to be sold. The viability of many smallholdings depends on their juxtaposition to a marketing chain.

Estates

Estates are notable for their hierarchical structure, consisting of a general manager, supervisors and a regimented workforce. They are also vertically integrated, with groups of estates being controlled from a central office, and with downstream market linkages which may extend to the processing of intermediate outputs into end-products. Such organisation can embody important economic advantages, in reducing the cost of market information, improving access to technologies, and in major economies of scale. But estates also have disadvantages, notably in the high costs of controlling and sustaining their workforces as well as the basically unsatisfactory nature of their workers' regimented lifestyles. Their reliance on one or at most two crops also makes them vulnerable to price changes. Then there are the incompatibilities with traditional lifestyles and arrangements including traditional land use practices.

Yet the estate system has shown its viability and flexibility over some 100 years in Indonesia. Estates have been successful with rubber, oil palm, cocoa, and tea, all crops where the advantages detailed are most marked. They have also been characteristically favoured by Indonesian political elites, especially in recent years, and large new areas of oil palm and cocoa have been established.

While most Indonesian estates are in the so-called 'public' estate or PTP sector, which is based on former Dutch enterprises nationalised in the 1950s, this may soon change if current privatisation plans proceed. Such changes should add dynamism to their activities, especially in respect of economically desirable expansion into further processing and making of various end-products.

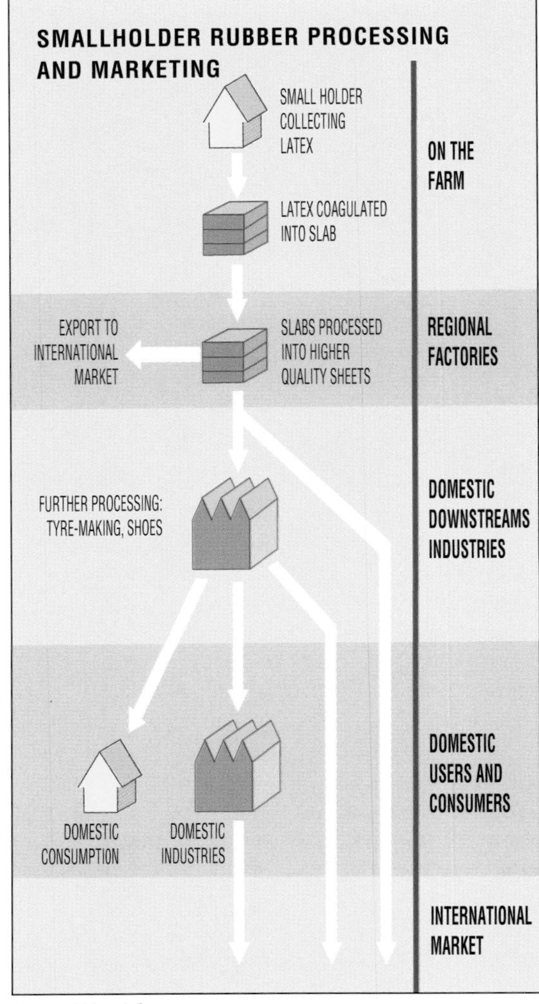

Smallholdings

Smallholdings, with their base in the farm household have a different structure, which does not possess the economic advantages of estates. Nor does it include workforce monitoring costs, and it affords its participants more independence. Traditional methods and lifestyles are reflected in this system. When tree crops were first introduced they were superimposed on traditional 'swidden' systems and planted along with the other crops, in a practice still widely followed today. In these systems, farmers take advantage of abundant land, and set that against a relative shortage of cash–resulting in an extensive production system where yields are comparatively low but so too are inputs. Production is geared to producing a cash

CONTRASTING LIFESTYLES

Work on rubber estates is very regimented. Work starts at about 5-6 am, when tappers assemble for instructions prior to going out to assigned 'tasks' of 300-400 trees per person (*right*). Their work in the field is then checked carefully by an ever watchful *mandor*, who strictly penalises those who tap carelessly, either 'consuming' too much bark or damaging the cambium so as to prevent bark renewal. Similar surveillance applies to those performing other tasks, including weeding and factory processing.The work of smallholders, in contrast, is far freer in that they can decide personally what to do. But the daily round is still difficult and the living wage of Rp 2,000-3,000 per day is not, like that of estate workers, more or less automatically paid. Hence the smallholder rubber tappers still have to rise very early to take advantage of the higher 'pressure' (and yield) of latex at that time. They also have many other tasks to perform, including tending other crops, processing, clearing jungle, and supplementary tasks such as gathering firewood.

««« A smallholder dries harvested coffee in front of his house, Bengkulu, Sumatra. Approximately 20 times more coffee is produced by Indonesian smallholders than is grown on estates.

An oil palm plantation in Sumatra. Plantations are more important for oil palm production, producing about twice as much crude palm oil as smallholders.

supplement to the subsistence crops which are cultivated in tandem. Environmentally the system is comparatively benign and sustainable–so long as population pressures remain modest. As well as utilising local knowledge and intermediate, low input methods, the system is also usually governed and regulated on the basis of customary laws and practices (or *adat*), outside the formal administrative system. Another feature of smallholdings is the range of activities that supplement the plantations. This feature buffers the smallholder against the problems of low prices for particular items. One crucial feature underpinning smallholding viability is their universal juxtaposition with a marketing chain of dealers, processors, and other traders who collect the crop, further treat it, and arrange its consignment to manufacturing consumers in Indonesia or overseas.

Like estates, smallholdings too have had to adjust to various changes. In both Indonesia and elsewhere, smallholders have grown far more than estates both in area and volume of product. However, despite their advantages in terms of crop husbandry, individual small producers still face some problems in accessing new technology and securing the capital needed to implement such technology successfully.

Government Intervention

The government has tried to provide information and credit through special services to individual farmers. However, from the 1970s, the emphasis switched to 'group smallholding' systems. Farmers were given plots of land–about two hectares in area–in large development blocks. They were provided with credit, advice and processing and marketing support so that new technologies could be applied under specialised management. Numerous variations of group smallholder schemes have been tried, and have all suffered from serious shortcomings ranging from excessive costs to insufficient technical guidance and under-budgeting. Overall they have been relatively ineffective, and now official policy makers are visibly seeking better means of encouraging improvement.

Useful public rural improvements in the last 25 years have been upgradings of roads, education, health, and other infrastructures, which have enhanced communications and given people better access to new ideas. The means of improvement favoured today comprise those executed under private auspices, a good example of which is the recent wide proliferation of small private nurseries providing high-yielding trees to smallholders.

Plantations in East Java

East Java produces about half the country's sugar, 80 per cent of coffee, and 40 per cent of cocoa. There has been a shift since Independence from estate to smallholder production while, during the 1950s the estates went from foreign ownership to state control. There is also a distinction between upland areas, where enclave, estate production of coffee and cocoa predominates and lowland areas where smallholders produce sugar and tobacco in conjunction with traditional crops like rice.

Although processing of sugarcane has benefitted from technological advancements, the harvesting is still largely done manually in the same way as the early 20th century.

Since Independence, the estates have declined in economic importance. They still exist but are now more like smallholdings in terms of organisation. At the same time, smallholders are becoming more commercialised and more technologically advanced–becoming more like estates. The result is that the sharp dualism between the enclave estates on the one hand and individual small producers on the other is becoming increasingly blurred.

The figures (below) indicate that cane sugar and palm kernel are not produced in great quantities on smallholdings.

PLANTATION CROP PRODUCTION,1989 & 1993, ('000 million tonnes)

ESTATES			SMALLHOLDINGS		
CROP	**1989**	**1993(est)**	**CROP**	**1989**	**1993(est)**
Rubber	27	335,0	Rubber	853,2	1,009,8
Coconut	28,5	39,3	Coconut	2,192,9	2,467,9
Crude Palm Oil	1,860,4	2,288,3	Palm Oil	183,7	833,7
Palm Kernel	410,4	524,6	Not Applicable		
Coffee	32,4	20,9	Coffee	376,6	418,5
Tea	122,2	98,8	Tea	24,6	28,9
Clove	3,3	2,8	Clove	53,1	64,5
Cane Sugar	2,071,4	2,336	Not Applicable		
Tobacco	4,1	3,1	Tobacco	76,8	139,2

Source: Biro Pusat Statistik 1994

Cultivating for the City

The continued growth of urban centres in Indonesia has led to increasing demand for fruits and vegetables. While horticultural production provides an important source of rural employment, the expansion of vegetable cultivation into upper mountain slopes has brought with it the threat of soil instability and erosion.

A landslide destroys a vegetable terrace.

Kangkung being collected, East Java. Because this plant is fast growing, reaching marketable maturity within a few weeks, people with very little land to convert to fish ponds or other profitable activities, can produce this crop

» *A farmer proudly displays his carrot harvest from the slopes of Mt. Lawu, Central Java.*

Features of Horticultural Production

Vegetable production in Java has increased considerably since 1970. With rapid population growth in Jakarta, Surabaya and other urban areas, large supplies of fresh food of all kinds are required daily. Outside Java, the cultivation of vegetables is particularly important in North Sumatra, not only for consumption in the city of Medan, but also for export to countries like Malaysia and Singapore.

Horticultural production comes mainly from small, family-owned holdings which are very often less than 0.5 hectare in size. But in some places, especially in the uplands, wealthy farmers may control as much as 50 hectares through rental agreements.

Crops Grown

Vegetables that have to be grown at low altitudes, like tomatoes, chilli peppers, red onions, aubergine and cucumber are usually cultivated on rice-land during the dry season. Many of these are multi-harvest vegetables that can be intercropped with each other or with non-irrigated crops like corn. By contrast, single-harvest crops like carrots, potatoes, cabbages and shallots are grown at altitudes over 1,000 metres. Farmers are normally able to obtain three and sometimes even four crops of these vegetables from the same land every year. With abundant rainfall in the uplands, they have few worries about water, although in the dry months from June to September hand-watering of crops is sometimes necessary.

Labour Requirements

The rapid expansion that has occurred in vegetable cultivation is important not only for urban food supplies but also as a source of rural employment. High-altitude vegetables require a large amount of labour during cultivation, particularly if they are grown on steep slopes. The most labour-demanding task in upland horticulture is field preparation. With lowland vegetable crops it is harvesting that demands large numbers of workers.

HORTICULTURAL PRODUCTION PROCESS

Seeding corn with cattle plough, East Java

Nursery of vegetables, East Java

Spraying pesticides on fruit trees, East Java.

Harvesting potatoes, East Java.

Cleaning harvested spring onions, Lombok.

Bringing spring onions to market, Java.

Although there are variations from one crop to another, on the whole more women than men are employed in vegetable production.

Capital Inputs

Horticulture is a capital-intensive, as well as a labour-intensive, form of land use. This is because of the large inputs of fertiliser and pesticide that are needed, especially on high-altitude crops. Although it is very profitable when climatic conditions are favourable, it is also risky in that crops can be lost because of insect pests, unexpectedly heavy rain or because of a shortage of water at critical times. Market fluctuations due to unusually large supplies of vegetables from other regions resulting in huge drops in prices of vegetables and fruits can also cause big losses to many farmers.

MAIN FRUIT AND VEGETABLES PRODUCTION, 1992 (TON)

FRUIT		VEGETABLES	
Banana	2,650, 841	Shallot	528,311
Mango	484,782	Beans	92,487
Pineapple	376,278	Cabbage	1,213,365
Waterapples/Jambu	107,130	Potatoes	702,584
Papaya	406,587	Mustard Greens	370,852

Sources: Biro Statistik Indonesia 1994

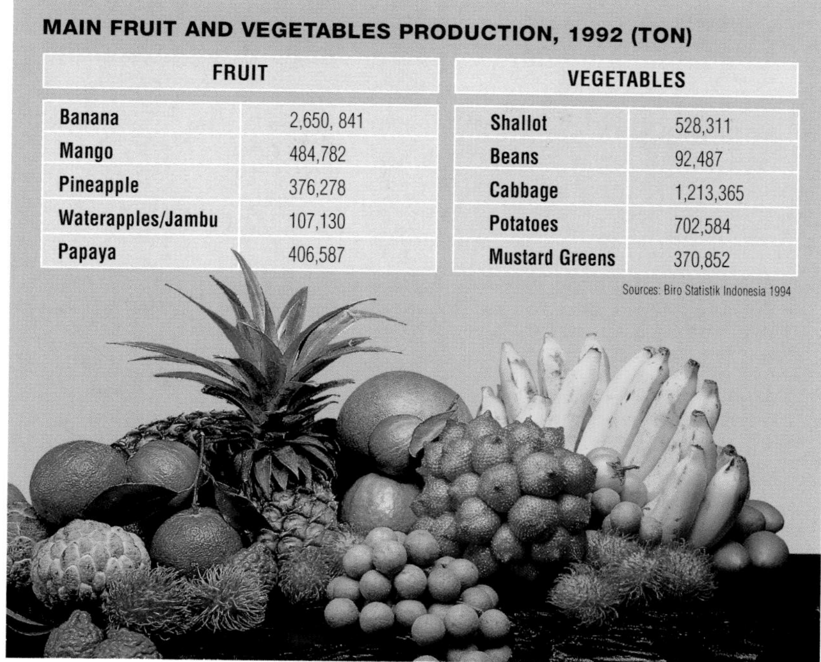

Developments in Horticulture

Increased vegetable output on the lowlands has involved greater intensification of cultivation, rather than extensification. In the case of higher-altitude crops, however, expansion has occurred in planted areas, especially in the more mountainous parts of West Java, which produces almost half of Java's single-harvest vegetable crops.

The origins of horticulture in this region go back to colonial times, when every large town had its vegetable production centre, often in association with dairying. Most of the highland areas now under vegetables represents an extension of these traditional centres. Some of this land was once part of Dutch plantations whose status remained unclear after independence. As local farmers moved onto the land, perennials like tea were replaced by vegetables.

High Altitude Mountain Cultivation

The cultivation of annuals on upper mountain slopes has implications for the environment. In places where horticulture has been practised for many decades, fertility is declining and increasing amounts of manure and chemical fertilisers are required to maintain productivity. At the same time, farmers do not normally terrace their land because natural slopes provide the good drainage that crops need. As a consequence, erosion of the topsoil is occuring in most high-altitude centres of vegetable production. In addition, landslides occur frequently, adding more sediment to the rivers that wind their way down to the Java Sea. To date, Indonesian government authorities have found it difficult to prevent the upward movement of cultivation, especially when this particular form of land use is a profitable one like vegetable-growing.

Poultry and Fish

City residents need other food commodities besides vegetables. The raising of poultry for eggs and meat can be found within trucking distance of most urban areas. Originally this was a small-scale activity in which farmers raised only a few hundred hens. Now a dramatic change has taken place, and the poultry industry today is characterised by large production units with more than 100,000 birds. Small producers find it hard to compete with large companies that not only have their own production and breeding farms, feed-manufacturing mills and slaughtering facilities but also control marketing outlets.

Fresh-water carp (*ikan mas*) form a popular supplement to the diet in both rural and urban areas. Since fish have proved to be a much more profitable crop than rice, farmers on the periphery of upland towns now deepen their rice-fields and strengthen the embankments around them to make fish ponds, which they fill with water from irrigation canals. Other people, who have less land and money to stock ponds with fingerlings, cultivate leaf vegetables such as *kangkung* (*Ipomoea aquatica*) on tiny plots, often within built-up areas. This plant grows readily on almost any land provided water is available. The *kangkung* plant takes only a few weeks to reach marketable size and requires no inputs of fertiliser or pesticide. The vegetable is the poor man's response to limited production resources and is always in demand among urban consumers whose household budget is also limited.

Tawangmangu village with the farmers' horticultural gardens, Central Java. The long mounds on which the vegetables are planted are clearly visible. Their preparation is one of the most labour demanding tasks. When one crop is harvested, the remaining stalks are dug back in. Manure from poultry farms near the city is also added to maintain soil fertility.

Fruit and vegetable seller in Jakarta.

Fishing boats returning with their catch, Bali.

Trawler with net, Maluku. In many parts of Indonesia fishermen are increasingly using modern and more efficient methods of catching fish.

Traditional boat building, Sulawesi. The skills necessary for building wooden boats may still be found among some groups in the archipelago.

Floating lift nets, South Sulawesi.

LITTORAL LIVELIHOODS

Few people in Indonesia are far from water. The archipelagic and tropical nature of the country makes water almost as important a defining characteristic as the land. By living on the coast or by the banks of a river, or on the shores of a lake, people hope to exploit multiple opportunities that exist at the interface between two 'worlds'.

In the remoter areas of Indonesia's larger islands, rivers were often the only avenues of communication. They facilitated trade and the interchange of knowledge. The widespread use of terms like *hulu* (upriver) and *hilir* (downstream) did not just describe geographical relationships; they also often demarcated (in general) different ethnic groups and cultural traditions and livelihood strategies. In this way *hulu* and *hilir* denoted different ways of life. The development of road transportation has, inevitably, broken down these former distinctions to some extent.

Rivers and lakes are also resources for modern economic activity. Rivers are dammed to generate power, control flooding, and irrigate lowland areas. Lakes may become, like Lake Toba in Sumatra, important tourist destinations. There can also be, however, environmental costs associated with their exploitation and development. As concentrations of pollutants in rivers and lakes increase so plant and animal populations are affected and biological productivity declines, undermining the livelihoods of those who depend on the resource.

Along the coast of north Java, north-eastern Sumatra and south-western Sulawesi, the intensification of production and expansion in the area of *tambak* (fish ponds) led to the destruction of the natural breeding gounds for fish as mangroves were dug up. Other side effects were an increase in coastal erosion, the infiltration of polluted water into neighbouring rice fields and vice versa, and the spread of disease among high density fish and prawn populations. Today the digging of new ponds is banned and the mangroves that were uprooted, are being replanted.

In Indonesian history the sea, like rivers, has usually not acted as a obstacle, but as a facilitator of contact between groups. The sea was an important conduit for the migration of people, and helped to determine patterns of warfare and human interactions in the wider sense. The shipbuilding, sea-faring and combat skills of the Bugis of Sulawesi for example became renowned–and feared–across the archipelago.

River Features

The Mahakam River in East Kalimantan is 920 kilometres long, and has many features common to Indonesian river systems. It is divided into three sections. The Lower Mahakam stretches from Samarinda to Muara Muntai and the Three Lakes; the Middle Mahakam to Long Iram and Long Bangun where a series of rapids make further navigation impossible. The Upper Mahakam stretches past these rapids and into the Muller Mountains.

The Mighty Mahakam

The source of the Mahakam lies in the Muller Mountains where the fast flowing rivers and their tributaries cut V-shaped valleys and gorges. At the edge of this range the rock becomes much softer, and the river flows through a series of rapids before entering the floodplain. This region

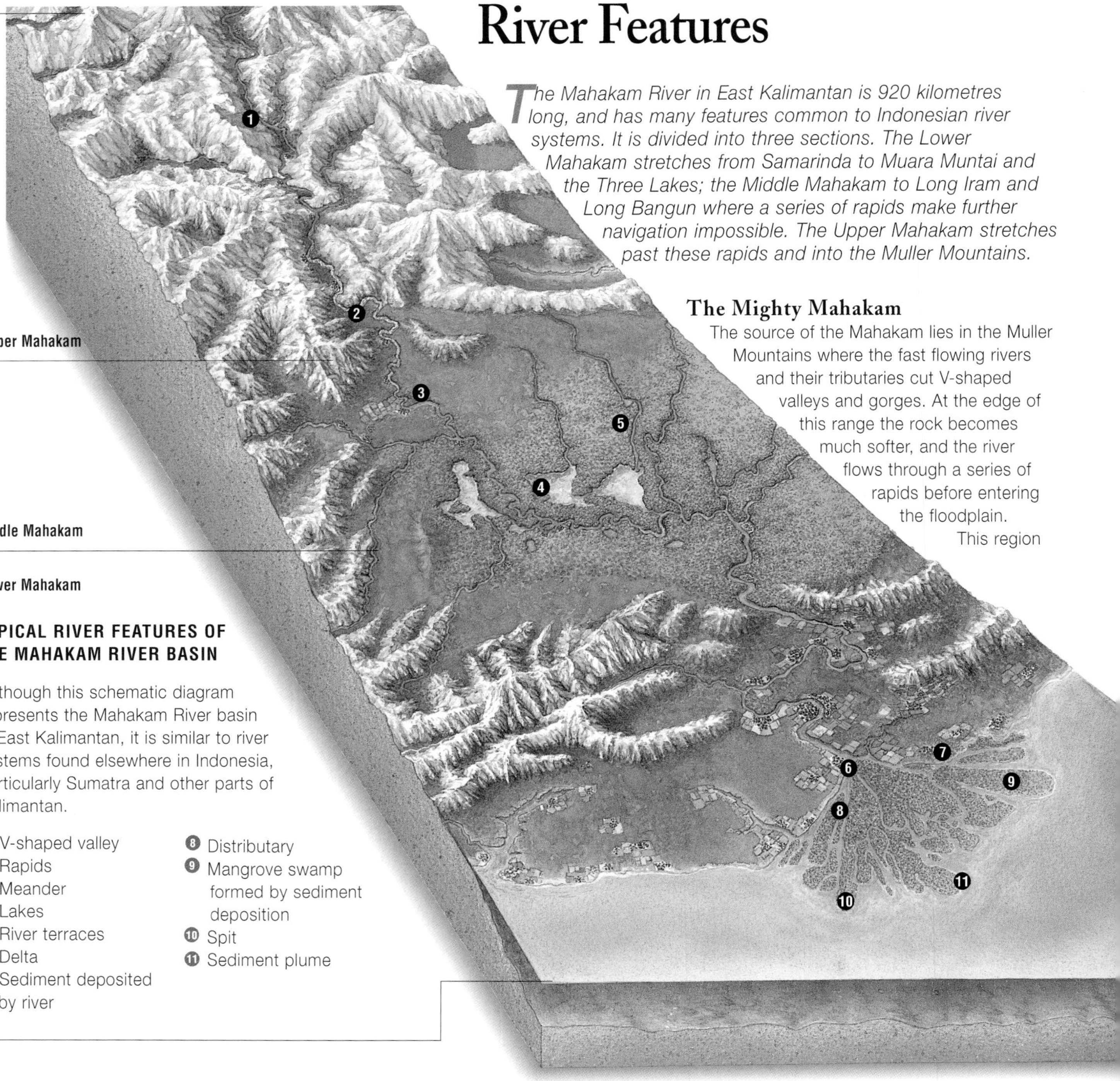

Upper Mahakam

Middle Mahakam

Lower Mahakam

TYPICAL RIVER FEATURES OF THE MAHAKAM RIVER BASIN

Although this schematic diagram represents the Mahakam River basin in East Kalimantan, it is similar to river systems found elsewhere in Indonesia, particularly Sumatra and other parts of Kalimantan.

1. V-shaped valley
2. Rapids
3. Meander
4. Lakes
5. River terraces
6. Delta
7. Sediment deposited by river
8. Distributary
9. Mangrove swamp formed by sediment deposition
10. Spit
11. Sediment plume

Example of river braiding in Irian Jaya. This feature is very typical of the lower course of the Baliem Sirets drainage system.

»» The Mahakam River in East Kalimantan displays typical meander features. The beginnings of an ox bow lake can be seen on the left.

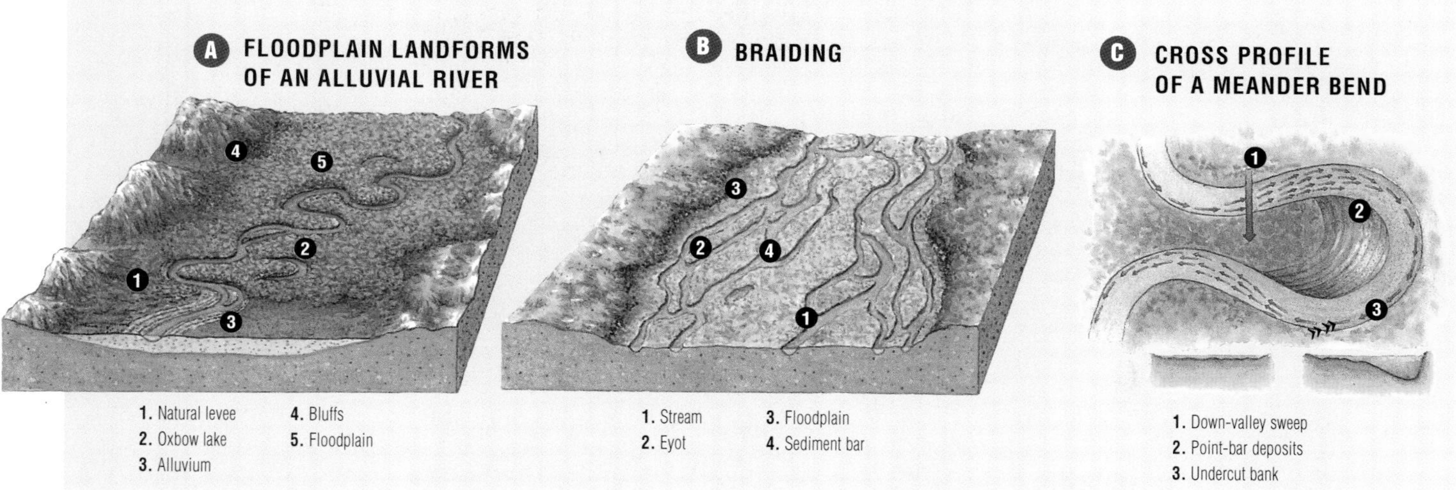

of the river displays many features of an alluvial floodplain (diagram A). The meandering river channel dominates the floodplain (diagram C). Abandoned reaches of former channels-caused when narrow necks between meanders are cut through-are also found. This event, a cutoff, may produce an oxbow lake. In Kalimantan this is often little more than a swampy area, where silt and sand are deposited. Not infrequently, villages may have to move when they are cut off from the river. Another characteristic of this region is the overbank flooding which once or twice a year innundates part of the floodplain, bounded on either side by rising slopes called bluffs. For this reason the dwellings on the river banks are built on piles along many of Indonesia's rivers.

Another river feature found along the middle reaches of many Indonesian rivers is braiding (diagram B). This occurs for short periods during the year, for example during the monsoons when rivers have to carry a heavy load in relation to their velocity. When the river level falls quickly, the channel may become choked with debris, causing the river to divide and converge in a series of channels, creating little islands called eyots.

As the river enters the sea it slows down and deposits large amounts of sediment. These deposits may form deltas, areas of sand bars, swamps and lagoons. Those deltas off the Kalimantan coast are usually covered in mangrove swamps.

People and Rivers

From a human perspective, rivers offer many benefits. They act as arteries of communication, sources of water for domestic use, they support fish and shellfish that may be caught for consumption and sale, and they may be dammed and manipulated for irrigation. Upriver communities are invariably found on river banks, and the largest downriver towns are usually also based on rivers, often close to the mouth, although swampy conditions on the coasts of Kalimantan and Sumatra sometimes precluded true coastal locations.

Banjarmasin, the capital of South Kalimantan, has grown up at the confluence of the Barito and Martapura rivers, about 22 kilometres from the sea. Pile and floating houses (or *lanting*) line the banks of the rivers and canals, and the inhabitants bath, shop, fish and play in the waters. The Pasar Terapung or floating market, throngs with boat borne stalls, and market-goers sample the wares from the *jukung* (canoes) and *klotoks* (motorised longboats).

Matahari rapids, East Kalimantan. Rapids usually mark the transition area between the mountains and plains.

Upriver communities use the river in much the same way, and for the same reasons. The lives of the approximately 40,000 Ngaju of Central Kalimantan, for example, are shaped by the rivers dissecting the province. They identify themselves according to these waterways, designating themselves as Dayak Kahayan or Dayak Katingan depending on which river they live. Houses are built on stilts on the river banks, and floating rafts (*batang*) used as bathing rafts, are permanently moored at the river's edge.

Fishing is an important occupation for many river dwelling Dayak groups. Along the Kahayan river, weighted cast nets (*jala*) are thrown into the river, trapping fish as they sink, or flat nets are stretched across the river and the fish driven into them from upstream. Three-pronged barbed spears (*salahewu*) are used for night fishing. A lamp attracts the fish which are harpooned when they rise. A variety of traps are used, and on the Upper Kahayan an unusual device called a *mihing* is employed. Measuring about 50 metres long and five metres wide, this trap is said to have been stolen from the spirits, and women are prohibited from having anything to do with it. Women fish with scoop nets with handles, and U-shaped baskets called *sauk* with which they ladle up small fish and crabs. Occasionally river turtles are caught and eaten.

Waterfall on the Boh river, East Kalimantan. Waterfalls are usually found on the upper reaches of the river where the harder rock of the mountain ranges give way to softer rock.

Indonesian River Systems

Indonesian river systems developed as important trade and communication routes where overland travel was difficult. The relationships that developed between different peoples, mediated by the river, are usually couched in terms of hulu *(upriver) and* hilir *(downriver). Even with the development of roads, these concepts remain important in describing very different societies and lifestyles.*

River-based Trade

Upriver groups generally distinguished themselves from the downriver Malay sultanates with whom they traded. The Batak of the interior of north Sumatra have a long history of trade with the Malay people on the coast. They used a network of paths following the river valleys, and transferred to canoes for the last stage of the journey downriver. John Anderson, described this ascent up the Asahan River in the 1820s by canoe as far as the first set of rapids and falls. Batak traders descended to the river using ropes, ladders and steep, narrow paths to trade cloth, salt and other commodities with Malay boatmen in exchange for swords and forest produce.

Seventh century Sriwijaya, at Palembang, was the first downriver port state, though others flourished after the 13th century. Their power was based on trade with and tax from the *hulu* communities. Their access to the sea enabled them to develop outside trade links. For example, the Batak of north Sumatra traded luxury goods like aromatic resins and gold, and after the 17th century, pepper, with the *hilir* states of Deli and Siak, who were able to trade them on. The presence of foreign trading communities of Chinese, Indians, Arabs and Bugis in these ports were also important. Jambi and Palembang in Sumatra, and Banjarmasin and Kutei in Kalimantan became very powerful states in the Indonesian Archipelago.

Indonesian Rivers Today

Most of Indonesia's river ports are located upstream (for example, Jambi 120 kilometres, Palembang 80 kilometres, and Banjarmasin 22 kilometres). This is because mangrove swamps and marshes preclude their establishment on the coast. Sandbanks and strong currents also form barriers. In Sumatra, before modern technology enabled the channels to be dredged, large ocean going ships could not ascend many of the rivers, and the sultan depended on the services of Orang Laut villagers who lived in boats in the swampy deltas. They acted as pilots and guides, transporting cargoes to and from ships anchored offshore in their smaller craft.

The Sumatran and Kalimantan rivers total 16,473 kilometres in length, with 10,437 kilometres navigable with a depth of one metre or more during the dry season. Roads and air routes are being developed in these regions, but rivers remain important to these islands' economies. With the disappearance of the sultanates and the development of a modern government and economy, there has been been an influx of other Indonesians to work in these port cities. New economic opportunities have enabled young Dayak, Batak and Minangkabau to move downriver to work or study. Government workers, police, teachers and health workers from other parts of Indonesia have also been sent upriver to work and intermarriage is breaking down ethnic differentiation.

Asmat warriors from Irian Jaya pose in their decorated dug out canoes, which were once used as fast war boats.

Settlements on the banks of the Samarinda and Mahakam River. With so few roads in Kalimantan, most settlements are found along the river banks.

River transport in Palembang. These boats are used for local transport.

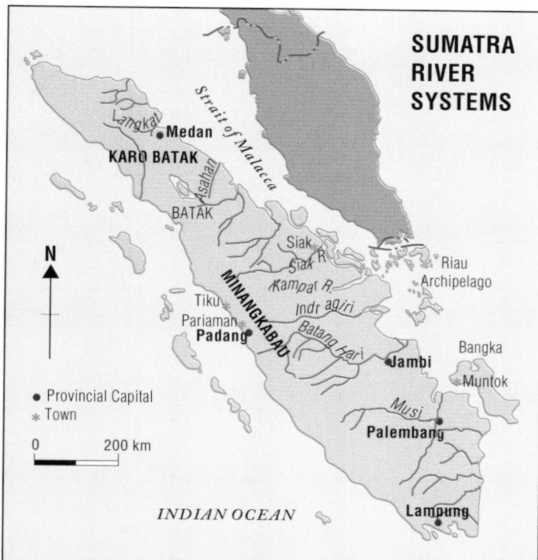

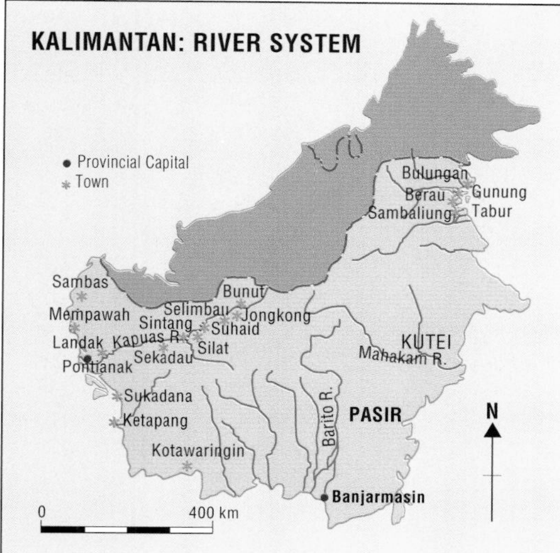

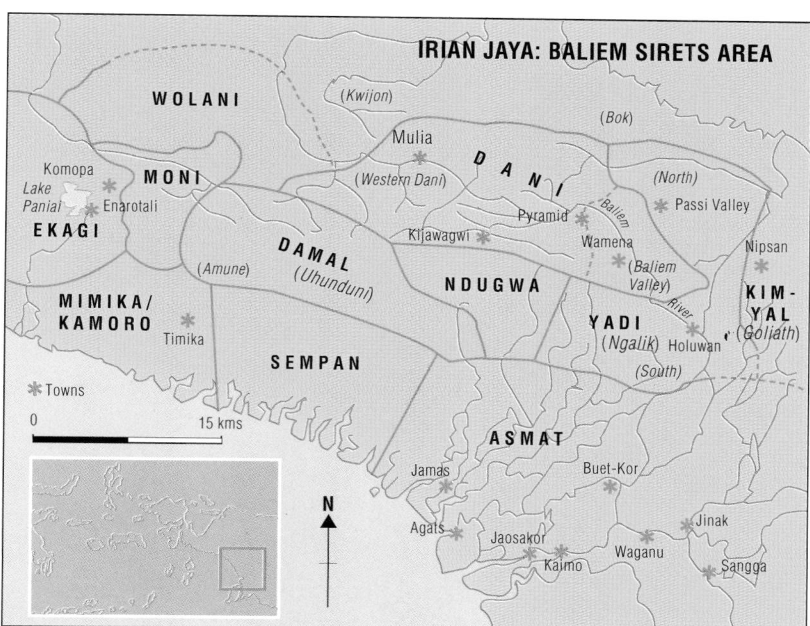

The use of navigable rivers in Kalimantan, Sumatra and Irian Jaya has a long history. These 'highways' formed links where thick forest and swamp form land barriers. In Sumatra, rivers flowing from the southern end of the Barisan range formed important trade routes, those flowing from the north being too small and fast flowing. The rivers of Kalimantan have always been, and still are, the main arteries of communication. The course of the Baliem Sirets river in Irian Jaya is so varied that up to four different ethnic groups support themselves using different survival strategies along its course.

Even with a well developed road and rail system on the island, Sumatran rivers have not been abandoned as methods of transport and communication. Passenger ferries ply between Palembang, Jambi and Medan, and smaller river boats take workers downriver from Palembang to Bangka Island. Passengers boat services link villages along the Musi River, and riverboats and motorised dugouts take people upriver from Jambi.

In Kalimantan economic activity is focused on the ports of Banjarmasin serving the Barito and its tributaries, Pontianak serving the Kapuas valley, and Samarinda serving the Mahakam valley. Although a number of roads have been constructed, the rivers remain the main means of communication with the population concentrated along their banks. Although river travel is slow, air transport remains too expensive for most people on the island.

The Baliem Sirets River

Irian Jaya comprises 410,660 square kilometres of swamp, marsh and rainforest. Over 31 major rivers drain north and south from the massif running along the centre of the province. The Baliem Sirets river system, one of the most extensive on the island, begins its journey over 2,130 metres above sea level in the Central Mountains, and flows 400 kilometres before reaching the Arafura Sea.

The river flows into the Baliem Valley 1,600 metres above sea level, home to the Dani. The sediment deposited by the river supports a vigorous agricultural system. During floods, crops may be harvested from rafts. The river drops 1,500 metres in less than 50 kilometres through the Baliem Gorge, being crossed at wider points by suspension bridges. At narrower places, bridges are constructed by building two overhanging wooden platforms on either side of the river, and extending lengths of wood out until they meet in the middle. The Ndugwa and Yali, who inhabit this part of the river, terrace the river slopes, and hunt wild animals, and gather forest produce.

Beyond the gorge the river flattens out and flows into a swampy coastal plain, some 100 kilometres wide, and home to the Asmat, who live in stilt houses built on the river banks, which are tidal for up to 90 kilometres upstream. Traditionally their villages were sited up defendable tributaries, though the government is encouraging them to relocate to the major rivers. Myriads of interconnecting streams form their highways and some villages have raised wooden walkways over the river. Little agriculture is carried out here, the bulk of their protein being obtained from the river. Women catch fish with nets while the men go after larger game such as turtles, crocodiles and sharks. They also collect drinking water at low tide when the river is less salty. Many Asmat now earn cash by selling ironwood trees. The trees are cut down and then floated to the coast for sale. Asmat wood-carvings are also important sale goods in the coastal towns such as Agats near the coast. Dug-out canoes, ranging from one and a half to fifteen metres long are usually used. The canoes are made using stone adzes. Although they are used mainly for journeys up and down the rivers, the larger canoes may also be used to travel along the coasts if required.

Crossing fast-flowing river in Irian Jaya highlands using a rickety bridge.

People and Lakes

Lakes can be natural or manmade (in the case of reservoirs, for example) features. They are often places where interactions between economy, society and environment become focused, as their shores mark the interface between land and water, and humans find it attractive to exploit opportunities in both. They are sometimes also seen to be imbued with spiritual and cosmological significance.

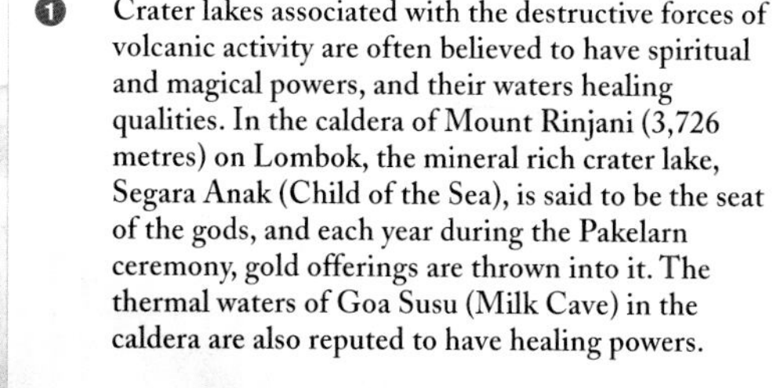

1. Crater lakes associated with the destructive forces of volcanic activity are often believed to have spiritual and magical powers, and their waters healing qualities. In the caldera of Mount Rinjani (3,726 metres) on Lombok, the mineral rich crater lake, Segara Anak (Child of the Sea), is said to be the seat of the gods, and each year during the Pakelarn ceremony, gold offerings are thrown into it. The thermal waters of Goa Susu (Milk Cave) in the caldera are also reputed to have healing powers.

2. The potential power of lakes has been exploited by damming. The three dams on the Asahan River, which drains eastwards from the southern end of Lake Toba in Sumatra, supply the energy for two power stations at Siguragura and Tangga. Artificial lakes created by dams may create problems. People's livelihoods disappear as villages and fertile land are inundated with water. Natural ecosystems are flooded and cultural sites are threatened. The Saguling and Cirata dams in West Java, for example, completed in the mid 1980s to provide electricity and water for industry and households in and around Jakarta, led to the displacement of several villages. Studies have shown that the displaced people had diminished adaptive capabilities and the compensation was sufficient to allow only 41 per cent of them to buy new land. At the same time as the dams and associated reservoirs were depriving people of land though, the newly created lakes were providing new opportunities in aquaculture.

3. Rice agriculture and plantations.

4. Many lakes teem with aquatic and lakeshore life and provide a living for lakeside inhabitants. The Ekari women of the Paniai Lakes in Irian Jaya harvest crayfish, dragonfly larvae, tadpoles, waterbugs, frogs and lizards from the lakes, and grow fruit and vegetables irrigated with lake water on the fertile lake shore. Lake Poso in Central Sulawesi contains a large number of endemic species, some of which are now threatened with extinction by carp and catfish introduced from Java. The lake is famous for its two metre long eels weighing up to 20 kilogrammes. When they migrate as elvers from the sea, the eels are caught using huge V-shaped traps set downstream from the bridge crossing the lake outflows at Tentena. Coffee and clove plantations surround the lake. Net fishing is carried out by the inhabitants of Lake Lindu, also in Sulawesi, who supplement this diet with irrigated rice and vegetables grown on its shores.

5. Fishtraps.

6. The natural beauty of lakes have made them popular tourist destinations, Lake Toba, for example. The culture of the Toba Batak who grow wet rice and other crops on its shores also serve to attract many tourists.

Coastal Aquaculture: an Environmental Lesson

Centuries ago, people living along the coasts of northern Java, northeastern Sumatra and southwestern Sulawesi developed a method of raising milkfish and prawns in ponds known as tambak, which they dug close to the landward edge of the mangrove forests. Channels were excavated, through which the tide brought in brackish water containing larvae, fry and natural nutrients, and which allowed drainage as fish and prawns needed a regular change of water.

Shrimps being harvested from shrimp ponds in Karawang, West Java. In the background an aerator can be seen in operation.

Developing the System

This traditional system was gradually modified as fish farmers found they could increase production by catching fry in the mangrove swamps to restock ponds and by adding both natural and inorganic fertilisers, and more recently manufactured feed, to pond water. This modification is often referred to as the improved extensive system. In northern Java, as aquaculture expanded away from the shoreline, fish farmers installed diesel-driven pumps to fill their *tambak* with brackish swamp water as the tidal range is less than 0.75 metres. At least a 1.5 metre drop is needed to ensure adequate water exchange.

When world prawn prices rose in the early 1980s, fish farmers in many areas of Indonesia turned to a much more intensive production system that no longer depended on brackish water. Rice fields a little distance inland were converted to ponds since the slight elevation made drainage easier. Pumps were used to carry salt water from the sea into deep pools where it was mixed with fresh water drawn from irrigation canals to obtain the desired degree of salinity before being added to the production ponds. The water was then diverted to the *tambak*, which had to be provided with paddle-wheel aerators because of the far greater number of prawns per hectare. In this intensive system prawns are raised entirely on manufactured feed. In fact up to 60 per cent of the variable cost of production is shrimp feed. As Indonesia does not have a comparative advantage in the production of prawn feed, low-cost feed will have to continue to be imported, for some time at least.

These developments were seen initially as an important way of creating productive employment opportunities for fishermen. It was, furthermore, a potential means of generating income and foreign exchange through the production and export of prawns. Other associated forms of employment could also be created: the related hatchery, transportation and processing industries, for example.

Unforeseen Problems

In most areas where a high level of intensification was attempted, the prawn industry soon encountered a number of problems. Producers found it increasingly difficult to obtain fry locally. This was because in removing the mangrove forests to make new ponds and to prevent shade being thrown over existing ponds (as it inhibited the growth of the prawns), they had done away with the prawns' natural breeding grounds and thereby broken the cycle of reproduction. This meant that farmers had the added expense of bringing fry from other regions. They also found that they could not always obtain the necessary amount and quality of fresh water in the dry season. At the same time, ponds were often flooded in the wet season because channels were inadequate for drainage on the scale required, especially where siltation had occurred. Where

Land near Denpasar, Bali being replanted with small mangrove trees. The tambak embankments have been removed and the Department of Forestry has planted mangroves under a reboisasi programme to halt coastal erosion.

Fish swarming at the inlet where fresh seawater flows into the tambak.

TRADITIONAL TAMBAK SYSTEM

1. Mangrove swamp protects the shore and ponds, and acts as a spawning ground for larvae and fry.
2. The tide carries nutrients through special channels into the tambak. The same channels also drain the ponds.
3. Tambak
4. The winding shape of the intake/drainage channels are determined by typography, as in the shape of the tambak.
5. Expansion inland is limited by the absence of tidal influence.

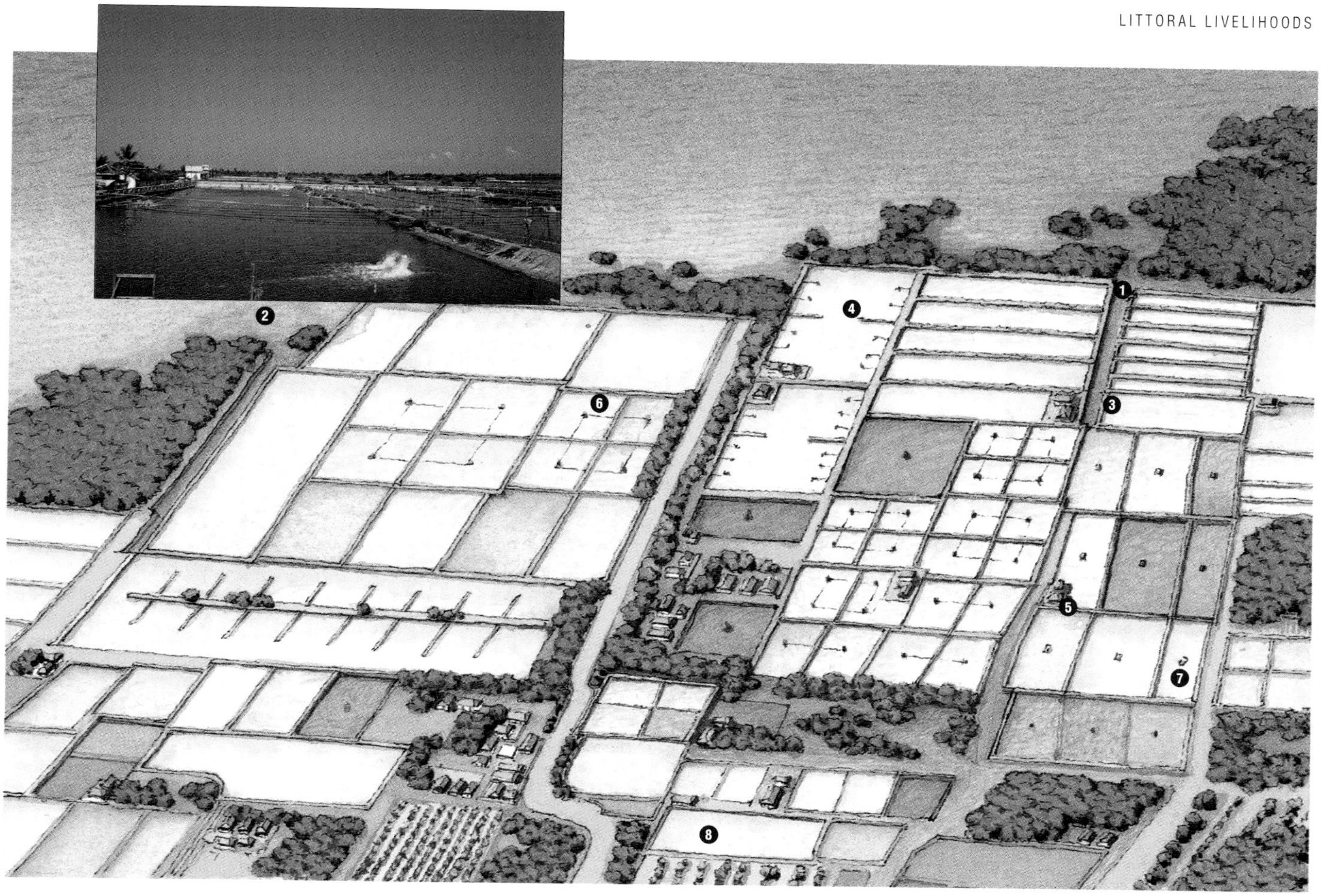

tambak depended on the irrigation network, water was frequently contaminated by fertilisers and pesticides used on agricultural land and by industrial waste from coastal towns.

Lack of experience in intensified aquaculture proved a major constraint as fish farmers, attracted by modern technology and high prices, moved further away from the traditional *tambak* system. The period of successful production lasted only until 1990 when, because of high densities in ponds, prawns were affected by a virus which caused them to decline in size and number. At the same time, many *tambak* became so poisoned by waste from excess feed left in the water as to be useless.

Wider Environmental Effects

Although environmental problems along the coast of north Java must be put down to multiple, rather than any single cause, poor *tambak* management can be highlighted as a key element in the equation for it has affected not only the pond ecosystem but also the immediate environment.

With the removal of the mangrove forests, the spawning grounds of many other marine species besides milkfish and prawns have been destroyed. Wave abrasion has increased dramatically along the exposed shoreline of northern Java, while the fields of rice farmers close to *tambak* have become contaminated by water discharged from ponds and also by the intrusion of salt through the ground water. Sedimentation has also adversely affected the coastal marine environment by reducing water clarity and inhibiting phytoplankton production and coral growth.

Environmental Measures

The government no longer permits new ponds to be constructed along Java's north coast. Mangroves are being replanted to repair some of the environmental damage, while contaminated *tambak* are being cleaned out in the hope that a less intensive system of aquaculture can be re-introduced. Further inland rice farmers are trying to bring thousands of hectares of once-productive agricultural land under cultivation again, although they know that yields will be low for some time.

Excessive expansion and intensification of a traditional system of land use over a short period of time without planning and consideration of long term sustainability of the system can lead to major environmental problems. Experiences with *tambak* illustrate the conflict of interests now occurring in resource utilisation in Java and also the delicate balance that exists within ecosystems.

INTENSIVE TAMBAK SYSTEMS

1. Mangroves removed to create more tambak leading to loss of shade, natural breeding grounds and protective strip along the shore.
2. Muddy flats lying close to the sea cannot be utilised.
3. Channels inadequate for drainage needs of tambak
4. Pipes to carry salt water from the sea
5. Pumps installed to pump salt water from the sea
6. Aerator
7. High prawn densities cause disease
8. Irrigation corral used to fill tambak, but which have become contaminated with agro-chemicals. At the same time brackish water from the tambak may pollute rice fields

An aerial view of tambak along the Sulawesi coast

Marine Fisheries

Indonesia has territorial rights over 7,893,250 square kilometres of ocean. In comparison, the country's land territory extends over 1,919,443 kilometres. Fishing is an important economic activity, providing work and an income for over 1.6 million fishermen in 1990. Indonesians consume 13.8 kilogrammes of fish per head each year, providing between 40 to 80 per cent of their dietary intake of protein. The government estimated in 1980 that its waters could yield over 6.6 million tonnes of fish each year. By 1992 only 23 per cent of this potential was being exploited.

In the Riau islands, and elsewhere, fish may be smoked for preservation

Landing a catch in the Riau islands. In 1990 there were 225,359 unpowered fishing boats and 73,144 fishing boats with simple outboard motors, operated by traditional fishermen.

Fish that cannot be consumed or sold immediately are dried.

The Fishermen

The main Indonesian fishing grounds are the warmer coastal waters, especially to the north of Java and Sumatra. Since the 16th century much traditional fishing focused on obtaining trepang for the Chinese market, and more recently, the fishing of sharks, simply for their fins–again for the Chinese market. The valuable shark species are being fished to extinction. Important export catches today are shrimp, tuna and skipjack. Sardine, mackerel, Chinese herring, sea bream, and sharks and rays are caught for the domestic market. Recently, Indonesia has become the world's leading supplier of live reef fish. About 90 per cent of the fishermen pursue traditional artisanal fishing using simple boats and equipment. They fish using hook and line, seines, traps and various forms of lift nets. The technology confines the fishermen to shallow, coastal waters, leading to overfishing in some areas.

Well under half the total catch is obtained in this way, most of which, however, is for home consumption. The remaining 10 per cent of fishermen are company based commercial fishermen in larger boats with inboard motors. They use more modern technology–lines, purse seines and drift gill nets. This latter form of fishing requires substantial capital investment in vessel and net but their productivity is much greater than that of the traditional fishermen Most of their catch is exported. The traditional fishing methods pursued by artisan fishermen involve less investment than commercial fishing and they are technically confined to limited areas, inevitably leading to overfishing in some regions, most notably the Melaka Straits and Java Sea. There are groups, such as the Bugis, Butonese and Bajau, however, who do fish large areas, covering up to 1,000 square miles in a single annual sailing trip.

UTILISATION OF FISHING AREAS

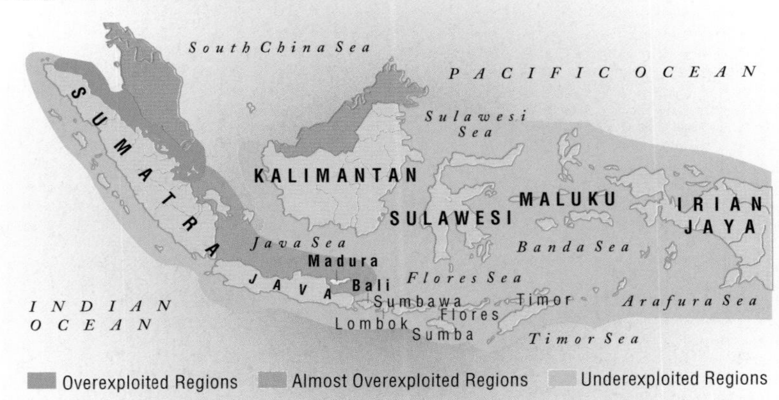

Developing the Fishing Potential

The government has recognised that investment in the fishing industry is needed if underexploited areas are to be developed to fill the growing demand for fish. Attempts to develop the traditional fishing sector in the 1970s by introducing Western technology have generally been unsuccessful. It has been pointed out that it was wrongly assumed that the resources upon which small-scale fisheries are based are infinite and that to increase the yields per fishermen and hence to raise his living standards, all that was required was to mechanise boats and introduce more efficient equipment. The introduction of improved technology

into this sector would increase productivity but may sometimes necessitate a drastic reduction in the number of fishermen in order to sustain fish yields. Local social and economic structures would also be adversely affected. Many analysts believe it is better therefore to aim at attaining maximum sustainable yields with existing traditional labour intensive technology rather than introducing modern, high labour saving devices. However, the need for cooling facilities and the improved storage and transportation of fish was recognised as crucial if Indonesia was to establish a major fishing industry. It has been estimated that up to 40 per cent of the catch is lost due to inadequate preservation and processing. It is difficult, though, for the traditional fisherman to obtain credit in order to develop these facilities. Bankers are generally reluctant to consider fishing vessels and gear that may be lost at sea as collateral, and the fishermen are forced to go to middlemen for credit.

Aware of these limitations, the Indonesian government has, since 1953, sought to develop fisheries for high-priced species in demand on the international market, through joint ventures, domestic companies and state enterprise. However, it is crucial that a tight control is kept on foreign fishing quotas to avoid overfishing. During the 1960s for example, before Indonesia declared if its Exclusive Economic Zone, Thai trawlers, having denuded fish stocks in

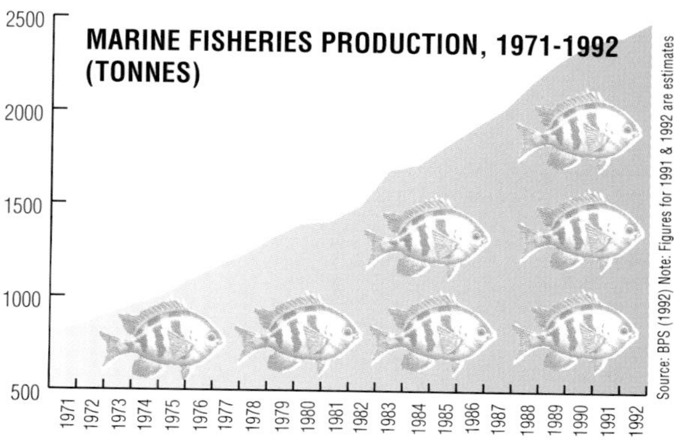

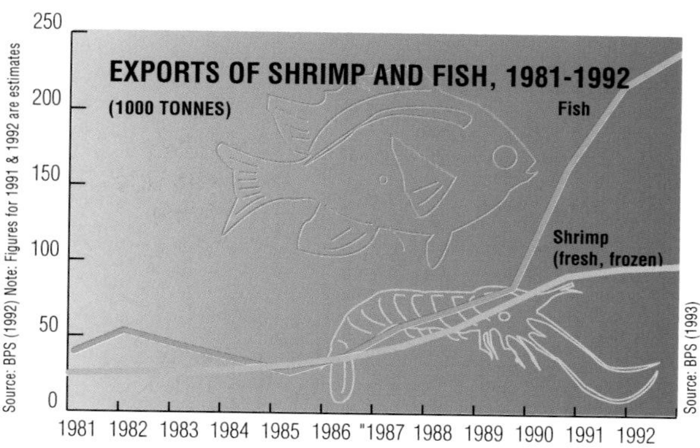

INDONESIAN FLAGGED VESSELS (FEBRUARY 1990)

Type of net	Number of licences
Gill line	39
Long line	120
Purse Seine	199
Fish net	203
Pole and line	88
Shrimp trawlers	237
Total	886

the Gulf of Thailand began exploiting the waters of the Java Sea, thus threatening the livelihood of Indonesian fishermen which often led to conflict. Such conflict is particularly acute when trawlers begin operating in the shallow inshore waters that traditional fishermen regard as their grounds. Furthermore, many kinds of fish and crustacea inhabit inshore waters during the first stages of their life and move offshore into deeper water as they mature. This means that without controls, breeding stocks are depleted and their future survival in commercial terms is placed at risk. The same fears apply to mangroves, important spawning grounds for many species. Their continual felling and destruction are also destroying the breeding grounds of many marine species.

The Japanese have been particularly keen to exploit Indonesian waters, and in the late 1970's applied to increase their fishing fleet from 82 to 300 vessels. Alarmed at the prospect of the indiscriminate taking of non-targeted fish species and age groups by trawling, thus affecting the regenerative capacity of fish stocks and the ability of artisanal fishermen to survive, Indonesia banned trawling in Indonesian waters after 1982.

Stiff penalties were imposed on those who were caught violating the law. Other forms of fishing were allowed, and by 1986, 51 Indonesian companies were operating in joint partnership or joint ventures with foreign companies. By 1990 over 1,048 foreign vessels had licences to fish in Indonesian waters. Licence fees brought the Indonesian government over US$26 million in 1990. The fishing industry also contributes significantly to agricultural exports. Exports of shrimp earned US$757 million in 1992, second only to coffee in terms of value. Fish exports, especially tuna and skipjack reached US$326 million in 1992. Japan is the main market for Indonesia's fisheries exports.

Problems faced by Marine Fisheries

Indonesia still has to deal with potential international conflicts over disputed or ill-defined marine boundaries. Malaysia has taken action against Indonesian fishing boats operating in the Melaka Straits and off the coast of Sarawak, where no agreement over international maritime boundaries has yet been reached for example. Pollution is also a threat. Conflicts have arisen between fishing and oil extraction and other industries producing waste material. Tanker incidents including oil spillage and bilge discharges have severely threatened certain waters in particular the busy Melaka Straits. Pollution has killed off the Chinese herring and teburak industry in Bagansiapiapi off the Sumatran coast. Even seemingly harmless occupations may also cause problems in isolated areas. Ambon Bay in Maluku, for example, has become polluted by the waste from numerous oil mills.

POLLUTED AREAS

Straits of Malacca, MALAYSIA, South China Sea, Sulawesi Sea, SUMATRA, KALIMANTAN, Makassar Strait, SULAWESI, INDIAN OCEAN, Java Sea, Sunda Strait, JAVA, Madura, Bali, Sumbawa, Flores Sea, Timor, Lombok, Flores, Sumba, Lombok Strait

Indonesian waters most affected by pollution from ships and off-shore oil drilling

Future Development

Four key areas need to be addressed if Indonesia is to ensure the management of its marine territories. Firstly, the administrative and institutional machinery dealing with fisheries needs reforming. It should ideally be a separate department rather than a part of the Department of Agriculture. Secondly, Indonesia needs to adopt an integrated approach to marine resources development and establish a uniform system of data collection, analysis and co-ordination of multiple demands. Thirdly, it needs to improve enforcement capability, and finally it must consider how a development and management regime can be structured to accommodate both national growth demands and the interest of the traditional Indonesian fishermen.

Artisanal fishing—a lone fisherman casts his net off the coast of Pangandaran, West Java.

Traditional Trading Boats

As recently as the early 1980s, there were relatively few commercial boats powered by diesel or even steam engines running from major Indonesian ports to smaller centres. Instead, a large fleet of sailing boats of several distinct kinds carried goods and produce between the islands of the Archipelago.

Butungese lambos unloading copra at Gresik, Java. This trade carries copra, salt, spices, dried fish and local produce to the main centres, returning with all kinds of hardware.

Repairing an old boat, Bugis village, Flores. As a result of the expansion of their trade and population, the Bugis have established new coastal communities in eastern Indonesia which depend on fishing, trading and boatbuilding.

Building a large hull, Gresik. Many craftsmen still build boats without the use of power tools, using adzes and chisels to cut planks and timbers from heavy beams of curved hardwood. The individually distinct designs of their vessels can be easily recegnised.

Trading Vessels

Nearly 1,000 Bugis schooners, called *pinisi*, of between 30 and 200 tonnes, with two masts and seven sails, were once common sights in Indonesian waters, being used to carry timber to Java and returning with cargoes of mixed hardware for the islands. But today, the *pinisi* has disappeared as a sailing ship; its masts have been removed, its hull made suitably stronger to withstand the vibration of an engine, and a large deck-house constructed aft. The crews now work for wages within a company structure.

Although the famous *pinisi* may be a vessel of the past, the Madurese still have a large fleet of lateen-rigged (triangular sail in the manner of an Arab dhow) *lèti-lèti* carrying timber to Java and general cargoes to more remote places. There is also a fleet consisting of hundreds of small (two to ten tonne) vessels sailed by Mandar crews based in west Sulawesi, the islands of southeast Kalimantan, and the island of Masalembo in the Java Sea, with lateen or fore-and-aft sails.

Another fleet with crews from Butung island and the Tukang-Besi islands off the coast of Southeast Sulawesi, and elsewhere, sail gaff- or sloop-rigged cutters, with counter-stern and centre-stern rudders. In eastern Indonesia, the trading boats under sail are usually locally owned. Although engines are becoming more common, they are frequently only temporarily attached, with the propeller sticking out over the stern on a long shaft.

The Boat Builders

Small boats are mostly built by restricted groups of specialised boat–builders belonging to one of the ethnic groups (*suku*) that sail and trade. These men, who have learned the art as apprentices, work in teams to build boats for sale. They are also prepared to travel to different regions of Indonesia to construct them wherever they are needed.

Building Techniques

Traditional hull shapes are built upon a curved keel that runs smoothly into the stem and stern pieces, with no place for a central rudder. The planks are carved to fit into position and are added one by one to the keel to form a shell. Each plank is attached to its neighbours, edge to edge, by a row of internal hardwood dowels. As the shell nears completion, curved floors and ribs are set in place crosswise and securely fixed with large tree-nails that run through the planks. Some of the ribs project above deck and are used to attach the stays that support the mast. The general plan of the floors, ribs, deck and deckhouse was copied from European colonial vessels. The unique way of building the shell first, and holding it together with internal dowels, however, dates from prehistoric times. This way of building boats highly influenced Chinese boat design: the Chinese 'junk' is actually a Southeast Asian-Chinese hybrid design, the term *jong*, from which 'junk' is derived, being a Malay word.

MADURESE JANGGOLAN

This type of boat comes from one small district on the island of Madura. It has double stems, two masts, *sokongan* supporting each sail, and deckhouse.

Boat Rig

The original Austronesian rig that assisted the colonisation of the Archipelago and the Pacific about 5,000 years ago was probably the two-boomed triangular sail, pushed up by a loose prop and supported against the wind by a stay. This is the only rig easily handled at sea without the use of a pulley–a device that was not introduced to the peoples of the Pacific until the arrival of Westerners. The rig is still used in Madura and has been adapted for large sailing boats such as the Madurese *janggolan*. The triangular sail is now used in a variety of rigs on fishing canoes and on the numerous *lèti-lèti* transport boats of the Madurese. The square or quadrilateral sail hung on a tripod mast is portrayed in relief at the 8th-9th century temple of Borobodur in Central Java, and probably spread from the ancient civilisations of Babylon and Egypt.

But the Western rig, with a stayed mast and fore-and-aft sails, was not introduced until the 19th century while the Bugis only adopted the two-masted schooner rig, with seven fore-and-aft sails, in the early 20th century. The latest innovation (post 1930s) has been the introduction of the triangular mainsail raised on a vertical spar, called a *layar nadé*.

Australian aboriginal drawing of an Indonesian (possibly Buginese) prahu, visiting Australia to collect trepang (seacucumber).

Hull Design

Progressively, from the late 19th century, the Western style of hull, with stem and sternposts set at an angle into a straight keel, has been adopted, along with the central stern rudder. Traditionally, rudders in Indonesia were on the side of the stern, held in place by a bar and pivoted on a rope so that they could be lifted over reefs and rocks. This design is almost identical to that used on boats in ancient Greece and Rome. The latest major change in hull design is the broad counter stern through which the rudder pivots in a tube. The virtues of all these sailing boats are their low running costs and their flexibility in responding rapidly to changing market needs.

Coastal Settlement

As a result of the increase of their trade and population, the Bugis people from South Sulawesi, and also the Butungese and Mandar peoples, have established new coastal communities, particularly in eastern Indonesia. This process of migration and coastal settlement is long established. Initially, a few houses are built on poles driven into a beach in a lightly populated area. Survival in the early stages of settlement depends on fishing, trading and boat–building, which in turn depend on the exploitation of 'free' natural resources. Coral rocks are mined to form the foundations for houses and paths, local timber is used to build and repair boats and buildings, and fish forms the main element in the diet. With their better technology, greater resistance to Western diseases as a result of their trading history, and supported by their trading network, the Bugis progressively have taken over local land, first for food and later for cash crops. The famed aggressiveness of the Bugis has also been highlighted to explain their ability to adapt to new, often harsh, environments.

TRADITIONAL BOATS

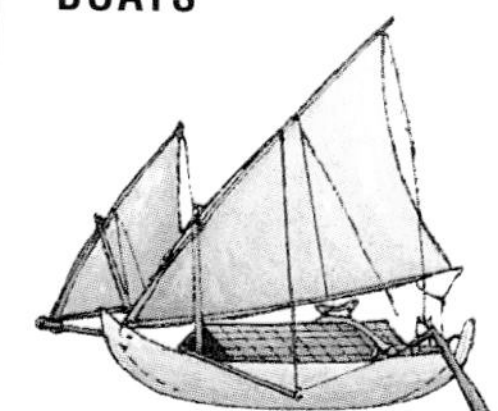

Lèti-lèti with fixed main sail. It differs from other boats in the use of a steering oar rather than rudder.

Butungese lambo, with nadé rig but with centre rudder and counter-stern (pantat bèbèk).

West Sulawesi quarter-rudder lambo with slope-roof deck-house and nadé rig.

A bustling market in Bali. The rapidly expanding urban population is supported by a complex food production and distribution system.

PERCENTAGE OF POPULATION IN URBAN COMMUNITIES BY PROVINCE

- 10 and below
- 11 — 20
- 21 — 30
- 31 — 40
- 41 — 50
- 51 — 60
- 61 and above

CITY AND TOWN LIFE

The obverse of rural and agricultural, is urban and industrial. The former is often viewed as 'traditional' in character the latter, 'modern'. This distinction between two Indonesian 'worlds' and the terms used to describe that distinction are in many respects inadequate and deceptive. There are degrees of rural and urban-ness, rather than a clear demarcation between the two. Many people and families have their feet in both these worlds; family members work for part of the year in urban-based jobs, and part of the year on the farm. There is thus also considerable cross-fertilisation and interaction between the two Indonesian 'worlds'.

Notwithstanding these difficulties, urban management and change is distinctive. The rate of growth of urban areas has in certain cases out-run the ability of local and national government to 'manage' change. This can be seen reflected in environmental problems such as water-borne pollution and traffic congestion, social problems such as inadequate housing, and economic problems rooted in a scarcity of jobs–or at least what are officially perceived to be the right kind of jobs. Urban issues are, however, being more effectively confronted though finding satisfactory solutions may take many years. The scale of the combined problem, the speed of change, the scarcity of funds, and the lack of skilled personnel pose significant challenges to planners.

But although the problems may remain severe, urban dwellers do cope–usually highly effectively–with city life. In addition, there is a continuing flow of people from rural areas, whether they be permanent or circular migrants, who arrive usually quite aware of the challenges they face. Most urban dwellers make their varied livings in a sector of the economy that, until recently, was largely ignored and which still defies easy categorisation and measurement. The so-called informal sector employs more people than any other and is a critical part of the urban economy. The role of small-scale, unregulated, almost invisible actors in the urban economy is seen, for example, in the supply of food to city dwellers. The threads which bind rural and peri-urban producers with market traders, brokers and wholesalers, and they in turn with *warung* owners, street vendors and small-scale home food processing enterprises are complex. The larger export-oriented manufacturing enterprises discussed in the next chapter which gain the most attention and have the highest profile, but the varied mosaic of small-scale, often family and home-based enterprises are in many respects, important to the urban population and economy.

The rapid growth of urban areas has led to the expansion of road networks. Traffic jams cause pollution and threaten the health of city kampung dwellers who live on public land near major roads.

Some streets like this one in Yogyakarta are reminiscent of Indonesia's towns and cities before modernisation.

Becak drivers are now banned from Jakarta, but there are still some who are able to make a living in places like Solo.

URBAN POPULATION BY PROVINCE AND ISLAND GROUP (percentage), 1990

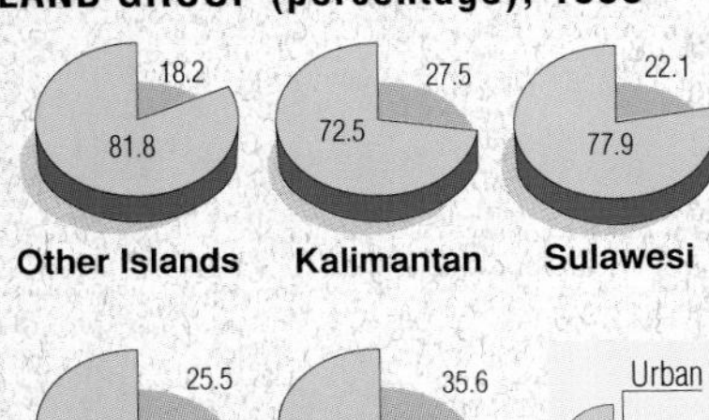

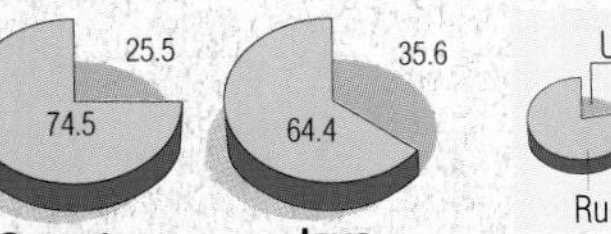

Modernising and Urbanising

Modernisation is often synonymous with industrialisation and urbanisation, the three components of 'development'. Indonesia's industrialisation rests firmly in, and on, Java. Although Indonesia's natural resources are concentrated in the Outer Islands, Java had 69 per cent of Indonesia's urban population of around 55 million in 1990 as well as many of the medium and large sized firms.

Goods being loaded for export at port in Java. Many ports rely on the vast pool of casual urban labour.

Measuring Change

A village or *desa* can be classified as 'urban' if it meets three criteria: first, if it has a population density of 5,000 people per square kilometres or more; second, if 25 per cent, or fewer, of its households are 'agricultural'; and third if it supports at least eight urban facilities, such as a school, hospital, cinema, shopping centre, bank or factory. However these criteria are highly arbitrary. For example, many people are only temporary residents in the city, and are recorded in the national census as rural residents. Yet they may work for long periods in modern sectors of the economy, while living in a city or town. Those who remain in the countryside may spend more time working at home than in the field, producing handicrafts and other 'manufactures', yet they are defined as farmers. Over large areas of Java, rural and urban are fused into a mosaic of interaction. This is seen as a general feature of development in Asia.

Structural Change: Modernising

Since 1970, Indonesia has experienced rapid and sustained economic growth. However, while agriculture has expanded at little more than three per cent, manufacturing has grown at a rate of well over ten per cent per annum. These different rates of growth have contributed to a fundamental process of structural change. Many of the fastest growing manufacturing industries have been geared to export. Although almost all of Indonesia's exports were

The red slat roofs of kampung communities can still be found in sprawling, modern Jakarta.

natural resource based–in particular oil, gas and timber products–until the mid 1980s, since then growth has been concentrated in non-resource based industries. From two per cent of total exports in 1980, manufactured products in 1992 contributed 39 per cent of total exports by value.

Urbanising

One of the clearest trends in Indonesia's development is a process of urbanisation. In other words, an increase in the proportion of the population who are living in urban areas. In 1930, there were only seven towns with a population of over 100,000, and a mere nine per cent of the population were classified as living in urban areas. At the last census in 1990, this latter figure had grown to 30 per cent, representing 55 million people. The rapid rate of urban growth, especially since independence, has severely taxed urban infrastructures and the planning efforts of municipal authorities and central government. In Jakarta, the authorities announced in 1970 that the city was 'closed' to all new migrants. Inhabitants were only issued with identification cards if they were able to supply proof of employment and an address for accommodation. This attempt at 'blocking' Jakarta's growth subsequently failed. Despite the failure of this policy, one of the key objectives of many rural development programmes is to keep people 'on the farm'. The failure to stem the tide of movement to urban areas demonstrates the relative powerlessness of the authorities to control and limit urbanisation.

Three metropolitan regions or 'mega-cities' dominate Indonesia's urban hierarchy: Jakarta, Surabaya and Bandung, all in Java. Jakarta, with a population of over eight million is already the world's eighth largest urban agglomeration. As a result, planning documents now talk of *Jabotabek*–an area which encompasses the adjacent *kabupaten* (districts) of Bogor, Tangerang and Bekasi, as well as Jakarta. Such areas have been termed 'Extended Metropolitan Regions'.

Some of the consequences of rapid and uncontrolled urban growth are burgeoning squatter and slum settlements, over-stretched transport systems, inadequate sewerage and waste disposal infrastructures, growing pollution, low levels of clean water provision, growing numbers of urban poor, and ineffectual planning. Migrants to urban areas are all aware of the challenges that await them: despite the obstacles, they still make the journey because opportunities are invariably that much better than in the countryside.

Before the war, Surabaya was already a major commercial and industrial centre in the archipelago, a role which it is poised to regain today.

DISTRIBUTION OF GROSS DOMESTIC PRODUCT (PER CENT), 1970 & 1991

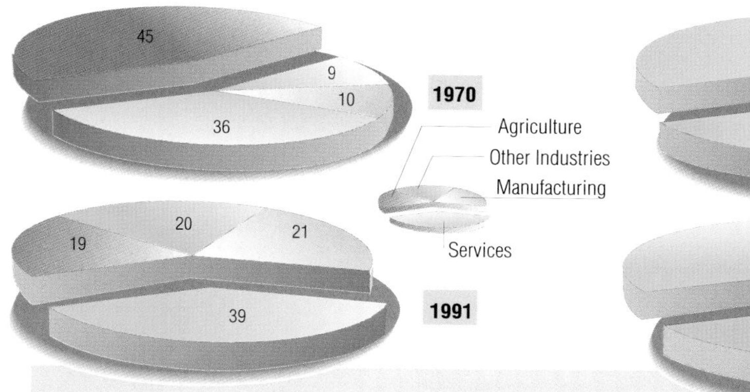

EMPLOYMENT BY SECTOR (1965 & 1989-1991)

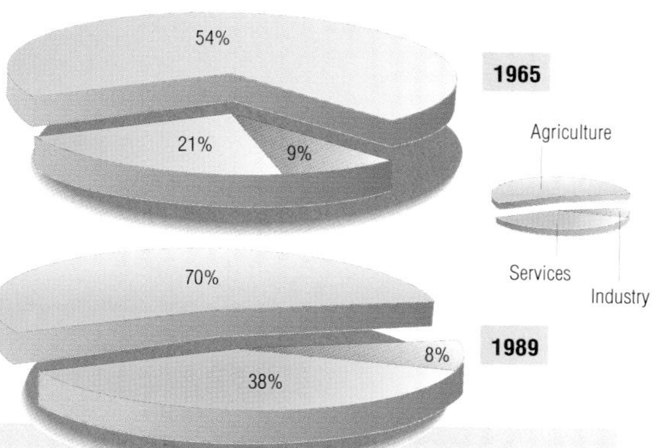

Cinema billboards in Jakarta. The presence of cinemas are one criteria used to classify urban areas.

Rapid urban growth can overstretch existing transport systems resulting in traffic congestion. The resulting pollution can also become a threat to the general health of urban dwellers.

KOTADESASI: URBANISING THE COUNTRYSIDE

Drawing on work initially conducted in Java, the geographer TG McGee has argued that Asia has a geographical characteristic which sets it apart from other parts of the world. That is, the presence of high-density agricultural regions based on the intensive cultivation of wet rice. Nowhere is this observation more apposite than in Java. These so-called Extended Metropolitan Regions (EMRs) or Desakota have:

- spatially concentrated pools of skill-orientated labour of considerable size.
- a varied and inter-locking range of land uses.
- a high level of accessibility and mobility associated with the development of modern transport and communications (in particular, cheap two-stroke engine-driven transport).

Cities in Java, and in Asia in general, are undergoing a process of kotadesasi. The term is taken from two Indonesian words - *kota* (town) and *desa* (village), and is used to describe the urbanisation of the countryside. The suffix *si* indicates that this is a process.

T G McGee writes that *Kotadesasi* is a:
'process involving the growth of distinct regions of agricultural and non-agricultural activity characterised by intense interaction of commodities and people. ... The *kotadesasi* regions are generally characterised by extreme fluidity and mobility of the population.'

In short, McGee maintains that Java exhibits not city-based urbanisation, but region-based urbanisation where formerly agricultural populations are drawn into the processes of urbanisation and industrialisation, *in situ*.

SPATIAL CONFIGURATION OF HYPOTHETICAL ASIAN AND WESTERN URBAN SYSTEM

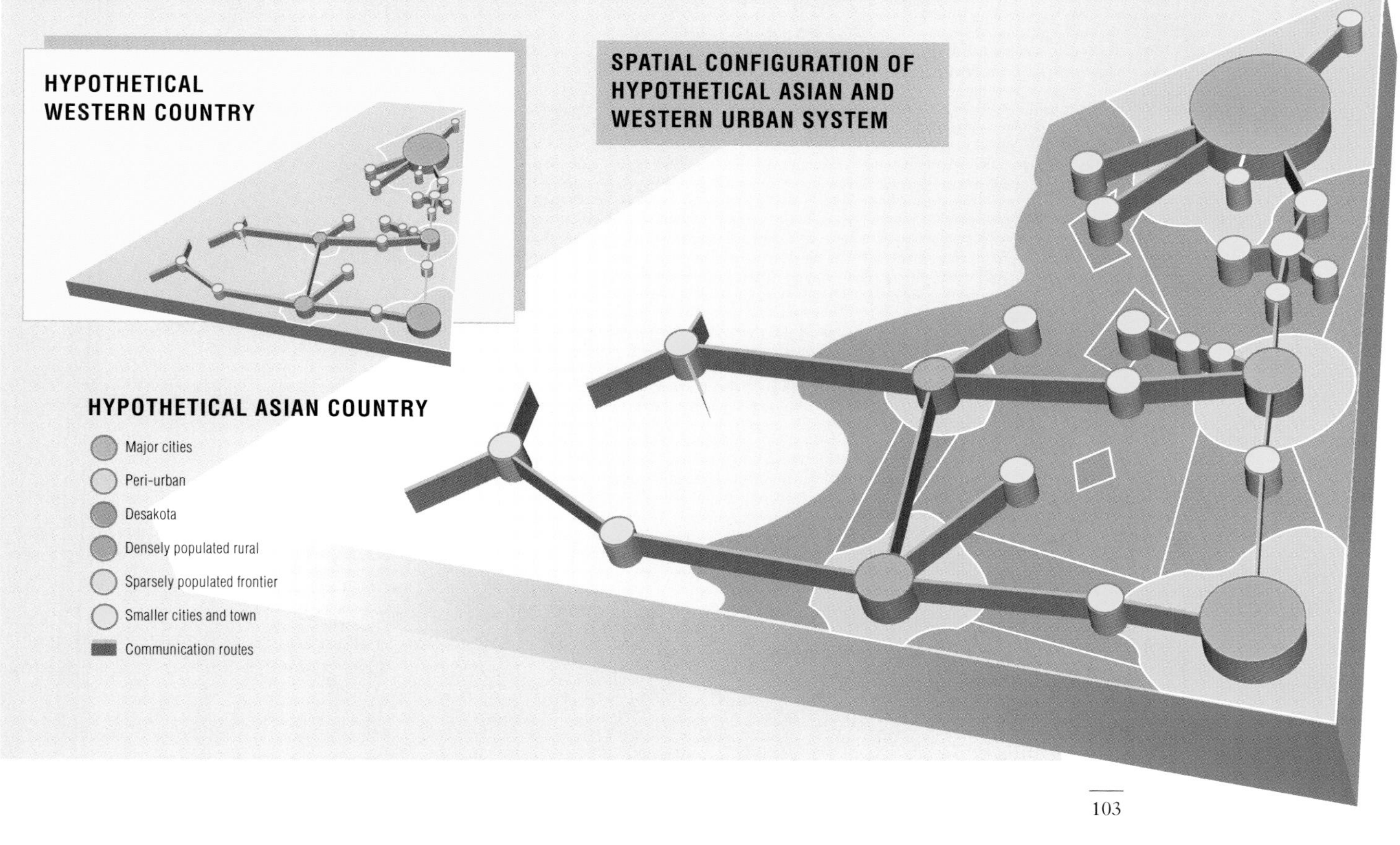

HYPOTHETICAL WESTERN COUNTRY

HYPOTHETICAL ASIAN COUNTRY

- Major cities
- Peri-urban
- Desakota
- Densely populated rural
- Sparsely populated frontier
- Smaller cities and town
- Communication routes

Urban Planning and Management

Although Indonesia's court cities, such as Yogyakarta, contained well planned central precincts, the first measures to systematically plan and to improve Indonesia's urban areas were introduced during the colonial period. Current planning legally falls under the control of the Planning Ordinance of 1948 and the Town Planning Regulations of 1949.

POPULATION OF THE LARGEST CITIES IN 1990 & PROJECTED POPULATION IN 2000 (Millions)

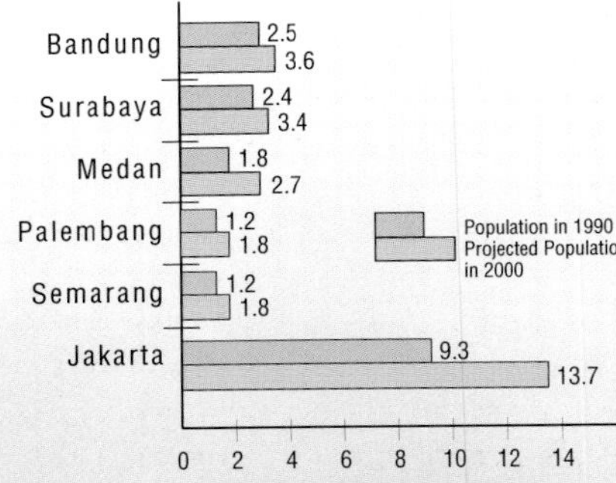

Indonesian cities are often a mix of the old and new. This old photo shows the PT Java Maluku Building in Surabaya, designed around 1900.

The Bandung Urban Development Project was responsible for the improvement of a number of urban kampungs or villages.

Urban Policies

Urban policy in the first years of the New Order focused on a handful of cities, Jakarta in particular, and a limited range of activities. Among them was the Kampung Improvement Programme (KIP), which in the 1960s concentrated on improving water supply and access to these urban villages or *kampung*. In subsequent years the range of cities targeted has increased, and new programmes concentrate on such areas as low income housing and market improvements.

An Integrated Urban Infrastructure Development Programme (IUIDP) was phased in during the 1980s in an attempt to provide a more coordinated and systematic approach to infrastructure development in Indonesia's cities.

During the 1980s the Indonesian government embarked upon the ambitious task of developing a National Urban Development Strategy (NUDS), with support from United Nations agencies. The final 1985 NUDS report identified 508 important urban centres throughout Indonesia, and advocated increased governmental support for the development of towns and cities, especially outside Java, where urban areas are often connected to resource-based export industries. While the attempt to develop a long-term strategic vision for Indonesia's cities is welcome, the difficulties of implementing a comprehensive spatial strategy are proving less tractable.

Apart from Jakarta, which has provincial status, the larger of Indonesia's towns and cities are called *kotamadya*. They are governed by a *walikota*, or mayor, and have the same status as a *kabupaten*. *Kota administratif* are administrative towns of lower rank. The remaining towns and cities have no special status, though they may be the administrative centre of the surrounding region. Physical planners with links to the Ministry of Public Works are responsible for land use planning and infrastructure development in urban areas, while economic planning comes under the offices known as Bappeda, which are connected to the Ministry of Domestic Affairs.

Managing Urban Growth

There are 55 million Indonesians living in urban areas, according to the 1990 Census. This represents 31 per cent of the total population, which is a low level of urbanisation by world standards. The number of Indonesians living in urban areas grew at a rate of 2.6 per cent per annum between 1980 and 1990. As Indonesia is urbanising at a fast rate, it will soon catch up with the rest of the world. Projections anticipate an urban population of 76 million (36 per cent of the population) in the year 2000.

In 1990 six Indonesian cities contained one million people or more. These were Jakarta, Bandung, Surabaya, Medan, Palembang and Semarang. Some commentators have speculated that the entire 200 kilometres corridor which connects Bandung to Jakarta will eventually become a massive urban region. Population growth in Bandung has been fastest on the fringes of the city, beyond the boundaries of the existing *kotamadya*.

The fringe area doubled its urban population to 1.3 million between 1980 and 1990 and resulted in the Bandung 'mega-urban' region growing to a population of 3.3 million in 1990.

Living conditions in Indonesia's cities range from good to very bad. The standards in the upper middle class suburban enclaves of the cities are very high. Yet other parts of these cities are among the poorest in the world, with people crammed into inadequately serviced squatter settlements, often located in environmentally degraded and unhealthy areas. Many of Indonesia's urban problems are due to the rapid growth of cities since Independence, and the difficulties planners have faced in trying to keep pace. With the urban population expected to grow by, on average, more than two million each year until the end of the century, providing jobs for the expanding urban labour force is a key objective. Urban authorities in Indonesia have generally been slow to appreciate the significance of the urban informal sector as a job-creating mechanism, instead reacting against its somewhat disorderly appearance. Compounding the issue is the high cost of providing much-needed infrastructure, and the difficulty of raising funds to support capital works programmes.

Challenges for Urban Planners

While Indonesia has received considerable support in improving the way cities are planned and managed over the last two decades, there are still major difficulties to be overcome. One notable challenge is a shortage of local government officers with the planning, financial and socio-economic analysis skills necessary to tackle new urban problems. It has meant that urban authorities have resorted to preparing quick plans, often using outside consultants and with insufficient input from local communities. Another problem has been the communication gap between those who prepare the plans and those who implement them, and city managers, which has sometimes delayed the implementation of planning initiatives.

Providing appropriate land for urban expansion is another specific challenge. Control of land use is exercised through local offices of the National Land Agency. However, land development has been left largely to the private sector and state companies (which include the National Urban Development Corporation, or *Perum Perumnas*), which has often led to the haphazard patterns of land use on the urban peripheral areas. Not infrequently, this has created, indeed even exacerbated, environmental problems as urban areas have been allowed to spread indiscriminately into environmentally-sensitive hinterlands.

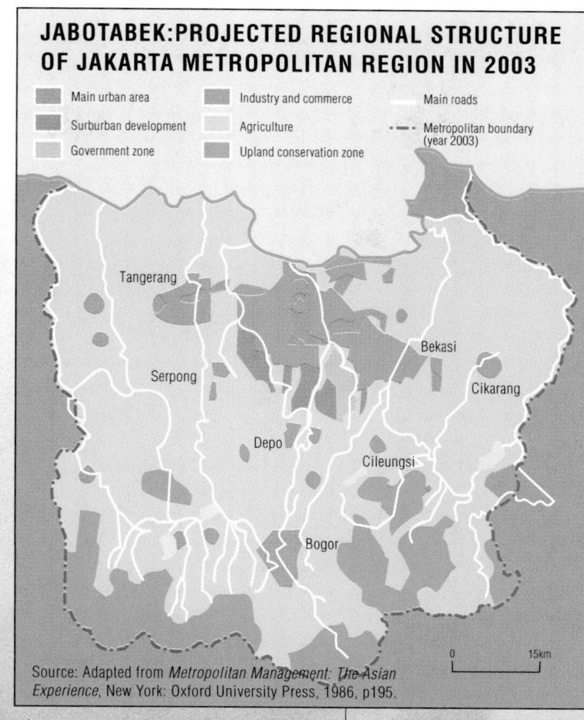

Providing housing for Indonesia's growing urban population continues to be a major concern. The Kampung Improvement programme and self-help schemes have addressed the needs of some of the poorer sections of the community, but public housing schemes in Indonesia have not worked particularly well. As a result, housing provision is increasingly being left to the private sector. Clean water and efficient sewerage systems have received considerable attention, generally with international support. In the larger cities chronic traffic and transport problems have had a high priority, but it has only been in the largest cities, such as Jakarta, that this has resulted in major investments in freeways and an elevated railway network. In the future, the effective functioning of the cities will provide a crucial support for Indonesia's industrialisation and urbanisation. This point is increasingly recognised by the present government, but the extent of current urban problems, and the cost of many solutions, will make better cities a long-term proposition.

In larger cities like Jakarta, transport problems have led to large investments in freeways and road networks.

New middle-class housing on the fringes of Bandung, West Java.

Modern skyline of Jakarta.

Kampung Life in Jakarta: Rural Feet in the City

Indonesian cities often contain smaller communities, living and functioning much as a rural community would do. Many of these 'urban villages' began spontaneously, some just after World War II, with migrants arriving from other parts of Java, or even from Sumatra, to try and earn a living as small traders in the city centre. The introduction of the Kampung Improvement Scheme has brought better infrastructural facilities and services to these urban village communities.

Boundary canal separating kampung from city

Sitting and chatting in the kampung.

Life in an Urban Kampung

Households in urban kampungs can be made up of very diverse groups. Some of the older inhabitants are established residents who settled in the kampungs during the 1950s and 60s. They may include married couples and their children, and relatives who live in rural villages that are within 30 to 50 kilometres of the city. These members come to work in the city when they are in need of money, and return home after a while.

Women frequently earn their living by running cooked food stalls, either on main city streets or smaller side roads. When trade is good, the stall owner may have several relatives staying with her to help her run her business. They will help carry raw food from the market, pluck chickens, dice vegetables, cook food, push the cart to its trade location, and serve customers throughout the night. Items offered at these kinds of stalls include banana fritters, fried chicken, beef, fish, cashew nuts and beer, among others. During the 1970s, however, many such traders saw their trade fall away as events such as the anti-trader campaign, the banning of becaks, and building developments forced them to move to less economically favourable positions. The anti-trader campaign forbids small traders from operating in the city centre. Errant small traders could have their equipment confiscated or be fined for breaching these regulations. Many stall owners were forced to get rid of their mobile stalls from strategic central-city locations, and resorted to carrying their wares on hip and head through the city streets.

Also to be found in these urban kampungs are communal lodging houses with up to 20 people living in them at any one time. The tenants who use these boarding houses generally live in cramped conditions with several people sharing one small room, their few possessions stacked in suitcases, or hanging from roof beams. These men tend to come to the city on a temporary basis, and in order to channel as much money as they can back to their families, they live as cheaply and frugally as possible.

HOUSEHOLD TYPES, 1975-1979

This schematic diagram of the case study kampung shows the location of household stalls and producers in this 77 household kampung. The goods and services that are offered are often classified as informal sector activities. Number of households in brackets. Diagram not drawn to scale.

Neighbouring house not in sample; Iced drinks, snacks; Prayer house; Gado gado; Dried foods, rice, mosquito coils, soap etc; Sweets; Fresh vegetables; Fried nuts, snacks; Cooked meals; Ice & lollies; Porridge; Rice, salted fish; Spices, tea; Padang empek 2; Dried foods, rice, krupuk, sweets; Noodle soup; Cigarettes; Coconut cakes; Fresh vegetables; Sweets; Kerosene, cooking oil; Cakes; Cooked meats; Breakfast food; Fruit pieces, cakes, sweets; Cideng Canal

- Nuclear households, total 34
- Extended households, total 21
- Communal lodging-houses, total 9
- Truncated households, total 13
- Regular stall (15)
- Occasional stall (7)
- Owner of stall
- Occasional deliveries of cakes (5)

A SECTION THROUGH A KAMPUNG IN JAKARTA

THE KAMPUNG IMPROVEMENT PROGRAMME

Indonesia's best known development intiative, targeting the urban poor, is the Kampung Improvement Programme (KIP), initiated in Jakarta in 1969. Its motivation lay in the recognition that Jakarta's burgeoning and densely settled kampungs lacked most services and were characterised by high levels of sickness and mortality. The KIP intended to provide an improved physical (roads, walkways, canals, piped water) and social (schools, health clinics) infrastructure at low cost by retaining most of the existing housing stock. This philosophy has remained a hallmark of the programme since its inception, although some emphases have changed.

The KIP programme has diversified to include a wider range of urban services such as sanitation, through the construction of bathing, washing and toilet facilities. The physical condition of the urban kampung was significantly improved under the programme which is generally regarded as a success. There has also been a gradual move away from shared, communal facilities like community standpipes (*left*), wells and latrines, towards individual or private facilities.

The spending of government funds has encouraged private investment. There are two reasons for this. Firstly, residents feel more secure in tenurial terms as a result of the official imprimatur represented by the KIP (although this was not an intention of the programme) and they have therefore been willing to invest private resources in improving their homes; and secondly, residents have felt obliged to bring their own houses up to the standards set by the KIP in the surrounding environment. The newest version of the KIP is the Community Infrastructure Programme or CIP which incorporates a greater recognition of the role that local communities and Non-Government Organisations or NGOs can play in designing and implementing projects.

The Founding of the Kampung

Some city kampung may include whole areas of families who are related to each other. These are usually areas where the residents have been there for several generations, their parents or grandparents having come to the city in the 1920s. These families tend to work in fixed employment as guards, electricians, sweepers and office workers. The kampung headman is likely to be chosen from this group, who view themselves as the founding clan. The position of headman is supposed to be an elected one, but in many cases it becomes a hereditary position, being passed from father to son. The headman communicates government programmes to the people and registers those who come to and leave the kampung. He is also expected to act as mediator in the village's dealings with government agencies and other external bodies. The religious leader is also likely to come from the founding clan. The mosque often provides the only large space where people can meet, and is the hub of the community.

Some of these established kampung were on the periphery of the cities when they were founded, and in market garden areas with only one or two large village houses. Rubbish dumps, swamps and rivers, and tree lined, unmade roads were often all that were in evidence. Vegetables were grown in these areas to be taken to the city by foot.

In one kampung study, it was found that after World War II, there was a rapid influx of people from West and Central Java. Later, more people came from East Java and Sumatra. Within 50 years, the population on this area consisting of 1.8 hectares of land grew from 50 to 3,500. Many villagers fled to the city from the ravages of war during the Japanese and Dutch occupations. Typically newcomers first stayed with relatives or friends. Houses were built from scavenged materials. Existing large village houses were subdivided into smaller units for aged parents and married brothers and sisters. Clusters of relatives and people from the same village lived in adjoining homes. Over ten to 20 years, single-storied houses were gradually converted into two storied ones. Temporary construction materials gave way to brick. Chicken wire windows were replaced by glass. Tiles and cement substituted earthen floors. Houses with few possessions were suddenly cluttered with sideboards of crockery, radios, televisions, refrigerators, furniture and motorbikes. Solid doors protected the new possessions inside.

Food being prepared by kampung traders.

« Improved kampung houses after the economic 'boom' of the early 1970s.

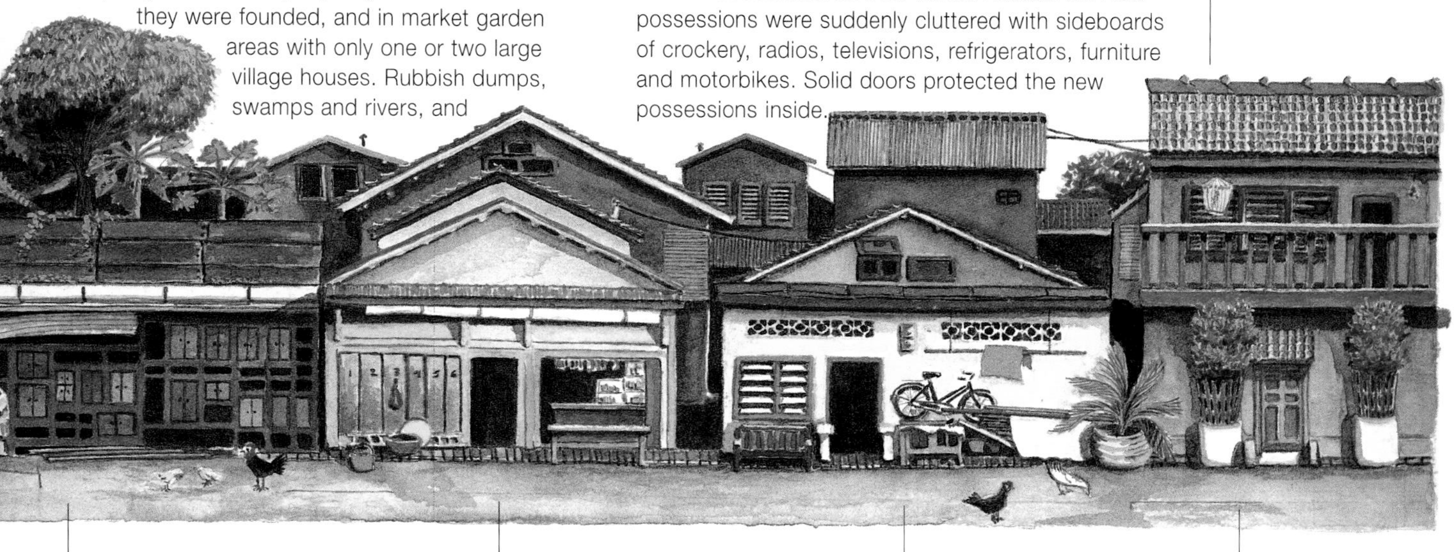

The Informal Sector

An informal sector exists outside the formal economy that provides a wide range of consumer services and home-manufactured produce. Although it may have had its origins in the colonial economy, it still provides an important source of income for most urban dwellers today.

»»Informal sector activities figure prominently in this Indonesian street scene. Becak and dokar drivers and street vendors pack the street plying their wares and services.

Informal Sector Diversity

Indonesian streets are frequently dominated by street traders, pedicab drivers and scavengers, but they certainly do not cover the whole range of activities that comprise the informal sector. Some commentators have estimated that approximately 25 per cent of rural and urban kampung dwellings not only house people, but are also used for small scale enterprises ranging from tailors and shoemakers, to potteries and repairshops. Another category of informal activities found in Indonesian cities are the numerous jobbers and casual labourers who are employed without contractual agreement on construction sites, and in harbours, factories and trading and traffic centres. A significant part of the female labour force also work as domestic servants.

The term 'informal' sector is usually used to denote a wide range of activities. The formal sector represents the more administratively visible part of the economy and society, namely the public and private corporate sector. The 'informal sector' is defined in terms of what it is not, namely 'formal'. Nevertheless, the informal sector represents the largest segment of the urban economy. Nationwide, one calculation estimated that in 1986 the informal sector employed some 72 per cent of the urban labour force.

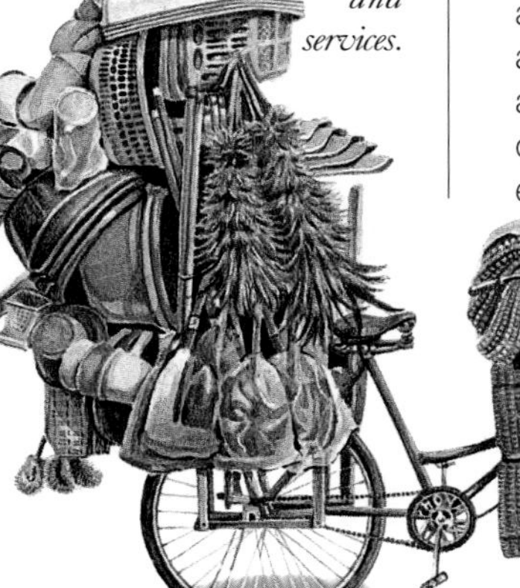

Common household items are often sold by mobile vendors on bicycles.

Like his turn-of-the-century counterpart, the modern basket-seller (below) still brings his goods to market by hand, slung on a shoulder pole.

Simple consumer items like wooden clogs and sandals are easily produced in small batches and can be sold at neighbouring markets.

Roots of the Informal Sector

The informal sector is not a recent phenomenon. During the colonial era, urban centres were strictly controlled and the non-European population was largely contained in separate ethnic *kampen* (quarters). These areas had a lively 'bazaar' economy which also formed the home base for the retail trade and functioned as a pool of cheap labour for the colonial economy. After independence, migration and settlement regulations were relaxed and a large influx of rural migrants began to move cityward. Other factors which contributed to the urban population explosion were the political unrest of the 50s and early 60s, stagnating employment in agriculture from the early 70s, and improved public transport in the 80s. As cities are perceived as centres of hope and prosperity, measures to slow down the rural exodus have generally failed and urbanisation appears to be an irreversible process.

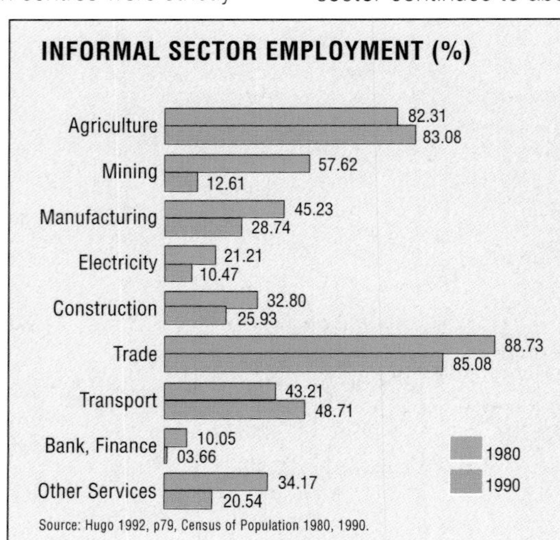

INFORMAL SECTOR EMPLOYMENT (%)

Sector	1980	1990
Agriculture	82.31	83.08
Mining	57.62	12.61
Manufacturing	45.23	28.74
Electricity	21.21	10.47
Construction	32.80	25.93
Trade	88.73	85.08
Transport	43.21	48.71
Bank, Finance	10.05	03.66
Other Services	34.17	20.54

Source: Hugo 1992, p79, Census of Population 1980, 1990.

Continuing Importance

Growth in Indonesia's industrial sector was supposed to 'trickle down' to the traditional sectors of the economy. Instead, urban industrialisation tended to widen structural inequalities between the handful of leading sectors and the rest of the economy. With the International Labour Office concluding in the 1970s that the informal sector was both economically efficient and profitable, there emerged the view that the informal sector be promoted as a strategy to tackle structural inequalities and to meet the basic needs of the poor.

Continuing rural-urban migration and the economic recession in the early 1980s reaffirmed the importance of the informal sector in terms of work and income generation. While the formal sector has a tendency to produce 'jobless growth', the informal sector continues to absorb the bulk of the estimated 2.4 million job seekers who annually enter the labour market. These jobs are created with little capital and without any subsidy from the state. Such informal enterprises often rely on indigenous resources, including recycled materials, and produce predominantly for local markets. The entrepreneurs mobilise their own financial resources via family networks, savings clubs and rotating credit

GENERALISED CHARACTERISTICS OF THE FORMAL AND INFORMAL SECTOR

FORMAL	INFORMAL
Description	
• Employee of large firm	• Self-employed
• Often a multinational	• Small scale/family enterprise
• Much capital involved	• Little capital involved
• Capital intensive with relatively few workers, mechanised	• Labour intensive with use of very few tools.
• Expensive raw materials	• Using cheap or recycled waste materials
• A guaranteed standard in the final product	• Often a low standard in quality of goods
• Regular hours (often long) and wages (often low)	• Irregular hours and uncertain wages
• Fixed prices	• Prices rarely fixed and so negotiable (bartering)
• Jobs done in factories	• Jobs often done in the home (cottage industry) or on the streets
• Government and multinational help	• No government assistance
• Legal	• Often outside the law (illegal)
• Usually males	• Often children and females
Type of job	
• Manufacturing–both local and multinational industries	• Distributive-street peddlers and small stalls
• Government-created jobs such as the police, army and civil service	• Services–shoecleaners, selling clothes and fruit
	• Small scale industries such as food processing, dress repairs and furniture repairs, among others
Advantages	
• Uses some skilled and many unskilled workers	• Employs many thousands of unskilled workers
• Provides permanent jobs and regular wages	• Jobs may provide some training and skills which might lead to better jobs in the future
• Produces goods (like cars and food) for the emerging middle classes so that profits may remain within the country	• Any profit will be used within the city or remitted to the rural areas
• Waste materials provide raw materials for the informal sector	• Uses local and waste materials–the products will be for local use by informal sector, the lower paid people

In some Indonesian cities, the informal sector can be an important source of foodstuffs–vegetables and fruits may be sold by roadside vendors.

Informal sector activities continue into the night, such as in the case of this peanut-seller in Jakarta.

systems. Accommodation for newcomers is provided and training given on the job. Many workers in the informal sector also maintain strong ties with their places of origin and often foster plans to return. Urban-rural remittances, particularly on Java, occur at a very large scale and for many village households this capital flow has even become the major source of household income.

There is a tendency to associate such informal sector activities with poverty. While it is true that many workers in this sector are poor, it would be wrong to assume that earnings are necessarily lower than formal sector wages. Budget studies carried out in Surabaya between 1977 and 1983, show that wages in local formal industry are some 25 per cent to 40 per cent lower than the incomes earned by street vendors. Apart from generating work and income for a large proportion of the urban population, the informal sector is also a major supplier and distributor of basic services and needs such as water, food, clothes and shelter. In urban areas the self-built housing sector meets up to some 80 per cent of housing needs. Without the informal sector the majority of the urban population could not even survive in the city.

«This mobile cigarette and drinks stall is a fully-fitted out business, complete with posters and loudspeaker for attracting customers.

INFORMAL GROWTH, A CASE FROM SURABAYA

At the beginning of this century, Wonokusumo north-east of Surabaya was a small village. It was bought and used as a dumpsite by the cleansing department. In the mid 60s, when the site was filled, the land was divided into 8 metres by 15 metres lots and allocated to 60 municipal sweepers. Provided with building permits and encouraged by security of ownership, the area became built over. Relatives and friends from the island of Madura came flocking in. Many sweepers let-out parts of their houses and when relatives could not pay the rent, the landlords tried to find them a job. Frequently, the villagers turned to informal sector activities for employment. A popular solution was to save money by means of an *arisan* (savings club) and to invest this in *becaks* (*right*). In 1978 there were 165 becaks. The becak-drivers, in their turn, patronised the other informal sector enterprises like the food stalls, cycle menders, houseshops and water vendors. The village at that time consisted of 320 households, many of them incomplete. Single males circulated frequently between Madura and Surabaya. If they could not afford shelter, they slept in their becaks. When it was raining, they moved to the porch of a relative or stayed in the *langgar* (prayer house).

Markets

Generally, small-scale local trade and wholesaling is run by local people who operate in a circuit of travelling markets that might encompass an 80 kilometre radius. Large-scale inter-market bulk trade is often conducted by Chinese, Indians and other ethnic groups with networks stretching across regional boundaries. The vast majority of market trading in Indonesia is within the monetised economy. Only a few exceptions remain. For example, in Lembata (Eastern Indonesia) pure barter can still be seen as a way of life.

Ox cart taking goods to the market. in Surabaya, East Java.

»An old painting of a market in Java.

Fruit and vegetable sellers.

Market System

In parts of rural Indonesia, including Java, Bali and Sumatra, periodic markets still operate, where traders' circuits will take them from one town to another in a regular pattern. In 1824 when the missionaries R. Burton and N. Ward travelled through the Silindung valley in Sumatra they noted the presence of periodic markets. A similar system can still be found operating in towns around Lake Toba today.

In rural central Java, farmers and artisans may retail their produce directly at local markets, but most of the trade is conducted by small-scale retail traders *(bakul)*, who are predominantly women. They deal in one type or a narrow range of produce such as dried foods, vegetables, copper ware or cloth, which they obtain from various sources including villagers and more casual traders as well as from manufacturers and whole-salers. Within the market place there is an acknowledged status hierarchy among the traders. Cloth traders are often accorded the highest status, largely due to the fact that their stock is of higher value requiring more complex finance and trade relationships with suppliers.

Within Indonesia, market prices are pitched so that customers are expected to bargain, with both buyers and sellers enjoying this art. At different times of the year prices fluctuate, not only reflecting seasonal supply and demand for foodstuffs, but also demand peaks associated with different festivals. At

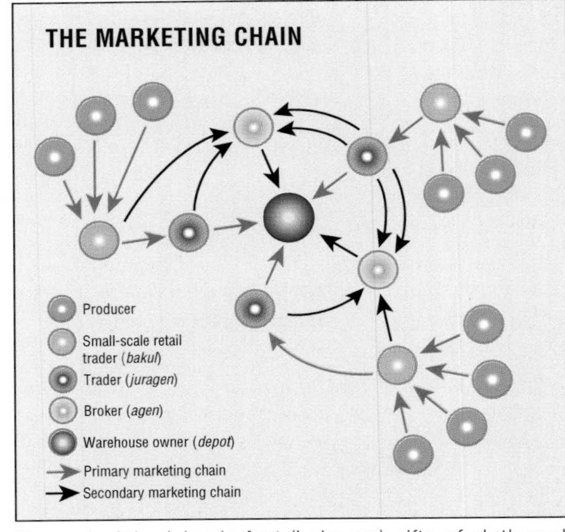

the end of the Islamic fast (Lebaran) gifts of cloth and food are widely given and demand forces up prices, which then fall back at the end of the festival.

The Marketing Chain

In certain parts of Central Java, *bakul* also sell on to traders concerned with bulking and who may store non-perishable goods before transporting them to bigger urban markets. These traders are almost always men. *Bakul* may also sell through brokers or direct to warehouse owners, who are often Chinese. They bulk goods before transporting them to distant markets where credit relationships and long-term contracts with buyers ensure regular supplies. Warehouses were formerly located in the local markets close to the vendors, but the now widespread use of lorries has led to them increasingly being located on the outskirts of town. This facilitates ready access by vehicles used to transport the goods to other regional centres.

Mixed Enterprises

The majority of Indonesian markets sell a wide range of products. However, more specialised markets are also found, dealing in song birds and animals, for example, and also in more expensive items.

Indonesian markets are a riot of colours, sounds and activities

Banjarmasin in South Kalimantan is a major gem market, and buyers and dealers from other parts of Indonesia will make periodic visits to acquire stock. Other markets sell only more expensive consumer items such as bicycles or mopeds.

Stall selling wide range of goods-from foodstuffs to drinks, to household products.

Service Providers

The market place is also the trading arena for artisans such as tailors, cycle repairmen and barbers, who sell their services to passers-by, usually operating from permanent stands or kiosks. Vendors providing identical services will cluster together, for example 20 or 30 small motorcycle repair shops will exist side by side. This serves a number of functions. It attracts clients without sophisticated advertising, and vendors can share raw materials and equipment as well as pooling their expertise. It also adds to the community atmosphere. Beggars and street entertainers also gravitate to the rural market place, often exacting a small payment from the traders to move them on.

Shops and Kiosks

Around and within the market place and warehouses are shops and kiosks, all linked into the market system, each selling to a different clientele and in different units. Shops tend to deal in more expensive consumer items and processed foods, or may specialise in a single commodity such as furniture, where prices are usually fixed. These shops may advertise locally, with goods being fairly standardised in price. Many customers in the larger markets are *warung* owners from surrounding villages who make their profit by breaking down commodities into smaller units, selling a single cigarette at a time, for instance. Similarly petrol is poured from bulk containers into open measuring buckets and then into the petrol tanks of cars and motorcycles.

Trading Relationships

Relationships between traders vary. Long term credit relationships may exist where traders buy items from depots supplying goods up to a fixed limit. For example, many cloth traders typically acquire their wares on this basis from factories, and replenish stock throughout the year for cash, any outstanding debts being settled at the end of the year. No social contacts between the traders exist outside of the market. Goods may also be supplied on short term credit, collecting goods in the morning and paying for them at noon for instance. Links between these partners are generally more personal.

Official Control

In large Indonesian towns and cities, particularly in Jakarta, government policy aims to abolish the more traditional, often unofficial street markets. Traders in these street markets usually set up under plastic awnings or on wooden benches. Such markets are viewed as obstructive. These street traders tend to block pavements and often make road transport down narrow roads difficult. Government planners aim to move them into official concrete built markets.

There is considerable opposition on the part of traders to this relocation policy. The street traders argue that these officially-built markets tend to favour large operators. The traders also claim that the officially-built concrete markets are poorly located. The markets are often built on the outskirts of urban centres of population where they often do not attract customers easily.

Specialised markets are also found in Indonesia. This bird market is located in Jakarta.

TRADE PARTNERSHIPS

Small-scale traders are often regarded as economically inefficient. Sales are *ad hoc* and on a day to day basis, with small quantities being sold to individuals whom the vendor knows only vaguely, or not at all, thereby limiting the possibility of bringing moral or legal sanctions to bear. In some cases, however, individuals, may repeatedly buy from the same vendor rather than seek out the best market price. A credit relationship may then be established with the vendor often selling to their trading partners a reduced price. Clifford Geertz and Alice Dewey see such economic behaviour as being embedded in social relationships. Geertz attributes it to notions of shared poverty, while Dewey attributes it to risk avoidance, trading off the opportunity for greater profit against the sureties of a regular outlet. S. Plattner, on the other hand, argues that these partnerships should be viewed as efficient adaptations to a lack of information in a market where goods are non-standardised, supplies vary, there are no sanctions against failure to complete a transaction, and abuyer's ability to pay or a seller's ability to supply is not always known. (*Right*) Woman trader going to market with home grown vegetables, Rantepao, Sulawesi.

Food in the City

The food needs of expanding urban populations in Indonesia are met by a wide variety of food outlets. While expensive foreign restaurants and fast food outlets cater to non-Indonesians and the affluent local middle class, a diverse mix of less formal warungs and mobile food vendors provide sustenance for many urban dwellers.

Fast food outlets are becoming increasingly common in Indonesian cities.

»»Padang food is now found in many Indonesian cities.

Food Distribution Networks

An important facet of urban life and the urban economy is the distribution and consumption of food. Before reaching the cities, much of the food will already have passed through a number of intermediaries. Some of these 'food chains' involve the direct movement of food from producer to processing firm, and then either on for export or for local consumption through retail outlets. Other 'chains' involve foodstuffs passing through a series of buyers which include markets, stores or hawkers as well as restaurants, before reaching the consumer. Limited storage and the perishability of many foods encourages rapid turnover and movement. When food arrives in the city it goes either to the main market places specialising in fruit, vegetables or meat, or to bulk buyers such as supermarket chains or processing factories. From the main city market places, food is delivered to the consumer in several ways. Housewives may visit these large specialised markets to buy fresh fish or fruit, for example, but most is purchased by smaller market traders or hawkers, and small store owners or restaurants. These small, city-based market traders sell on to still smaller traders, to cooked food stall holders, or to housewives. They deal in small quantities, usually buying only as much as they can physically carry.

Roasted chicken in Yogyakarta .

»»Fried tempe fermented soya bean cake .

Local Processed Foods

Commonly eaten, processed foods such as shrimp paste, *tempe* (soyabean cake), *krupuk* (a kind of cracker) and *tahu* (beancurd) are usually manufactured locally, in small factories or by city-based homeworkers.

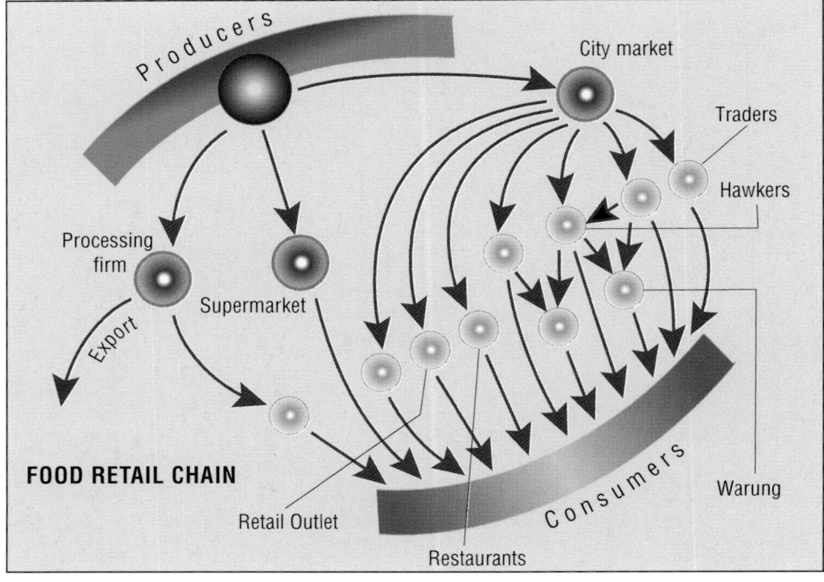

Krupuk are eaten either on their own, as a snack, or else as an accompaniment to meals–to dip in sauces or scoop up food. They are made from fish flakes, crab claws, shrimp paste or fruit, mixed with rice, dough or sago flour. This is rolled out to form thin wafers which are dried and then deep-fried before being eaten.

Another important ingredient in Indonesian cuisine is *tahu*, a major source of protein. It is made by first soaking soya beans in water for up to six hours until they become mushy. They are then mashed to a semi-liquid pulp. The pulp is then cooked for several hours in a large vat and must be constantly stirred. While still boiling, it is poured through cheesecloth into another vat to screen out impurities. Vinegar is added causing the liquid to curdle, and the separated liquid is siphoned off. The curds are placed on a bamboo tray to dry. The dried curds are then shaped into blocks by enclosing them in a piece of cloth which is folded into a flattened cube and then pressed with a board. The curd is then sold to restaurants where it is deep fried.

Warungs and Restaurants

Restaurants and less formal eating places are an important feature of Indonesian cities. Cheap eating stalls (*warung*) cater to poorer city dwellers, and provide one of the few economic opportunities for the women who usually run them. *Warung* owners may set up stalls outside their house, or nearby, commonly selling the kind of food eaten at home. They adopt a place that is unoccupied for at least part of the day, sometimes paying a small rent or bribe to a local official, of about Rp.500 a month. These food stalls may open from early morning until late at night, or for only part of the day, depending on the clientele they serve. As food preparation is time consuming, and fuel expensive, it is often cheaper for poorer people to buy snacks and meals on the street. In the densely populated wooden shanty areas of big cities like Jakarta, room for cooking is limited, and cooking stoves have been responsible for serious fires in the past. Although a valuable source of employment, large numbers of food stalls mean that competition is stiff, and margins wafer-thin. Sometimes temporary restaurants (*rumah makan*), appear under awnings along the streetside.

Diverse Cuisines

Most Indonesian cities, and especially Jakarta, have a diverse ethnic mix, and this manifests itself in the wide range of cusines available. This is partly due to the tendency for individuals of the same ethnic affiliation to live in the same area. Usually, those specialising in similar cuisines are found clustered together in particular streets or areas. Minangkabau-run establishments serving Minang or Padang food have become so successful that chains have been established throughout virtually the whole country. Successful restaurants often trace their roots to street hawkers. One famous Soto Ayam Madura stall in Surabaya serves everyone rice from baskets slung from the bamboo carrying poles of the restaurant's founder. Indonesia's foreign communities, by their patronage, also support their 'own' restaurants; the increasingly affluent domestic middle class too have acquired new and exotic tastes. This has led to the growth of pizza houses, hamburger outlets and doughnut bars, as well as more expensive Vietnamese and Japanese restaurants. Foreign department stores such as Sogo have also established supermarket outlets for expensive imported foods.

Traditional food outlets are an important social and culinary focus for most Indonesians. To many city officials, however, these food vendors are a nuisance. They clutter up streets meant for traffic and pedestrians, block emergency accessways, and pose threats to health and hygiene by their methods of food preparation as well as the debris they leave behind. Clearance programmes have attempted to relocate them to approved sites, usually purpose-built covered markets. Rents and overheads, however, are high, and the location is often unsuitable. Many vendors thus drift back to their old street haunts.

FOOD VENDORS

A wide range of street vendors (*kaki lima*) may be found in Indonesian towns and cities, selling fruit, vegetables and prepared food (*clockwise from right*: apples, grapes, ice kacang, bakso, cut fruit). With the exception of women who sell tonics (*jamu*) the *kaki lima* are predominantly men and generally cater to lower income groups. Some sell from carts (*roda*) which they wheel along the road side, while others balance portable kerosene stoves at the end of shoulder poles, stopping at suitable places to cook and sell for example, fried bananas (*pisang goreng*). The *pedagang pikulan* are hawkers–mainly men–who sell vegetables from baskets slung at either end of a long pole. Other hawkers sell fruit, vegetables, eggs or spices from mats or baskets set out at the side of the street. These are more likely to be women. Usually individuals selling the same produce cluster together along the same stretch of road. The etymology of the term *pedagang kaki lima*, or 'PK5' as it is often abbreviated in newspapers and reports, is usually translated as 'trader with five feet or legs'. The five legs would seem to refer to the two legs of the trader, the two wheels of the push cart and the leg at the front of the cart. But the term is also used for stationary vendors or hawkers peddling their wares via a shoulder pole. Another meaning of *kaki lima* is 'pavement' which formerly had a width of five feet. This is considered the more likely origin of the term.

Fresh chillies in Pasar Beringharjo, Yogyakarta.

This new N250 Commuter Plane is the first aircraft to be designed and built in Indonesia. The project was designed to serve both commercial and national development interests.

The Palindo Jaya 500 is an Indonesian led design project, initiated to provide transportation connecting the numerous sea ports of the archipelago.

One of the most important developments in Indonesia has been the improvement and expansion of the country's transport and communications network, both at national and international level. Most of the larger islands, for example, have experienced the rapid growth of road and inland waterways transportation for both passengers and goods. Devlopment has also led to an increased growth in Indonesian exports, including foodstuffs and other goods. This has resulted in the upgrading of outdated port facilities, and the appearance of new container ports (above), as well as the expansion of airports and air facilities.

DEVELOPMENT AND CHANGE

Until the 1960s 'development' was equated with 'economic development' or, to use that older term, 'material progress'. Development was about modernisation–about increasing national income and industrial output. In the 1960s as economic growth began, this focus on development as economic growth began to come under scrutiny world wide. It was clear that economic expansion was not always contributing to a raising of people's standards of living. Economists started to argue that development should be seen as a multi-dimensional process incorporating social as well as economic progress.

Many of the spreads in this chapter illustrate the ways in which the Indonesian government has 'intervened' in people's lives in order to promote social development–through a nationwide health infrastructure, through mass education, and through specifically targeting the poor, for example. As the spreads also make clear, these programmes have generally been highly successful. There have been striking improvements in such key measures as life expectancy and literacy rates, and a sharp drop in the incidence of poverty. This is not to say that there are no problems, only to observe that considerable progress has been achieved, especially during the New Order period.

In addition, the process of economic development has itself created new problems. The widening inequalities between different regions, and particularly between Java and the rest of the country, are a growing cause for concern. Development has sometimes shifted problems of poverty from rural to urban areas, for example. Development has also facilitated the emergence of a wealthy class of Indonesian set against a large percentage of the population who remain mired in poverty. Most obviously, though, unrestrained economic growth has created massive environmental problems in some areas. This has raised the question of whether development is sustainable.

Implicit in much of this chapter, and in this introduction, is the view that development is something that is done to people. In this way, people are seen as the objects of state-directed and state-inspired programmes of development. But just as important, development is also something that people do themselves. People are not just victims of events beyond their control; they are actors in their own right, who play a critical role in shaping their destinies. Men and women struggle and devise innovative strategies to increase their income and to escape poverty. They may be the subjects of the development process, but they are not its prisoners.

The Development Process

Early attempts to promote Indonesian development by the Dutch were cut short by the war. Economic stability was only achieved under the New Order regime in the 1960s. With industrial development, living standards in Java have greatly improved and attention is now being turned to developing other regions.

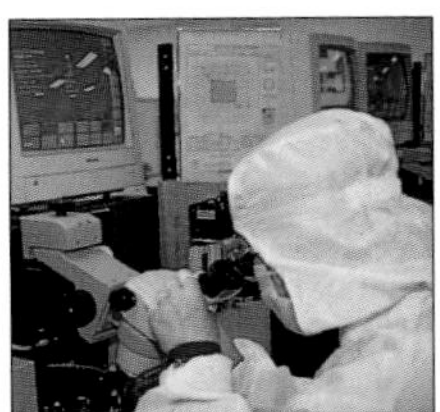

Manufacturing now commands a large share of Indonesia's GDP. A worker in a high-tech electronics factory on Batam Island, Riau Archipelago.

» As the economy becomes more sophisticated, the availability of a large pool of skilled labour becomes even more critical. A heavy emphasis has been placed on education, particularly in science and technology.

The benefits of modernisation–Indonesian youths sampling the latest pop releases in a Bandung shop.

Early Development

Concern with economic development as a policy goal began in Indonesia at the turn of the century. Dutch colonial authorities were worried about the problem of what they termed 'diminishing welfare' in Java, and in a speech in 1901, Queen Wilhemina announced the intention of the Government (dominated by the Clerical Party) to enquire into the problem. A number of influential officials argued for an accelerated programme of public expenditures, partly to repay 'the debt of honour' incurred as a result of the payments made by the colony to the home budget in the 19th century. Between 1900 and 1930 government expenditure on a range of activities increased. Emphasis was placed on government-sponsored emigration from Java to the Outer Islands, extension of irrigation facilities, provision of agricultural credit, and expanded access to education. It was also recognised that the government had a responsibility to 'encourage industry'–indigenous and European–through fiscal concessions, the provision of infra-structure such as transport, and the provision of a guaranteed market for output.

Accelerated government expenditure on these programmes was combined with an improvement in the world market price of major export staples leading to an acceleration in rates of economic growth in Indonesia after 1900. One recent estimate puts the growth of real GDP in the three decades between 1900 and 1930 at almost three per cent a year, higher than the growth of population. Indeed, it has been estimated that between 1898 and 1928, real per capita GDP grew by around 65 per cent, although it proved impossible to sustain these growth rates after 1930. The Indonesian economy was severely hit by the world

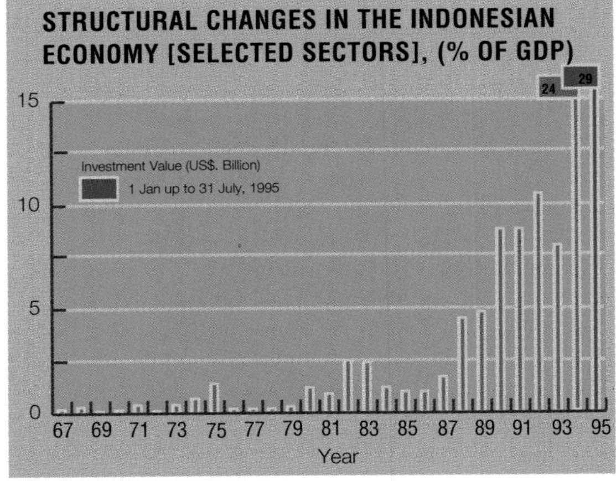

depression as prices for its main export commodities fell more rapidly than prices for its main imports. Even more seriously, overseas export markets contracted as a result of growing protectionism and international commodity agreements. As a result of this experience, the colonial government became increasingly convinced that Indonesia would have to industrialise if the living standards of the great majority of the population were to improve. Foreign investment in a range of manufacturing industries was encouraged and technical and vocational educational facilities were expanded.

This experiment in colonial economic planning was suddenly cut short by the German occupation of the Netherlands and then by the Japanese invasion of Indonesia. In 1945, Soekarno and Hatta declared independence, triggering a protracted and often violent confrontation with the returning Dutch colonial authorities. It was only in 1950 that full independence was granted and there followed a succession of short-lived governments with little continuity in policy-making. Although a five-year plan was drawn up for the period between 1956-60, which emphasised the rehabilitation and expansion of infrastructure and increased access to education, growing political and economic instability made implementation of the plan increasingly difficult. The economy deteriorated further during the Guided Democracy era (1958-65) when economic

DEVELOPMENT TIMELINES

This chart outlines the major events, both national and international, and Indonesian government legislation that have affected the country's development process.

1901	Ethical Policy
1914-33	WW I; World Depression
1942-49	Japanese Occupation. Independence
1958	Guided economy; direct state control of production and trade nationalisation of Dutch enterprises. Centralisation of power after regions' unsuccessful attempts to secede. Guided democracy
1965	Attempted Coup
1966	Hyperinflation
1967	**Pre-oil period**: Operation of subsidiary branches of foreign banks. Reincorporation to IMF and World Bank. Some nationalised firms returned to previous owners. New foreign investment law; balanced-budget law
1968	Ban on entry of foreign banks. Debt rescheduling. Adjustments in tariffs; abolition of import licensing system
1969	**Repelita 1**
1970	Unification of exchange rates
1971	First oil price rise. More devaluation liberalisation of capital account
1973	**Oil and commodity boom**. **Growing inward orientation**
1974	**Food crisis**: Programme of direct credit control and allocation. State dominance of the financial sector

DEVELOPMENT: WHAT'S IN A WORD

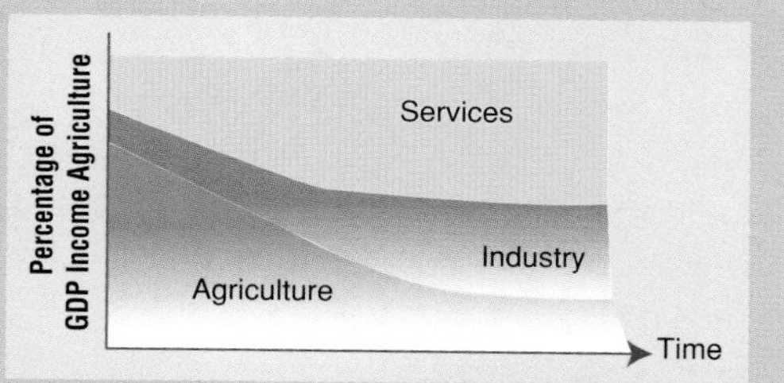

Most economists agree that economic growth refers to a process of sustained increase in real per capita national income or output over time. Furthermore, following on the work of scholars such as Simon Kuznets, there is widespread agreement that such a process, if sustained over a period of decades, is almost certain to bring about a marked structural transformation in the economy, leading to a steady decline in the share of the agricultural sector in gross domestic output and a steady increase in the share of manufacturing industry and the modern service sector. Some economists would go further and argue that such a structural transformation should be equated with economic development.

However others would argue that economic development should refer to those changes in society which facilitate a sustained process of economic growth, or indeed enable such a process to get underway. Such 'enabling' factors are often considered to include access to education and to infrastructure including improved transport infrastructure (roads, ports, airports) and improved public utilities (electricity, gas, water and sewerage).

In addition, certain institutional changes are also considered prerequisites to sustained economic growth along capitalist lines. They include free markets for both goods and factors of production (land, labour and capital), and a legal system which supports a market system of production and exchange. Development today is seen as a multi-dimensional process embodying social as well as economic progress. Issues of health, education and environmental standards are now recogised as integral to development.

policy making was completely subordinated to political objectives. By the mid 1960s, per capita Gross Domestic Product (GDP) was falling, there were shortages of basic necessities, smuggling was rife and inflation was out of control.

Economic Stabilisation

After the attempted coup in September 1965, President Soekarno was eased out of office by a military-backed group led by Lieutenant-General Soeharto. The stabilisation of the economy moved to the top of the policy agenda, and after the inflation rate was reduced to single figures and the exchange rate set at a realistic level, it was possible for the New Order regime to implement the first of a series of five-year plans. Economic growth over the period of the first three plans accelerated to more than six per cent a year, and although there was some deceleration in growth after 1982, as a result of falling oil prices, real per capita GDP continued to grow at over two per cent per year. Between 1965 and 1990 World Bank estimates indicate that real per capita GDP grew at 4.5 per cent per year, implying a trebling over this period. By 1990 the share of agriculture in GDP had fallen to below 20 per cent, while the share of manufacturing industry exceeded 20 per cent. President Soeharto, who is intimately associated with this record of economic progress–known as the 'Father of Development'.

New Challenges

The New Order concept of economic development is broadly similar to that of the Dutch colonial government during the last four decades of colonial rule. Heavy emphasis has been placed on the development of physical infrastructure, the provision of agricultural support services (including credit) and improving access to both education and health facilities. The problem of overpopulation and poverty in Java has been tackled by a mixture of policies designed to improve agricultural productivity, encourage industrialisation and move the landless poor to other parts of the country through government-sponsored land settlement schemes. There can be little doubt that the cumulative impact of these policies over almost a century has been to improve living standards and reduce the extent of poverty especially in rural areas of Java. At the same time, however, new development problems are gradually beginning to emerge. Java is now no longer the poorest part of the country, and as industrial development accelerates in Java it is likely that regional differences in the pace of development will become increasingly pronounced.

Economic development has improved living standards and reduced poverty even in relatively remote places like Nias.

«Major investments have been directed to improving infrastructure like transport facilities. Before being taken over by Tanjung Priok (Jakarta) after WWII, Surabaya was arguably the premiere port in Indonesia, a position it is trying to recover today.

Year	Period	Events
1978		First big devaluation
1979		Second oil price rise
1981		Requirement of approved-importer license
1983	First adjustment period	Rephasing of capital-intensive projects; Flexible exchange rate; Second major devaluation (28 percent)
1985	Tax reform; Freeze on civil salaries	Reduction in import tariffs; Duty exemptions for exporters
1986	Second adjustment period	Reduction in NTBs; Promotion of Non-petroleum /gas exports; Third major devaluation
1987		Austere budget
1988		Southern Growth Triangle launched; Application of floating system; Full financial sector; Liberalisation
1989-1990	Non-oil led recovery	Definition of bank capital; Deregulation of investment licensing; Liberalisation of the maritime sector
1991		Offshore borrowing limitations
1992-95		New banking law; Freeing up of investment and banking; Technology for national development; Soaring foreign investments

Development in Practice

One of the major concerns of development policy in Indonesia since Independence has been infrastructural development as well as provision of basic needs. In the early post-independence years, development policy in Indonesia concentrated on overcoming what was perceived as the unfavourable colonial legacy: inadequate infrastructure, especially outside Java, very low levels of educational attainment and undeveloped market institutions.

Oil revenues from the exploitation of Indonesia's vast reserves have allowed the government to substantially raise development expenditure since the 1970s.

A sugar processing factory in colonial Java.

The Nineteen Fifties

In addition to the lack of infrastrucutre the government was concerned about the absence of a robust class of indigenous entrepreneurs. In the early 1950s programmes were initiated which were intended to promote indigenous entrepreneurship. Unfortunately these programmes often amounted to little more than the establishment of companies by politically well-connected indigenous Indonesians, who used their positions to acquire import licenses and other privileges while the companies were managed by Indonesians of Chinese origin.

The first five-year plan which began in 1956, and which was scheduled to run until 1960, emphasised the rehabilitation and extension of rural infrastructure such as irrigation and roads, and the rapid expansion of educational opportunities. Some progress was made in achieving these objectives, but mounting inflation, the economic dislocation which followed the expulsion of all Dutch enterprises in 1957-8 and growing political instability prevented most of the plan targets being met.

The Nineteen Sixties

The seven-year development plan, which was initiated in 1961 and intended to run until 1968, was largely political in motivation and, in the increasingly disturbed conditions of the early 1960s, little attempt was made to implement it. After the successful stabilisation plan of 1966-69 when, with foreign assistance, inflation was reduced to single figures and the supply of basic needs increased, the government embarked on the first of a series of five year development plans or *repelitas* (standing for *Rencana Pembangunan Lima Tahun*). These were, and continue to be, exercises in top-down planning. The plan documents are drawn up at the National Planning Bureau in Jakarta, and production targets are set for different sectors of the economy. Although provincial governments are consulted, and increasingly provincial and and sub-provincial levels of government are involved in plan implementation, the key decisions are made in Jakarta. This reflects the highly centralised nature of the financial system, with almost all the important taxes accruing directly to the central government. Provincial and sub-provincial levels of government have little financial autonomy, and little scope for implementing projects funded from their own revenue sources. This is particularly true for the resource-rich areas outside Java. In provinces such as Aceh, Riau, East Kalimantan and Irian Jaya, much of the revenue generated from the exploitation of oil and gas, other minerals and forest products accrues directly to the central government and the producing provinces have little control over their use.

GOVERNMENT REVENUE AND EXPENDITURE, 1992-93

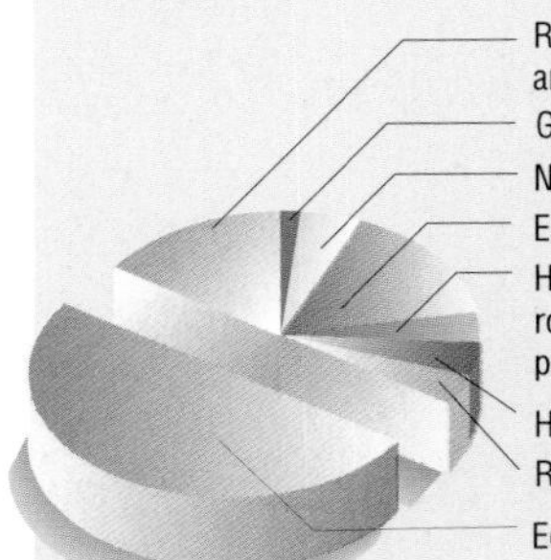

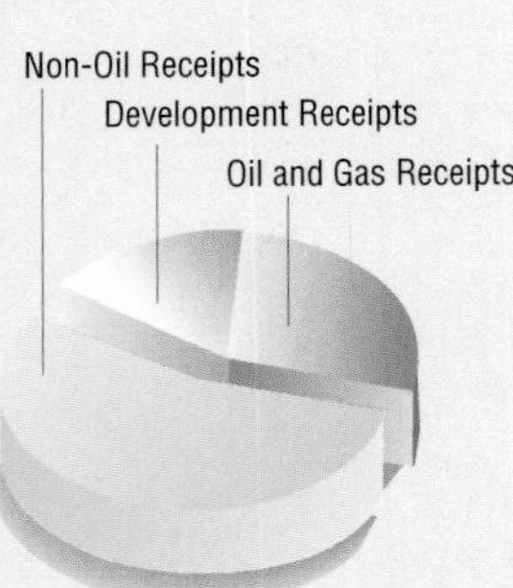

The pie chart on the left shows Indonesian development expenditure by sector. By far the largest share goes to the economic sector, which includes agriculture and irrigation; transport and tourism; information, press and communications; and trade and cooperatives. The righthand pie chart shows government revenues for the same year. The greatest percentage came from non-oil receipts which include income tax, value added tax, import and excise duties, export tax, and land and building tax. (n.b. Development Receipts = money for aid projects).

The Nineteen Seventies

The first five-year plan (Repelita I) of the New Order period ran from 1969 to 1974, and emphasised the rehabilitation of infrastructure, and accelerated production of basic needs, particularly foodcrops. During these years the first of a series of regional development programmes was initiated; cash grants were made to every village unit in the country to encourage them to repair roads, irrigation works, community halls and so on, and to build a new infrastructure. It was intended that these cash grants be combined with contributions of labour and materials from the villagers themselves. In addition, a development grant based on population was paid to each *kabupaten* (the level of government below the province) for expenditure on road-building, construction of irrigation infrastructure and other approved public works projects.

The second five-year plan, Repelita II, which ran from 1974 to 79, was drawn up at a time of rapidly increasing world oil prices, and the extra resources enabled the government to accelerate public expenditure on a range of infrastructural projects.

INDONESIA'S GROWTH TRIANGLES

It has been argued that the economies of Indonesia, Singapore, Malaysia and Thailand are complementary. Singapore and Malaysia are both comparatively rich in financial, technological, communications and marketing infrastructure and expertise, while Indonesia and Thailand can provide low wage rates, an abundant workforce, and ample land resources. It is on this basis that two so-called 'Growth Triangles' have been promoted. As Singapore's Trade and Industry Minister Lee Hsien Loong explained in 1991, the triangles offer 'a unique mix of resources and infrastructure, labour and skills.' For Indonesia, and in particular for the provincial authorities, the two growth triangles also offer an opportunity to decentralise industrial activity away from Java and Jakarta.

The first such 'triangle', which essentially dates from 1988, links the Indonesian province of Riau with Singapore and the Malaysian state of Johor. Activity has been concentrated on Batam Island which has seen investment rise from US$65 million to US$300 million between 1988 and 1990. Over the same period, Batam's official workforce rose from 9,600 to 16,300, the value of exports from US$44 million to US$150 million, and the island's population from 80,000 to 107,000. The more recent growth triangle links Aceh and North Sumatra with the five provinces of South Thailand and the four northern Malaysian states. The combined population of the area exceeds 20 million, with output in 1988 of US$12.4 billion.

Despite the apparent economic logic of these growth triangles, doubts still exist. In the case of the Indonesia-Singapore-Malaysia triangle, the dominant role of Singapore in the ostensibly equitable triangular relationship has caused concern. Indeed, the promotion of the Indonesia-Malaysia-Thailand triangle is partly an attempt to sideline Singapore. Other problems include the differences in the regulatory environments in the three countries and the absence of a combined coordinating agency which crosses national divisions.

The development grants to regional governments were increased and widened to include programmes designed to accelerate provision of elementary schools, and rural health clinics. The Elementary Schools Programme for example, financed the construction of some 6,000 schools each year.

The Role of NGOs in Indonesia

Since the early 1970s there has been a considerable growth in the role of non-governmental organisations (NGOs) in Indonesia, many of which are involved in community development projects. Some are affiliated to Islamic groups, while others are backed by one or other of the Christian churches. Projects favoured by NGOs are typically small, community-based projects, and do not involve much expenditure on imported, capital-intensive technologies. Their principle aim is to encourage people to adopt new, more efficient production methods in both agricultural and non-agricultural enterprises. The government attitude to such 'bottom-up' methods of planning and project implementation has been varied; in some cases local governments have been very supportive, but in others there is suspicion of development activities outside the direct control of government, and especially those which are dependent on foreign financing.

The Nineteen Eighties

The emphasis on infrastructure development continued into the third five-year plan, Repelita III (1979-84), with accelerated expenditures on the mining and energy sectors, and on the transmigration programme. However the budgetary and balance of payments problems caused by the fall in world oil prices in the early 1980s forced the government to curb spending on some more ambitious projects. In addition the transmigration programme, the largest government-sponsored land settlement programme in the world, ran into numerous difficulties both at home and abroad.

The generally conservative nature of Indonesian economic policy during the New Order has often been put down to the influential role of the so-called 'Berkeley Mafia'–a group of reform-minded, largely US-trained, Indonesian economists. Although it is too simplistic to think in terms of coherent groups with common ideas and ideals, whether a generally conservative–as opposed to a nationalistic–economic programme remains dominant, is likely to be a key issue in determining the pattern and process of future growth.

Infrastructural development-road construction in East Timor.

Regional Development

Indonesia is spatially varied in its resource endowments and unevenly developed between regions. Several Indonesian provinces, such as Irian Jaya and East Kalimantan, remain highly underdeveloped and with a high incidence of poverty, all issues of continuing political concern. In some cases, the sustainability of regional development has been questioned. Using conventional indicators of development, western Indonesia appears overall to be more developed than the east, with greater industrialisation, a lower incidence of poverty and a higher income per head.

Logged timber, natural resource-based industries like forestry are important in East Kalimantan.

Jakarta and its environs has attracted many of Java's non-oil manufacturing industries.

Location of Industries

Regional development in Indonesia is closely linked to spatial differences in the location of agriculture, industry and services. While the term 'industry' is used in Indonesia to cover a range of activities such as manufacturing, mining (including oil and gas), construction and utilities, manufacturing activities are in fact, highly concentrated regionally. Investment in industry is highest in the west of the country, and in those provinces rich in oil and liquified natural gas (LNG). In Java, investment has gone into manufacturing; in Irian Jaya and Kalimantan, extractive industries such as timber. In Bali, Medan and Jakarta tourism investment has been significant. The service sector, more widely, has also expanded, mainly in the Jakarta region. Consequently provinces such as Aceh, Riau and East Kalimantan, although classified as having 'industry', in effect, have virtually no non-oil manufacturing activities.

Roughly three-quarters of non-oil manufacturing, in terms of value added, is based on Java, and over two-thirds of this is in and around the cities of Jakarta, Surabaya and Bandung. Sumatra contains about 14 per cent of such industry, Kalimantan 7.5 per cent and Sulawesi, 2.5 per cent. Eastern Indonesia as a whole accounts for only 1.2 per cent.

When oil and gas are included in industrial output, the share of the oil rich islands in the value of Indonesia's industrial output rises dramatically. For instance, Sumatra's share rises to 24.4 per cent and Kalimantan's to 19.5 per cent.

Industry in Sumatra and Kalimantan mostly involves natural resource extraction and processing, especially of LNG and oil. There are also very large fertiliser and plywood plants in East Kalimantan. Nearly all manufacturing outside Java involves either the processing of local primary products such as oil and gas, timber, coffee, tropical fruits and coconuts, or the manufacture of a product for a very localised market, for example, ice. The growth of processing facilities has often been supported by the Indonesian government. For example, legislation banning the export of logs, has encouraged sawmills and timber processing plants to be established in the Outer

The Gross Regional Domestic Product (GRDP) per capita, as a unit of measurment, is roughly equivalent to the average annual output of each resident in a province. The map shows the GRDP per capita for all 27 Indonesian provinces. In some areas, such as East Kalimantan, the high values are partly due to the extraction of natural resources. In such instances, the money earned often does not stay in the province, but goes to those who financed the development, leaving the local population bereft of benefits: compare this map with the graph on the facing page.

Islands. An exception to this emphasis on natural resource-based industries in the outer islands is Batam Island in Riau, close to Singapore. Here there is a thriving textile and garment industry. On Java industries such as textile manufacturing are most important, as are those producing 'modern' sector consumer goods and involving light engineering.

Major Determinants of the Pattern of Regional Industrialisation

The concentration of non-oil manufacturing industry in Java is partially a result of the large population and market there. In addition, the need to be near the seat of government to obtain appropriate licences has also been important. Once a large industrial concentration develops, as has happened in and around Jakarta, it tends to attract even more industrial activities. The political strength of such an area increases and agglomeration economies, like spreading the costs of public services and easier contact between buyers and sellers, reinforce its growth. Of course, at the same time, congestion costs like pollution are also likely to emerge. Nevertheless, in this case, the forces favouring regional industrial growth are stronger.

The industries in the natural resource-rich provinces such as Aceh, Riau and East Kalimantan are capital-intensive and create comparatively little local employment. In most cases they have few direct linkages with the local economies although some downstream processing may occur. There is a tendency for these industries to form an enclave, and a dual local economy often develops where extractive industries and the traditional economy exist side-by-side but rarely interact.

Differences in Gross Regional Domestic Product per Capita

Gross Regional Domestic Product (GRDP) per capita is highest for the mining/oil rich provinces. However, if mining is excluded Jakarta has the highest GRDP per capita, followed by East Kalimantan, mainly due to its fertiliser and plywood plants. Irian Jaya's relatively high position is due to the importance of its extractive industries. A high GRDP per capita does not necessarily translate into high levels of disposable income and a high standard of living for locals in the provinces where it occurs. Furthermore, if mining is discounted, there is a tendency for GRDP per capita to be lower in those provinces where agriculture predominates.

PERCENTAGE OF THE POPULATION BELOW THE POVERTY LINE IN THE OIL AND LNG-RICH PROVINCES AND IN IRIAN JAYA, 1980 and 1990.

Province	1980 Urban	1980 Rural	1990 Urban	1990 Rural
Aceh	11.2	11.7	16.3	13.7
Riau	13.5	23.1	16.0	8.8
South Sumatra	9.8	33.4	14.0	23.6
East Kalimantan	25.6	42.0	34.8	34.4
Irian Jaya	37.0	53.8	67.0	33.0

*1987 figure

Sources: Based on Booth (1992) and Poverty and Income Inequality in Indonesia 1976-1990, Central Bureau of Statistics, Jakarta

Since the early 1970s, growth rates in GRDP per capita have been uneven between provinces. Generally, the relative position of oil rich provinces has improved, while provinces in Java have remained unchanged. The relative 'losers' have been many provinces in the eastern region–with the significant exception of Bali which has fared relatively well, mainly because of its tourist industry.

With the development of manufacturing in Java, agriculture has become less important than in the eastern islands. Higher wages in manufacturing industries, textiles and clothing for example, are attracting large numbers of people away from the land.

Regional Aspects of Income Distribution and Poverty

GRDP per capita is a poor indicator of differences in living standards between regions. It does not allow for income transfers between regions and other factors such as investment. The incidence of poverty is relatively high in those provinces with a high GRDP per capita reliant on extractive industries such as oil or mining. Indeed, rural poverty is actually on the increase in many areas while the majority of the local population seems to have benefited little or not at all from the resource boom. The relatively high level of GRDP in Irian Jaya for example, is based mainly on logging but 67 per cent of its rural people live in poverty. It is possible that the main benefits have been enjoyed in Java, particularly Jakarta, via income transfers and the opportunities which the oil boom has provided for further industrial development there.

In areas where economic growth is largely based upon extractive industries such as logging in Kalimantan and Irian Jaya, there is the added fear that growth may not be sustainable at its present rate. Also, industries based on the use of non-renewable resources such as oil and LNG mining are not sustainable in the very long term and there is a need to develop alternative industries in these areas.

« Pertamina oil terminal, Labuhan Batas, Sumbawa. Oil terminals may be sited away from their origin point, thus creating jobs in other regions.

Natural Resources for Human Use

Indonesia's huge and diverse natural resources have formed the basis for the country's development. These resources include extensive mineral and energy deposits, forests and fisheries, as well as land for agricultural development. Their importance lies not only in their contribution to export earnings, but also to local subsistence and usage.

Clearing the forest for nickel mining, Sulawesi.

Timber being floated down the Mahakam River, Kalimantan. The rainforest also yeilds numerous other valuable resources, including rattan, resins, turpentine and bamboo, among others.

»»An open cast nickel mine in Sulawesi. Given that current estimated reserves are likely to be exhausted in 40 years, sites like these could become abandoned wastelands.

Panning for diamonds in South Kalimantan. Various gems are obtained in this way, often by small scale operators and private individuals.

Mineral and Energy Resources

Even though the exploration and development of Indonesia's resources has proceeded on the basis of known reserves, only a relatively small proportion of the country's total area has actually been surveyed for minerals. In many cases, even the deposits that are known have not been quantified, although it is widely believed that the country's potential mineral reserves far exceed these known deposits These include both hydrocarbons such as oil, natural gas and coal, and hard minerals such as tin, bauxite, copper, nickel, iron sands, gold and silver. Unfortunately, many of these deposits are to be found in remote areas, making their extraction both difficult and very expensive. This means that production is very sensitive to changes in international market conditions.

Tin mining is mainly carried out in the Riau islands of Bangka, Belitung and Singkep, which lie off the coast of southeastern Sumatra. Estimates of tin reserves here have been pegged at one million tonnes. Bauxite can also be found in the Riau islands, particularly on Pulau Bintan which lies further north, not far from the coast of Singapore, as well as in the province of West Kalimantan. Copper is mined mainly in Irian Jaya, although deposits have also been found in Sumatra, Kalimantan, Java and Sulawesi. Nickel is mined in several places on the island of Sulawesi, the chief of which is Soroako in the south. Indonesia's reserves of nickel ore have been estimated at 40 million tonnes. These deposits are expected to last approximately another 40 years at current rates of consumption. Nickel has also been discovered on several island groups between Halmahera and the north-west tip of Irian Jaya. Asphalt mining has taken place on the island of Buton off Sulawesi. In addition to these major resources of mineral wealth, gold and copper in north Sulawesi, and iron ore in the middle of the island promise to be major future revenue generators. The Freeport-Indonesia mine in the highlands near Tembagapura in Irian Jaya is exploiting the largest gold reserve in the world, and represents the world's second largest open cast copper mine-with reserves of US$15 billion and US$23 billion (at 1994 prices) respectively.

Indonesia is fortunate in being an energy-rich country, with substantial oil, gas and coal reserves. These coal reserves in particular are of largely unexploited potential although some exploration and mining has begun. Most of Indonesia's commercial energy needs have traditionally been met by oil, although the rapid rate of increase in consumption has led to the threat that the country may need to import oil in the near future. This possibility has led to the government promoting alternative sources of energy consumption. Indeed, estimates suggest that Indonesia's proven recoverable reserves of crude oil total some 8.3 billion barrels, could be depleted in well under 20 years if current levels of domestic consumption are sustained. Nevertheless, the figure cited underestimates available resources since a large number of known oilfields have not been explored and still less developed. In addition to oil, coal is mined principally in Sumatra and Kalimantan. One estimate is that there are 15,000 million metric tonnes of coal reserves in the country.

Forests and Fisheries

Indonesia's status as an archipelgo means that it is endowed with considerable fisheries resources. At the present time the waters that are encompassed

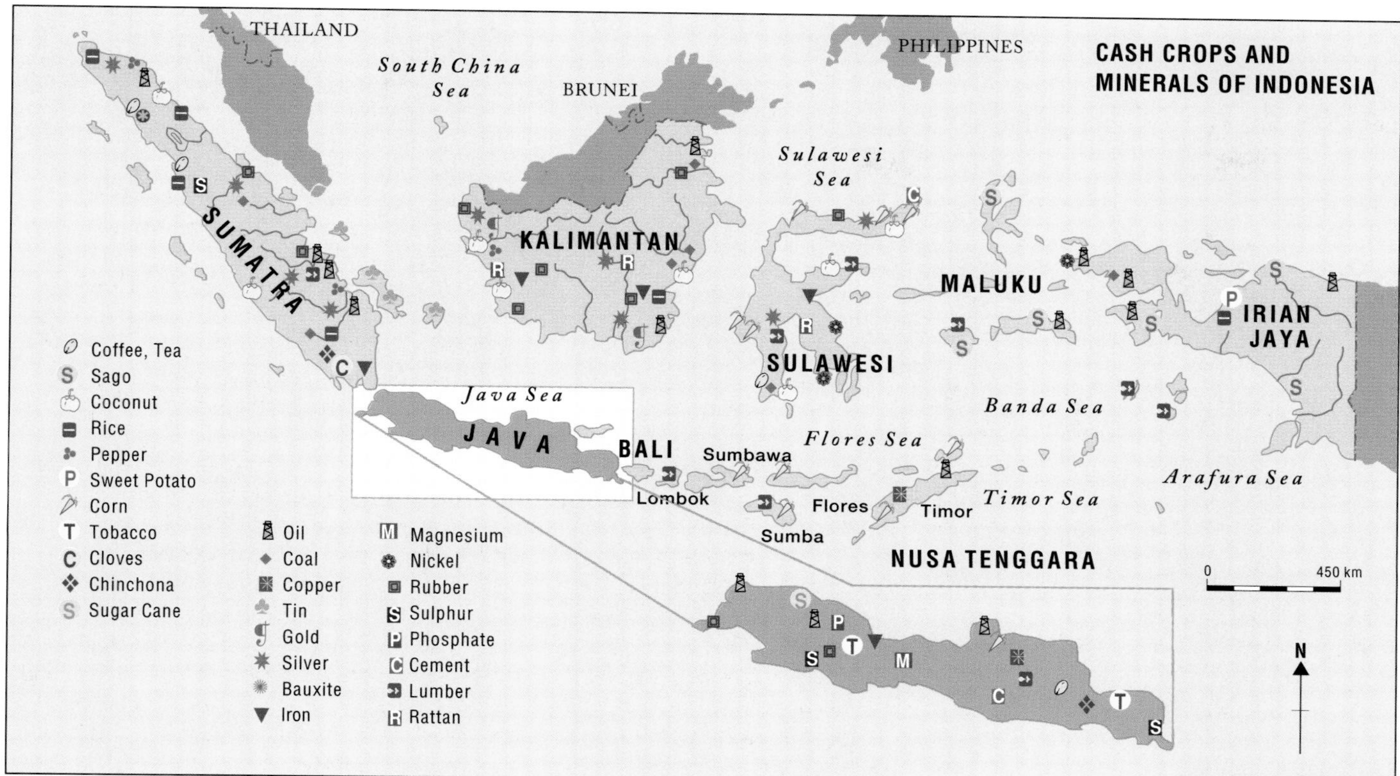

within the country's Exclusive Economic Zone are only partially exploited, although in some local areas, particularly in fishing grounds lying close to the coasts, over-fishing has increasingly become an issue of growing concern. However, through the gradual modernisation and expansion of the trawler fleet, the government is aiming to more fully and effectively exploit this resource.

Indonesia has the largest tropical area of forest in the world after Brazil. In real terms this represents almost 60 per cent of all tropical forests in Asia, and approximately 90 per cent of Asia's remaining virgin forests. Indeed, the world's most valuable diptero-carp forests can be found in Kalimantan. Forests not only provide lumber for domestic construction and wood products for export, but also other forest products (so-called non-timber forest products-NTFP) such as rattan, resin, turpentine and bamboo, to name but a few. In addition, the rainforests also represent a genetic resource of considerable potential economic value and a valuable tourist resource.

The areas under forest cover are mainly concentrated in Sumatra, Kalimantan and Irian Jaya. These forests are being exploited at unsustainable rates. Whereas it is estimated that Indonesia's tropical forests would support a sustainable cut of 22 million cubic metres per year, the current rate of harvest is over 33 million cubic metres per year. In addition, forests are also being lost through shifting cultivation and smallholder agricultural conversion, as well as clearance for development projects.

Land Resources

The general availability of suitable land allows for the cultivation of subsistence and cash crops. The former include rice, and other cereals like maize and pulses, tubers and roots. Cash crops are varied and include rubber, oil palm, cocoa, tea, tobacco, coffee, sugar cane, coconut, pepper, cloves and sago. Land as a resource is of singular importance in Indonesia's development. The availability of land allows for agri-cultural expansion, and agriculture continues to employ over 50 per cent of Indonesia's population. Land availability is not a simple question of physical availability but is tied to cultural and social systems. Traditional land tenure systems play a crucial role in determining availability. In parts of Sumatra, for example, virtually all land (cultivated or otherwise) is claimed by local clans or *margas*. In Kalimantan, on the other hand, only lands which have been previously cultivated or otherwise harvested by local people are claimed.

These traditional laws or *adat* are often complicated by legislation. For example, the Basic Agrarian Law of 1960 allows the government the right to reallocate under-utilised lands for public benefit, provided the local people consent. This has resulted in the acquisition and redistribution of land for development purposes, for example in the well-known case of the transmigration programme, although in many cases local protests have delayed, even curtailed development.

An industrial timber plantation of meranti trees, Kalimantan. The government is aware of the need to replant large tracts of rainforest that have been cleared. Indonesia has a thriving furniture industry, and with the rise in demand for fine wooden products, it is becoming necessary to plant trees, like meranti, which can be used to produce a wide range of products.

Kuda kuda sledge and rail being used to transport felled trees out of the forest. These trunks may be dragged for several kilometres before reaching a river for the final stage of their journey downriver to the timbermill.

Tourism: Investing in Culture

Since 1988 Indonesia has quadrupled its income from tourism, earning US$3.2 billion in 1992, making tourism the country's third largest foreign exchange earner. While international tourism was initially directed towards North Sumatra, Java and Bali, planners are increasingly attempting to market the cultural attractions of more remote areas like Sulawesi.

The tabuik procession in West Sumatra is a great tourist attraction. Derived from religious sources, it is also a spectacular display of dance and drama.

The cultural sights of Bali have been recognised for decades, this pre-war tourism poster depicts the legong dance. Many of the dances enjoyed by visitors to Bali were actually choreographed in the 1920s and 30s for tourists using elements and themes from more traditional performances.

First Five Year Plan

In 1969, the First Five Year Plan or Repelita I of the New Order emphasised the role of international tourism in economic development. Because of geographic accessibility, initial investment was directed to North Sumatra, Java and Bali. Part and parcel of this tourism initiative was the restoration of the ancient monuments of Central Java, particularly Borobudur, which was closed for 10 years while US$25 million was spent on it. Since reopening in 1983 Borobudur has attracted over one million visitors a year–testament to the value of Indonesia's material culture. Yogyakarta, the cultural heart of Java, has been developed, and new hotels, theatres and art galleries constructed. The Hindu temples of Prambanan, near Yogyakarta, provide a backdrop for tourist productions of the Ramayana, while a thriving craft industry–geared to tourist demand–produces batik, silverware and puppets.

Second Five Year Plan

At the beginning of Repelita II in 1974, the economic planners sought ways of attracting tourists to more remote areas. Believing that the ancestor ceremonies of the Toraja people of South Sulawesi (an integral part of their traditional *aluk to dolo* religion) could become an important attraction, tourist agencies began promoting the region. Despite the long drive from the airport at Ujung Pandang, and the minimal facilities in Tana Toraja, tourist arrivals increased dramatically from 422 in 1973 to 6,008 by 1975. With the opening of an airstrip, they now arrive in their tens of thousands. For many tourists, the greatest attraction of the area is the lavish funeral ceremonies of the Toraja people. Although the Toraja are nominally Christian (in 1981, 65.96 per cent were Protestant, and 11.80 per cent were Roman Catholic), and the colourful funerals essentially an aspect of their 'pagan' past, these ceremonies began escalating in scale and extravagance in the 1950s when the growth of salaried jobs provided many Toraja with disposable incomes.

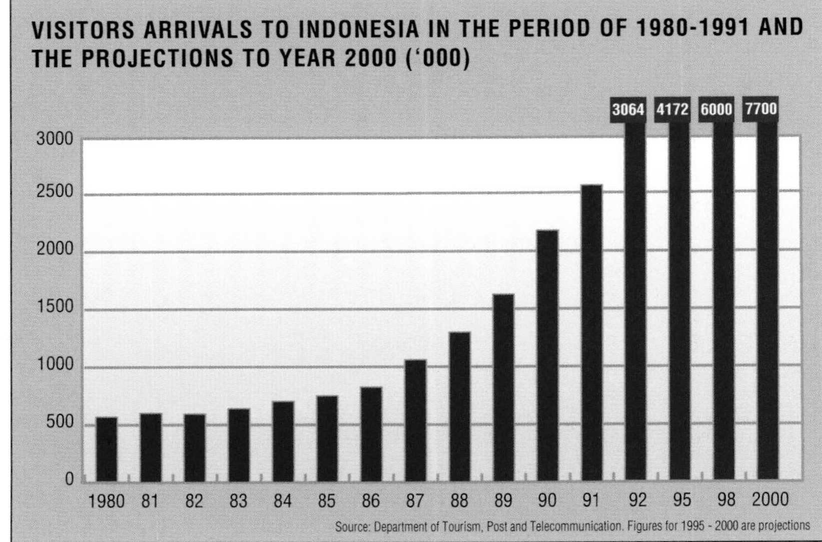

Bali's Tourist Experience

Bali is the most developed of Indonesia's coastal tourist sites, and tourist arrivals have increased from 47,000 in 1969 to nearly one million by 1992. Initially, the planners aimed to confine tourism to the southern resorts of Sanur and Nusa Dua, building luxury hotels that would provide work for locals. A small group of Balinese businessmen run some high quality hotels. Local Balinese entrepreneurs have been instrumental in the development of sites like the beach resorts of Kuta and Legian and

TOURISM AND DANCE

The promotion of cultural tourism is a part of national development policy and has played a major role in the revitalisation and preservation of certain cultural forms. This trend is illustrated in the development of various Central Javanese dances in Yogyakarta. The Sultan's palace (*kraton*), regarded as the focus of Javanese court culture, was opened to tourists following the Proclamation of Independence, and quickly came to be regarded as a place where culture was demonstrated in the name of nationhood. The classical palace dances (*above left*) are performed by dancers chosen from those in training at the academies in Yogyakarta and are popular with tourists.

Villages in the area of Yogyakarta, particularly those along the tourist routes leading to the popular temple sites, have now begun staging their own dance performances for tourists. Dances such as the hobby horse dance (*kuda lumping/jatilan*) (*bottom*), which was once regarded as a folk dances, and hence outside the sphere of high culture, have become immensely popular.

the mountain town of Ubud, where the scope for local involvement and employment is much greater. Most high quality hotels on the island are however, owned by foreign and Jakarta-based companies.

With the large increase in tourists since the 1970s farmers have sold off agricultural land and prices have soared, increasing 500-fold between 1970 and 1984 when they reached US$8,000 per 100 square metres. Seafront sites, formerly of no commercial value, were acquired mainly for restaurants, while souvenir shops mushroomed along resort streets. Javanese and Australians invested in bars and restaurants, burdening the existing infrastructure and often creating friction with local entrepreneurs. Foreign investors

were able to circumvent laws prohibiting ownership of land by non-Indonesians, either by selecting Balinese 'sleeping' partners or by marrying local women. By 1983, 44 per cent of restaurants and bars in the Kuta region were effectively foreign-owned. In response to this rapid and haphazard development, the Balinese authorities imposed their own controls on tourist development. For example, they stipulated that buildings could be no higher than the palm trees, that tourists must adopt suitable dress when entering temples, and that cultural officials should maintain standards by licensing dancers and musicians who entertain tourists. Today, tourism accounts for over 30 per cent of the island's Gross Regional Product (GRP).

Recent Developments

The long term plan is to gradually develop selected areas of Indonesia, from Sumatra to the eastern islands, and the government is beginning to invest in the necessary infrastructure–transport, hotels, airports and roads. In eastern Indonesia, Lombok is rapidly developing its tourist infrastructure. Hotels are displacing fishing communities in some places and enterprising fishermen now use their outrigger canoes to take tourists on coastal trips, or to the nearby Gilis. Gradually, tourism is spreading beyond Lombok to more remote islands such as Flores, Sumba and the Banda islands. More than ever, it is the cultural attractions of these regions which are being stressed. Meanwhile, the government has established a cultural park, Taman Mini,10 kilometres from Jakarta. It was built both to foster a national identity out of many cultures, and as a tourist attraction, bringing together the cultures of Indonesia on a single 120 hectare site. The park has been a great success with foreign tourists, and also with many thousands of Indonesians. Indeed, with rising incomes, domestic tourism is likely to be the tourist wave of the future.

These houses were specially built to accommodate the thousands of guests that would be invited to a Torajan funeral. In recent years, these events have become important tourist attractions. Indeed many observers argue that they have lost their religious and ritual meaning, and are nothing more than a form of tourist entertainment

TOURISM REVENUE (MILLION $US)

Year	Revenue
1987/88	1002
1988/89	1431
1989/90	1630
1990/91	2199
1991/92	2602
1992/93	3218
1993/94	3502
1994/95	3671

Source: BPS

Transport and Communications

The rudimentary transport and communications network established by the Dutch colonial government deteriorated during World War II and the political struggles of the following decade. Since the 1960s, however, massive investments in transport and telecommunications infrastructure have helped to link up the sprawling Indonesian archipelago.

In many rural areas of Indonesia, horse drawn transport, like this bendi in Java, may still be seen carrying local passengers on short journeys. These were once common sights in many Indonesian towns before motor traffic became commonplace.

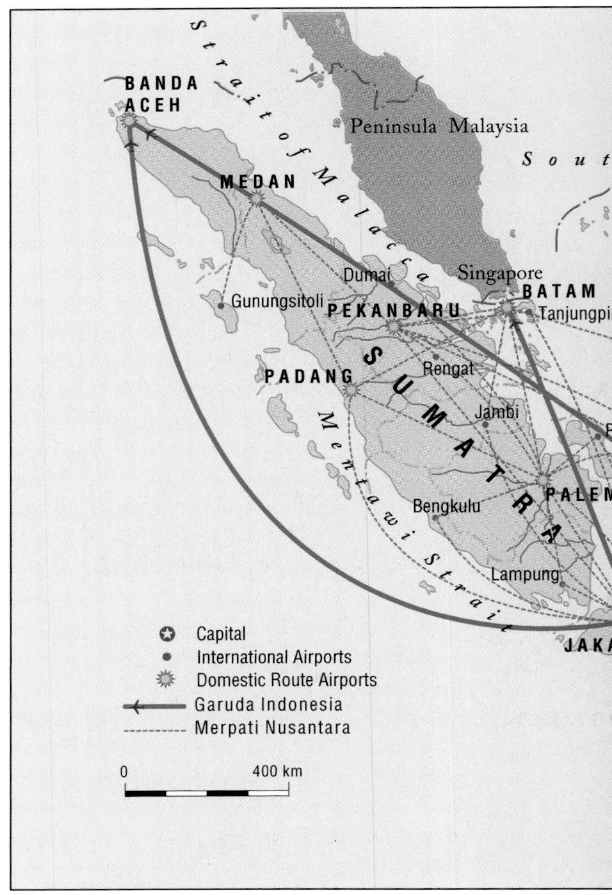

Colonial legacy

The transport infrastructure of the Archipelago at Independence reflected the turbulent politics of the time. During the period of colonisation, the main networks were those providing basic links between the export producing regions and the major ports. The Dutch invested in railways, ships, ports and roads, much of which was damaged during World War II, and deteriorated further during Indonesia's struggle for independence. The first two decades of independence saw little improvement. The rehabilitation of basic infrastructure had a low priority, the seizure of Dutch-owned transport enterprises in 1957 caused disruption, and the regional rebellions which broke out in the late 1950s hampered transport developments in places such as rural South Sulawesi.

Recent Developments

Since the late 1960s Indonesia has experienced rapid growth in its transport system. Repelita I focused attention on the rehabilitation of the existing infrastructure. Repelitas II and III shifted the priority to upgrading and expansion, and Repelita IV coincided with the government's attempt to deregulate and/or privatise parts of the transport sector. First steps were taken in 1985 to reform inter-island shipping–a critical transport component in a country of over 13,000 islands. It was followed up in 1988 with a package designed to deregulate domestic shipping. It gave more operators the opportunity to participate, and greater freedom to choose their own routes and schedules. The privatisation process has been applied rigorously to Indonesia's customs services. For six years customs inspections of imports were contracted to a Swiss firm because of the inefficiency of the customs service. Having made its point, and reformed parts of the bureaucracy, the government began to phase back direct control of customs in late 1991. Under Repelita V the principal emphasis has remained on roads. In 1990, 22 per cent of Indonesia's roads were classified as damaged and 17 per cent as badly damaged. Telecommunications development has become an important focus in recent years. As of 1994, and despite some improvements, the Indonesian telephone system is still inadequate, even in places such as Jakarta, where it sometimes takes hours to make a successful local call. Key communications infrastructure projects include a fibre optic cable installed to connect Jakarta and Surabaya, following the southern route of the railway. A second fibre optic link is being constructed between Surabaya and Banjarmasin, along the southern coast of Kalimantan. Another fibre optic cable connects Jakarta to Singapore. The current plan is to provide 1.4 million new subscriber telephone lines and a new central digital telephone switching system. The successful relaunch of the Palapa B-2R satellite in 1990, which had been put into incorrect orbit in 1984 and retrieved by the Space Shuttle, has added significantly to Indonesia's satellite communications capacity

Travelling village post office, Selat Panjang, Sumatra. With the rapid rise in literacy levels in Indonesia, far more people are able to read and write. In addition far more people are working away from home, often for long periods, and letters are often their only means of staying in touch with their families.

Air travel in Indonesia is provided by government-owned carriers including Garuda Indonesia, Merpati

LOADING AND UNLOADING OF INTER-ISLAND AND INTERNATIONAL SEA BORNE CARGO (000 Tons) 1993 estimate

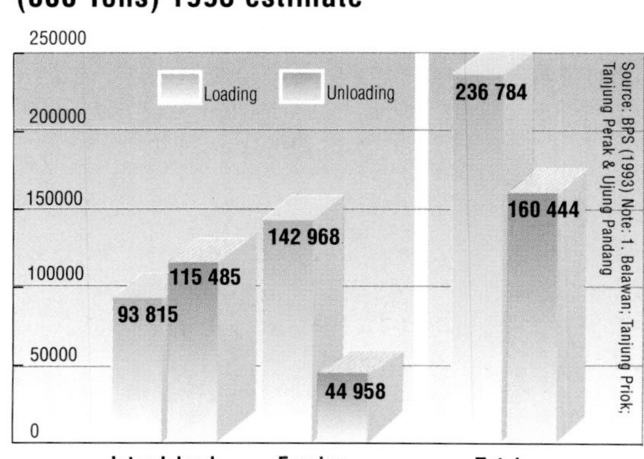

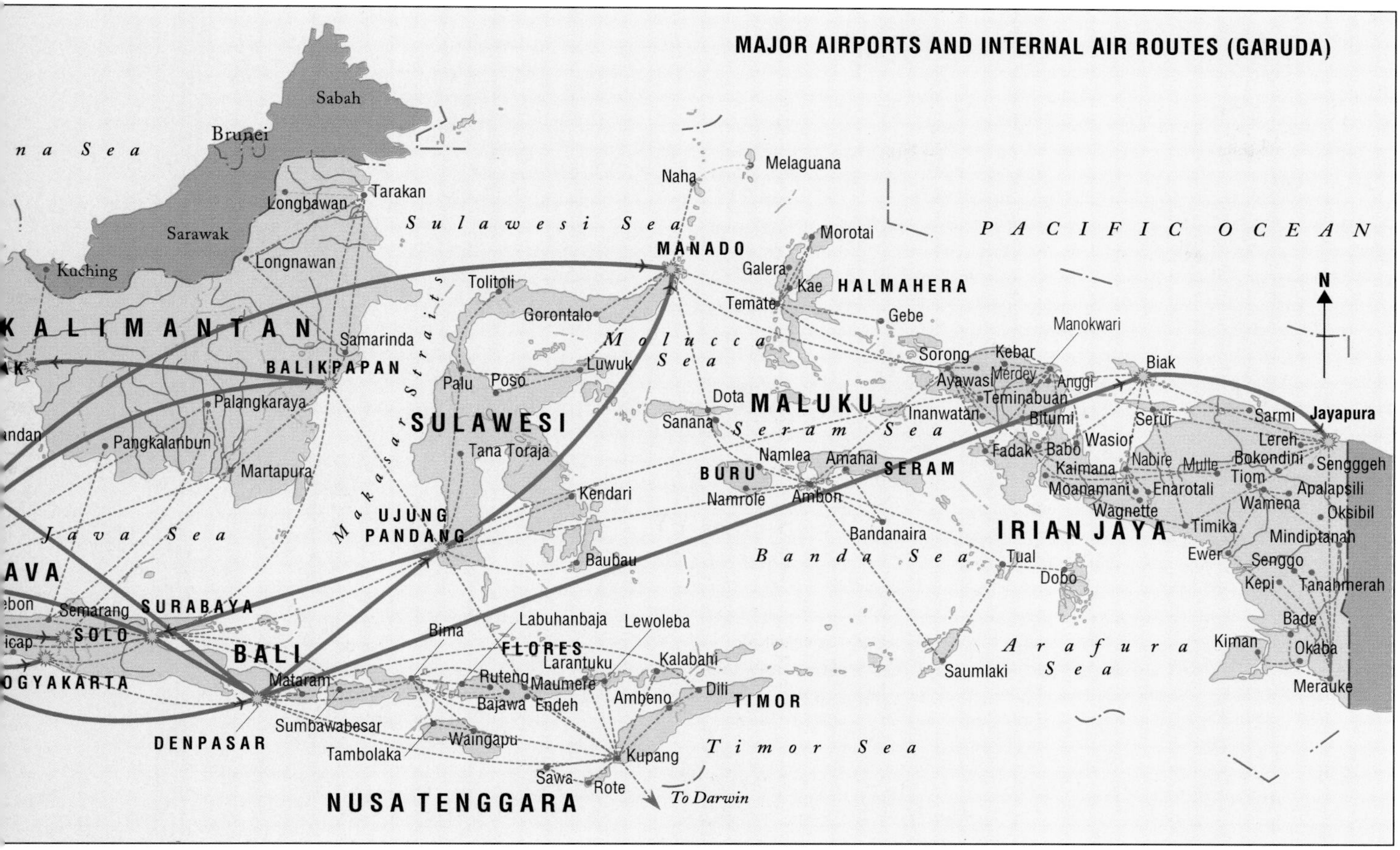

MAJOR AIRPORTS AND INTERNAL AIR ROUTES (GARUDA)

Nusantara Airlines (MNA) and Pelita Air Services, together with four privately owned companies, Seulawah, Bouraq, Mandala and Sempati. Government-owned aircraft provided 14.9 million passenger kilometres of international and domestic air travel in 1991, whereas private airlines accounted for only 1.1 million passenger kilometres, mostly on domestic routes. Garuda Indonesia is the flag-ship carrier responsible for the bulk of international travel and the main domestic routes. International aircraft arrivals in Indonesia almost doubled between 1987 and 1990. Domestic feeder services are provided by private airlines. Through Merpati, Indonesia has operated a pioneer air services programme serving remote areas in the east of the country which would not justify the provision of commercial services. Along with some missionary services these represent important communications links with more out of the way spots.

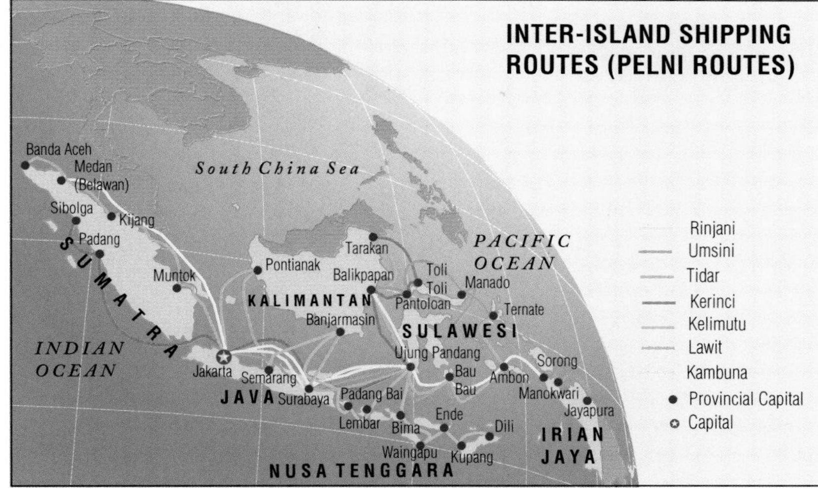

Social Impact

The social impact of Indonesia's transport development in both the village and the city has been remarkable. The 'Revolusi Colt' or 'Colt revolution' has brought micro-buses to just about every village, and the use of motor-bikes (*ojek*) for public transport has further diversified the range of very cheap motorised transport options available to villagers. Together these have accelerated changing lifestyles in the villages by increasing the frequency of travel and contact with urban areas.

In the larger cities private motor vehicle ownership is rapidly escalating, leading to ever increasing problems of traffic congestion. The public transport emphasis has been on large buses, while urban administrations have sought to phase out pedicabs (*becak*), successfully in much of Jakarta. This has deprived unskilled workers of jobs, and eliminated a relatively cheap, and highly flexible, form of transport which was in strong demand by urban *kampung* dwellers. Finally, fostering a sense of national integration has been a government concern. However, while air and sea services link the major urban areas, the transport system in peripheral regions such as Irian Jaya remains inadequate. The province accounts for 22 per cent of Indonesia's total land area, yet contains only three percent of the country's roads. Integrating such peripheral regions remains a political and economic priority of the government.

Micro-buses like this one in Flores, are to be found carrying passengers and goods throughout Indonesia.

Health of the Nation

In 1900, many Indonesians were facing high infant mortality rates, malnutrition and other deficiency disorders, as well as a host of infectious diseases. One of the most striking achievements in 20th century Indonesia therefore, has been the increase in life expectancy brought about through improvements in infectious disease control and health care services.

An educational poster in the window of a health clinic encouraging people to bring their children to be immunised

» A baby being immunised in West Java. The Expanded Programme of Immunisation aims to give every child protection against fatal childhood diseases. Brides are also required by law to have a tetanus taxoid immunisation, to prevent neo-natal tetanus, a major killer of newborns.

A fleet of mobile clinics, like this one in Yogyakarta, brings health care to people in more remote areas.

Colonial Health Care

The Dutch colonial government's 'Ethical Policy' to improve the welfare of the Indonesian masses concentrated heavily on medical intervention. Many of these were what would today be called 'high tech', including the construction of hospitals, laboratories and medical training institutions. They had little direct impact on the masses, who could ill-afford the cost of access to these facilities.

Programmes to fight plague, malaria, tuberculosis and a broad spectrum of tropical diseases were first initiated by the Dutch colonial government. The first schools to train Indonesian medical personnel were also started by the Dutch. The training of paramedical cadres called 'Doktor Djawa', succeeded in bringing modern medicine to the villages, and had an immediate impact on disease and mortality. By the late 1930s life expectancy had begun to rise steadily and programmes of disease control and hygiene were being established throughout the archipelago. These efforts were interrupted in the 1940s by the Second World War and the struggle for independence, and were slow in being re-established in the 1950s and 1960s.

Health Care Innovations

Health priorities in 1950 were the control of infectious diseases, the provision of basic care and nutrition for mothers and children, and the establishment of a system of local health centres. Programmes in each of these areas were handicapped by a lack of skilled staff and investment, and were disrupted by political chaos and regional rebellions.

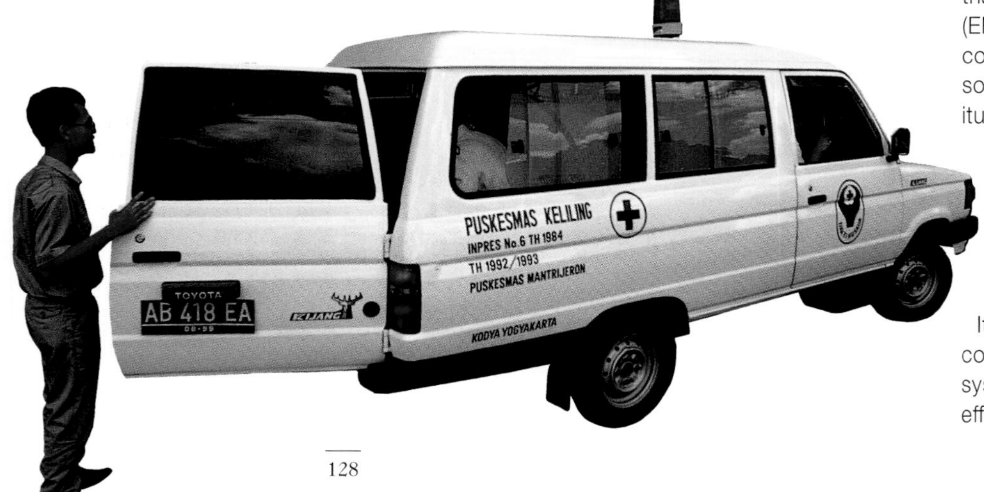

TEN MAJOR CAUSES OF DEATH IN 1992 (Percentage)

Cause	%
Cardiovascular disease	17.8
Tuberculosis	10.8
Pneumonia and other Respiratory Diseases	9.9
Diarrhea	8.0
Gastrointestinal Tract Disorders	6.7
Other Infectious Diseases	6.6
Bronchitis, Emphysema, Asthma	5.5
Injuries, Accidents, Violence	5.4
Neoplasms (Cancer)	4.8
Neuropsychiatric Disorders	2.6

In 1966, Indonesia entered a period of political stability and economic improvement. Nutrition levels rose, and living conditions became easier and healthier. Growing demands for modern diagnosis and treatment of disease were built upon local health centres, augmented by mobile and satellite clinics. By 1991 nearly 6,000 *Puskesmas* (Community Health Centres) had been established. Attached to them were over 4,000 mobile clinics and 16,000 health sub-centres. A network of 250,000 *Posyandu* (Integrated Health Service Posts) run by village volunteers has brought basic services to hamlets on a monthly basis.

Health Care Personnel

In 1970 there were under 6,000 doctors in Indonesia; by 1991 there were 25,000, who were backed up by 200,000 nurses and other trained paramedical workers. In villages throughout the archipelago people with minor or chronic conditions also have access to unregistered traditional healers (*dukun*) who can sometimes provide some help, though the first resort for most ill people is self treatment, or treatment by a relative. There are also numerous *tukang suntik* giving injections of dubious substances to gullible patients. It is not unusual for people to use both traditional and modern medicines to deal with their problems, but, often these attempts lead to iatrogenic, or practitioner-induced illnesses, when the combination of cures is too strong, or inappropriate.

Immunisation

Working on the principle that prevention is better than cure, the Expanded Programme of Immunisation (EPI) aims to give every child protection against common diseases. The budget for immunisation, some eight per cent of rural health center expenditure, has been called 'possibly the most cost-effective intervention in terms of reducing mortality and morbidity.' The challenges of immunising a dispersed and diverse population are formidable. It is costly to keep refrigerated medicines in stock. Disposable syringes are often in short supply and often boiled and reused. It is not unusual to see vaccinators using the large contraceptive syringes, merely because the logistics system of the family planning program is more efficient than that of the health department. Mothers

TOTAL (CUMULATIVE) NUMBER OF HEALTH CENTRES, 1973-1993

FACILITY	1973–1974 End PELITA I	1978–1979 End PELITA II	1983–1984 End PELITA III	1988–1989 End PELITA IV	1989–1990 PELITA V Year I	1990–1991 PELITA V Year II	1991–1992 PELITA V Year III	1992–1993 PELITA V Year IV
Health Centre	2,679	4,353	5,353	5,642	5,742	5,978	6,229	6,588
HC with Beds	838	838	966	1,052	1,052	1,107	1,232	1,371
Sub- Centre	6,636	6,636	13,562	13,562	14,303	15,944	17,465	18,816
Mobile Hc	—	604	2,479	3,124	3,424	4,023	4,618	5,285
HC with Radio Communication	—	—	—	310	350	420	712	1,318

frequently do not understand the principles of immunity, and sometimes fail to bring their children back for the necessary follow-up injections later on.

Nonetheless, the efforts are beginning to bear fruit. Incidence of many infectious diseases are falling. At the same time, the institutional structures created to provide immunisation can be also used to educate people about hygiene and nutrition.

Making Motherhood Safe

Childbirth is dangerous for mothers and babies. A mother dies in nearly five out of every 1000 births in Indonesia. In another 30 to 40 cases, the baby dies within days or weeks of birth. The causes of such deaths are varied, but simple: bleeding, obstructed labour, and infection. Skilled birth attendants with access to advanced technology often save the lives of mothers and children in such situations, but the better option is to prevent their occurrence. Mothers need to be well-nourished to deliver healthy babies. Their pregnancies should also be monitored to detect problems before they become critical. Women at risk should be quickly referred to hospitals with the specialists and equipment to handle the problems.

In 1992 three quarters of deliveries were attended by one of the 170,000 traditional birth attendants. Mostly women, they are often trained in the basic principles of hygienic delivery, and supplied with a kit of clean dressings and a knife for cutting the umbilical cord, but they are not fully integrated into the maternal health teams based in clinics. As a result the maternal mortality rate remains high. Recently the government has placed emphasis on training nurse mid-wives to take responsibility for antenatal care and delivery. In 1987 there were only 13,000 midwives for 66,000 villages. From 1988 to 1993 18,900 nurse midwives were trained and deployed as *bidan di desa* (village mid-wives), and the target is to have one midwife in every village by the year 2000.

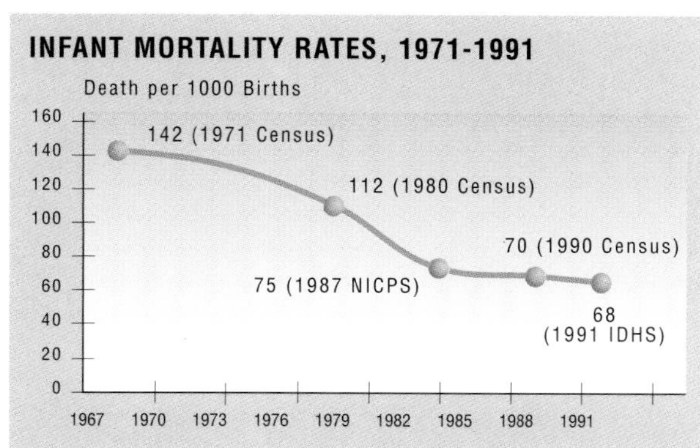

Challenges for the Twenty First Century

While life expectancy has risen, there are still health problems which are difficult to overcome, especially the high static maternal mortality rate. Beyond this is the 'invisible epidemic' of reproductive tract infections, including a wide range of sexually transmitted diseases, which are seldom diagnosed by doctors. Common reproductive tract infections are treatable, but commitment from patients and doctors has not yet been forthcoming. Up to half of Indonesian women have one or a number of these infections, which not only affect the women's fertility, but can make sexual relations painful, and facilitate the spread of HIV. On World AIDS Day in 1993, the government announced that 175 Indonesians had been found to be HIV positive, while 42 had developed full blown AIDS. Most of the victims were male, but increasingly women were listed among those individuals who have tested positive.

The decline of immunisable infectious disease has been offset by a rise of chronic and degenerative diseases. Lung cancer is widespread and growing rapidly, but treatment is available only to a few. With smoking an established habit among men, and a growing practice by women, cancer, and other tobacco-linked diseases, will increase. Indonesians are also concerned about heart disease, and growing numbers of Indonesians are exercising and changing their diets.

The government is confident in facing these challenges. The Minister of Health recently noted that improved nutrition has already added 15 centimeters to the height of Junior High School students within two decades. This is a simple measure of the health of the population. It is what gives officials confidence that the 'human capital' of Indonesia is improving.

A puskesmas poster promoting the health care programme. The government's aim is to encourage people to use the growing number of health care facilities that are increasingly being made available.

«« *An old Dutch military hospital. Although health care was available, only those Indonesians with money could afford it.*

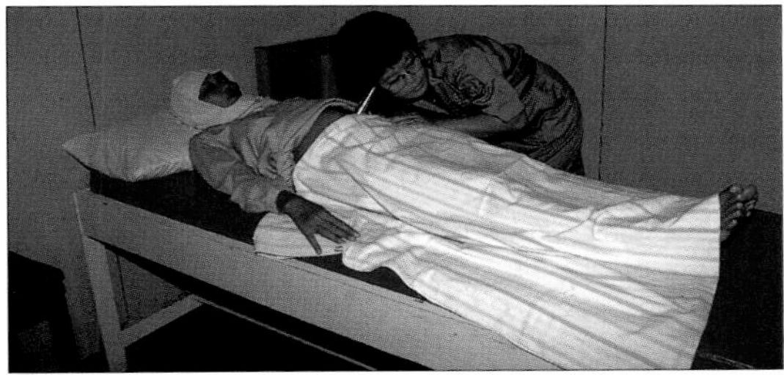

«« *Puskesmas have been built across Indonesia to bring health services to remote areas, a patient being examined in a puskesmas, Kalimantan.*

Educating a Population

Since the clarion call to literacy enunciated by Kartini nearly a century ago, education has been one of the foremost preoccupations of Indonesia nationalists and advocates of cultural development and women's rights. The Dutch colonial government made important but limited steps to open schools for native peoples but real commitments to mass education came only with Independence in 1945. The organisational ability to achieve those ambitions constitute one of the most important achievements of the New Order government

Raden Ajeng Kartini

Muslim schoolgirl from a Yogyakarta school.

The Beginnings of an Education System

In June 1903 Raden Ajeng Kartini opened the first primary school in Indonesia specifically catering for indigenous girls. Prior to this event education was designed to prepare Dutch and elite Indonesian males for positions of power, and seldom provided training for women. After Kartini's death, her admirers established the first of a series of 'Kartini Schools' in Semarang in 1912, the Taman Siswa (Student Garden) movement. Various efforts by Islamic teachers led to the construction of schools and the opening of opportunities for growing numbers of students. By 1940 a dualistic system had become entrenched, with separate hierarchies of schools for European and select elite students, and for indigenous students. In both cases, there were private and public schools. Some of the private schools had religious backing.

The Japanese Occupation had three major impacts on education. First, enrolment rose dramatically setting a precedent for large class sizes and compromises in the quality of facilities. Second, all schools were subject to a common requirement to teach Indonesian, Japanese and local languages. This marked the first time that Indonesian was treated as a national language in the national school system. Third, the Japanese set regulations concerning government employees and village leaders promoting literacy, skills and loyalty among a broad range of officials. The Kartini dream of schooling for self-fulfilment was thus replaced by a formulation stressing service, loyalty and nationalism.

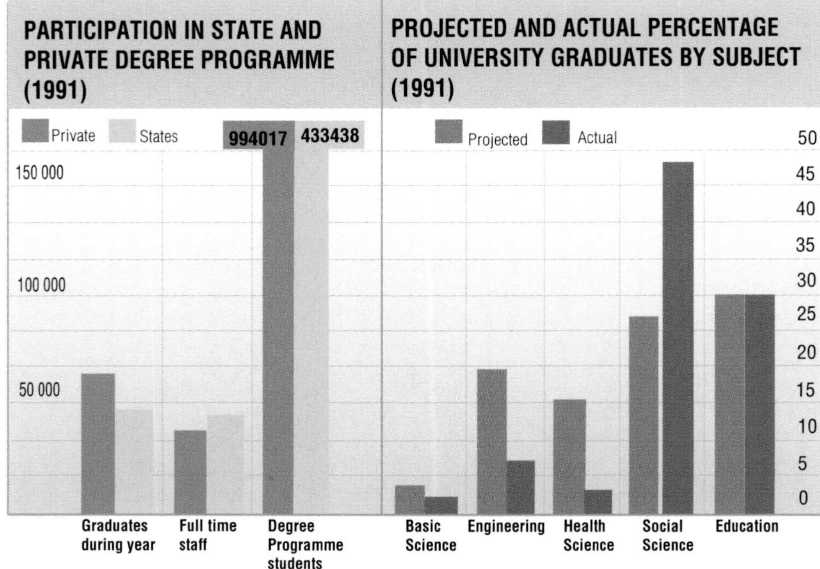

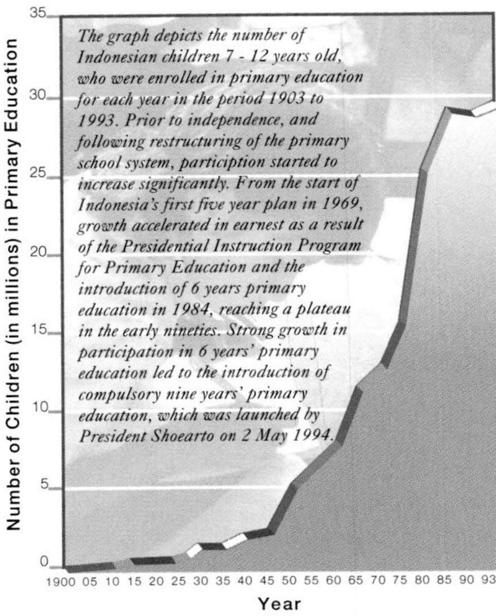

Education for Independent Indonesia

After Independence in 1949, the nationalist government took on the challenge of providing education under conditions of grim economic stringency. It was decided to have six years of primary education, followed by three years of lower secondary, and three years of upper secondary school. At the secondary level there were schools specialising in particular types of skills, such as mechanical education, economics, and paramedical skills. All schools, public and private, were regulated by the Education Department. Indonesian became the major language of instruction but regional languages were often used in the first three years of instruction. Education was promoting a national identity, but the process was slow because so many children were denied the opportunity to attend school for even a few years.

New Order Education

When the New Order government came to power in 1968 it repeated earlier commitments to educate the people, but it backed up these words with actions. The education budget was rationalised and although top priority was placed on elementary education, the government also worked to rebuild the severely dilapidated secondary and tertiary sectors. Using the facility of the Presidential Instruction (INPRES), thousands of elementary school buildings were constructed in villages across the country, to ensure that education was within easy reach of every primary-age child. Teachers were trained and sent to these new schools, and equipped with revised curricula to improve the content of education.

In the early 1970s, pupil numbers were rising much faster than the population growth rate. There were also difficulties in establishing systems to deliver books to pupils, equipment to schools and salaries to teachers. Gradually these problems were addressed and by the end of the 1980s, not only were virtually all primary-aged children attending school, but facilities had markedly improved. At the time of the 1990 Population Census just short of eight million children aged 13 to 15, and 4.7 million children aged 16 to 18 were attending school. Ninety one per cent of both males and females in the age group seven to 12 years old were attending school, compared to less than 62 per cent of males and 58 per cent of females 20 years earlier.

Tertiary and Vocational Education

The first universities in Indonesia grew out of medical and engineering schools established early in the 20th century by the Dutch colonial government. By 1993, there were 51 government, and 1,035 private universities listed by the Department of Education. In 1991, the country produced 109,000 degree graduates. Between 1988 to 1993, the Department of Education identified a need for 580,609 graduates. Not enough students were graduating in engineering, health and basic sciences to meet the demand for them.

The government also finances vocational training centres, and determines the accreditation status of privately funded centres. In 1991/92 over 70,000 workers received training in state institutions, while in the four years beginning 1989, over half a million trainees were reported to have attended private institutions.

Achievements and Challenges

The growth of primary education led to a rise in literacy rates. Illiteracy among those aged ten and over dropped from 29 to 16 per cent between 1980 and 1990. More importantly, among those between ten to 44 years old, who constitute the heart of the workforce, literacy rose in ten years from 80 per cent to 92 per cent, and women in this age group recorded a literacy rate of 89 per cent, up from 74 per cent ten years earlier.

In 1990 the government issued a regulation which provided the foundation for compulsory education through nine years of primary and lower secondary school. This will be more difficult to implement than universal primary education, because the basic infrastructure at the lower secondary level is more limited, the curricular demands are more demanding, and the cost of necessary buildings and equipment are greater than was the case with primary education. It is commonly estimated that the lower secondary school pupils will come from children aged between 13 and 15 years old. In 1990 about one-third of this group were not enrolled in schools, and a large portion were active in productive pursuits at home or in the workforce. It will be difficult to attract them back to school, even if the facilities become available.

The New Order has succeeded in achieving many of Kartini's most precious ideals. In practical terms, the population can read. Females have benefited from the development of primary education and currently have enrolment rates equivalent to males.

The dream of early nationalists for a national language is rapidly being achieved. Where a third of Indonesians could not speak Indonesian in 1980, ten years later that indicator had dropped to 17 per cent. By 1990, nearly three-quarters of the population were regularly listening to radio and watching television for entertainment and news, and the bulk of the programming was in Indonesian.

« Graduation ceremony at the University of Indonesia.

Literacy rates have increased dramatically in recent years and readership of newspapers and magazines are increasing.

« Technical and vocational education is now seen as vital to help meet the increasingly sophisticated labour requirements of an industrialising economy.

A class in progress at a Kartini school in Pekalongan. These schools were the first to set out to provide education for girls. Schools, up until that time education was designed to prepare Dutch and elite Indonesian males for positions of power.

Poverty and the poor

Although considerable poverty continues to exist in Indonesia, its incidence has declined dramatically since the 1960s primarily because economic growth has outstripped population increase. The geographical distribution of poverty has also changed. The incidence of urban poverty relative to poverty in rural areas has risen and the problem of poverty in Java has declined relative to that on some of the Outer Islands, where it remains a very serious problem.

Poverty alleviation programme logo.

A scavenger at a rubbish dump in Pekanbaru. Scavengers are part of the urban informal sector.

Identifying the Poor

The first step towards alleviating poverty is to identify the poor. This is a more complex task than it may at first seem, and several poverty lines have been devised in Indonesia to delimit poverty. Those below the poverty line, however it is defined, are considered to be poor.

In Indonesia, the most widely used poverty line is that estimated by the Central Bureau of Statistics (*Biro Pusat Statistik*, BPS). This is calculated on the basis of what it costs to buy a basket of commodities considered to be just sufficient to meet basic needs, namely the cost of food purchases to supply 2,100 calories per day and the purchase of essential non-food items. The urban basket differs from the rural one in that it includes a greater allowance for transport. Using the BPS poverty line the percentage of the Indonesian population in poverty has declined from around 40 per cent in 1976 to 15 per cent in 1990. Using this measure, about 54 million Indonesians were considered to be poor in 1976 but by 1990 this had fallen to about 27 million. Although still a substantial number, indications are that the trend is continuing its downward movement.

Geographical Distribution of the Poor

While it is still true that the number of people living in poverty in rural areas is much greater than that in urban areas, the incidence of poverty in urban areas has fallen at a somewhat slower rate, while the proportion of the Indonesian population living in urban areas has increased rapidly. Significant rural to urban migration has in effect resulted in a geographical shift of poverty.

THE POVERTY TRAP

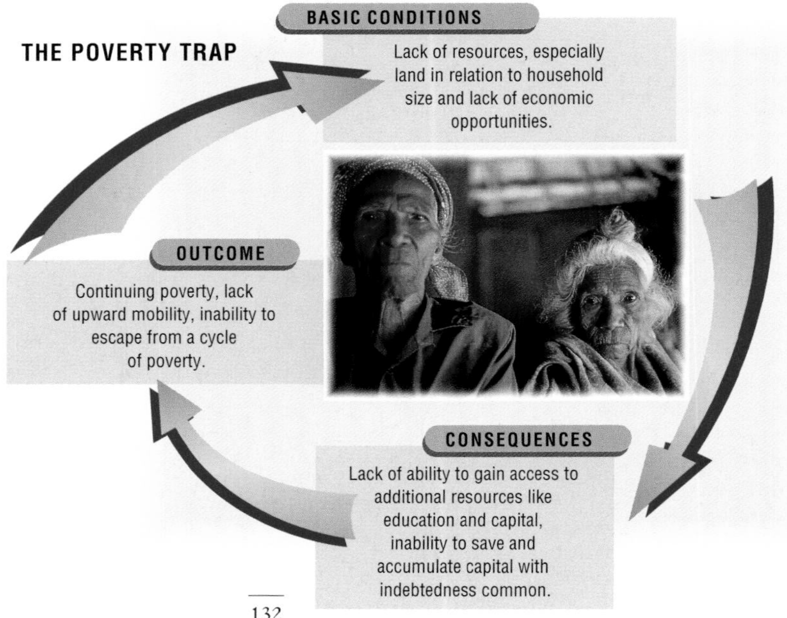

Elderly poor in rural areas, Ranggasé, Flores.

RURAL AND URBAN POVERTY AS PERCENTAGE OF TOTAL POOR POPULATION, 1976 AND 1993

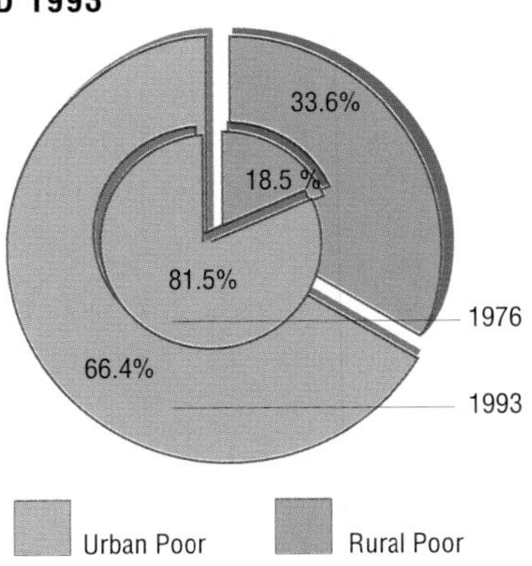

Formerly, it was commonly believed that of all the regions in Indonesia, Java had the most serious poverty problem. Certainly, this used to be the case. However, the incidence of poverty in Java may now be below the national average in both urban and rural areas. Regionally, the incidence of poverty is now greatest in the eastern provinces of Indonesia. In many eastern provinces, more than one in three households live below the poverty line.

Poverty and its Alleviation

The causes of poverty and the reasons for its persistence are often complex. However, most of the poor lack ownership or possession of sufficient productive resources to meet their basic needs. This may be because they are physically or mentally disabled; unable to obtain sufficient education to raise their productivity significantly; or lacking in ownership of, or access to, sufficient quantities of resources such as land and capital. In Indonesia, according to the World Bank, the largest proportion of the poor are in the agricultural sector and typically have little or no land.

The educational attainment of the poor also tends to be very low with household heads usually having no more than a primary school education. Studies by the BPS indicate that the incidence of poverty in male headed households is higher than for those headed by females, and, that on average, households in poverty tend to consist of about six members. However, the average disguises important differences. For example, a household made up of a single elderly woman is likely to be in poverty and similarly, a very large family with restricted access to resources.

Many different strategies exist for alleviating poverty. These include increasing the access of the poor to productive resources–improving their access to capital for example; raising the productivity of the resources which the poor already have through such means as the transfer of technology or improved education; increasing access for their produce or

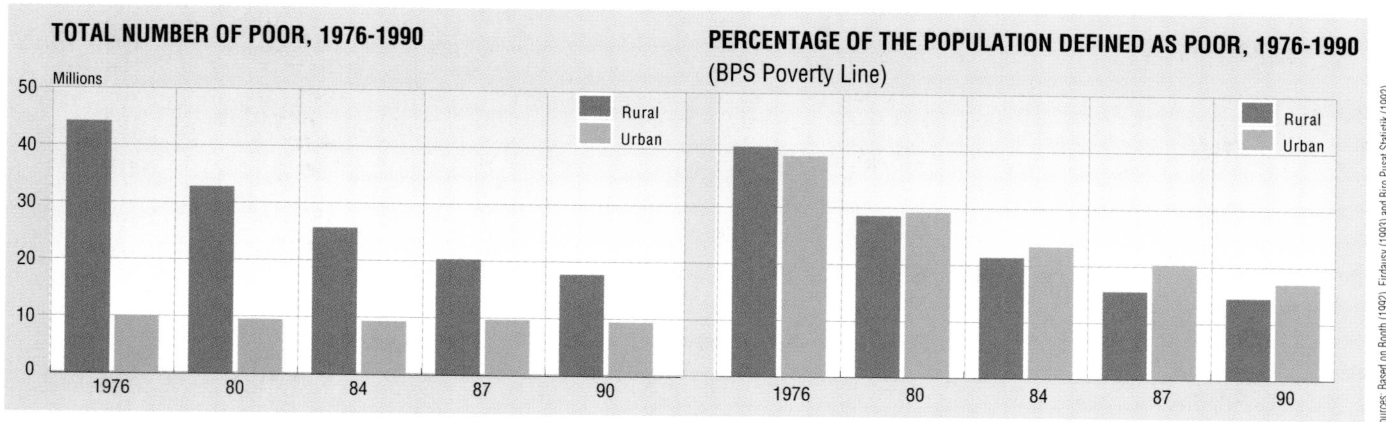

Sources: Based on Booth (1992), Firdausy (1993) and Biro Pusat Statistik (1992)

labour to higher-priced markets; and by the transfer of income to the poor, for example by subsidising the prices or supplies of necessities. Indonesian policy has attempted the latter by supporting the transfer of Green Revolution technologies, thereby boosting rice production. This has helped keep rice prices stable and relatively low, and also helped the urban poor and rural landless labourers who must spend a significant proportion of their incomes on food. The extent to which Indonesia's rice policies have helped the poor is, however, still controversial. At the same time, in urban areas, while the government provides some subsidised housing for the poor, it is far from adequate in quality or quantity. It is also true that there are instances where 'low income' housing becomes used by those on middle incomes. Thus, measures to help the poor may end up helping the better-off.

The government, aware of such problems and criticisms, has recently undertaken a bold programme of poverty alleviation called *Inpres Desa Tertinggal*. The basic strategy works through two stages. First, the government determines the villages with high concentrations of poor people, the *desa tertinggal* or 'backward villages'. These constitute about a third of the nation's villages. Then the poor within the village are organised into groups under the coordination of the village welfare institute. The regulations concerning the definition of poverty and the procedures for joining groups are flexible, and locally controlled, but government agencies are charged with ensuring that the core of each group includes the poor with the potential to become economically active. The 1994 government budget included a provision of Rp. 20 million for each backward village, to be used by the poor group in the village to establish viable, sustainable, environmentally friendly and appropriate enterprises. Funds are channelled through the Bank Rakyat Indonesia (People's Bank) directly to the groups, thus by-passing laborious and potentially wasteful bureaucracy. While this is the largest direct credit programme ever attempted in Indonesia for poverty alleviation, it builds on the experience of the Family Planning Progamme credit schemes which have helped poor villagers establish successful enterprises in animal husbandry, food processing and garment manufacturing. It is hoped that these fairly large injections of interest-free, unsecured loans, will help families break out of the poverty traps they face due to their lack of access to land and capital.

Poverty: a Case Study

A poor area of Jakarta. A food-seller dries fish amidst filth.

In 1980, Bali had one of the highest incidences of poverty in Indonesia. Since then it has declined significantly especially in rural areas, and in 1990 estimates by the BPS placed it as low as 16.6 per cent in urban areas and 9.3 per cent in rural areas. However, such figures disguise significant local differences. Nusa Penida is an island off Bali with poor soils and a long dry season. The island has little of the cultural and other attractions that make Bali so attractive to tourists. In 1990, the percentage of households in poverty in one village, Batumadeg, exceeded 90 per cent while in another two, Jungut Batu and Ped, it was less than 10 per cent and 20 per cent respectively. Batumadeg villagers depend on dryland agriculture using traditional methods and are semi-subsistent. The villages of Jungut Batu and Ped, meanwhile, produce seaweed for sale. The latter has proven to be economically profitable and requires little capital investment. The differences in poverty between the villages can therefore largely be explained by the differences in the natural resource base available to the villagers and the favourable market for seaweed compared with a crop such as cassava.

These children at Candi Sari, Central Java, are typical of many of Indonesia's rural poor. Small children often have to work to supplement their family income.

Environmental Costs of Growth

The 1980s and 1990s have seen the growth of environmental awareness in Indonesia, along with other Southeast Asian countries. Groups like the environmental pressure group Wahana Lingkungan Hidup (Walhi) have emerged while, in turn, the government has also paid greater heed to emerging environmental concerns.

Timber extraction by skidding destroys the forest drainage system.

Water polluted by detergent, Surabaya, East Java.

Farmers in the Dieng region of Java have adapted to lands prone to erosion by upland terracing.

Environmental Concern and Economic Growth

The Indonesian government fully recognises that environmental degradation can retard the economic growth of the country. Most significant in marking this 'greening' of the government was the appointment in 1983 of a Minister of State for Population and the Environment. In 1993 a further refinement saw the creation of a sole Ministry for the Environment while Population merged with Family Planning. The growth of an environmentally-aware middle class has done much to lead this transformation.

Taking into account the loss of 'natural capital' and considering only oil depletion, soil erosion and deforestation, Robert Repetto and his colleagues at the World Resources Institute have estimated that in real terms, Indonesia's economy only grew by four per cent annually between 1971 and 1984, rather than the 7.1 per cent as conventionally stated.

Causes of Environmental Degradation

Indonesia's enormous population has often been identified as the root cause of environmental deterioration: the 1990 census recorded the total population of the country as being 179 million while it is estimated that by the year 2000, it will have grown to somewhere between 210 and 216 million. This population will have to be clothed and fed, and this means more land will need to be cleared for such purposes as agriculture, expanding cities, and industrial development.

It is now considered, however, to be much too simplistic to equate environmental degradation simply with a large population as has been the tendency in the past. Although Java, with an average population density of over 800 people per square kilometre, does suffer from degradation, it is, in fact, often more severe in the Outer Islands where the population pressure is much less. For example, deforestation of marginal uplands with fragile soils has created severe problems in provinces like South Sumatra, Lampung, Bengkulu, South Sulawesi, North Sulawesi and East Nusa Tenggara. In the last of these provinces, the population density is 'only' 68 people per square kilometre, yet 37 per cent of its land is classified as degraded. In complete contrast,

LAND DEGRADATION IN INDONESIA (PERCENTAGE OF AGRICULTURAL LAND)

upland areas of Java such as the agricultural lands of Gunung Kidul in Yogyakarta are able to support a much higher population density of 500 people per square kilometre. In this instance, farmers have adapted by progressively introducing new crops and techniques in order to rehabilitate formerly highly eroded lands and to raise production. Nevertheless, one estimate put the on-site and off-site costs of upland soil erosion on Java alone at US$373 million per year.

Of Indonesia's total land area of 193 million hectares, 144 million is classified as 'forest'. Of this, 48 million has been earmarked for protection as national park land, 30 million for settlement and the remaining 66 million for 'selective' logging. Yet a 1990 Forestry Department report observed that on only 22 out of 578 logging concessions were guidelines for replanting and selective logging being adhered to.

Environmental problems in urban areas are just as severe. Cities like Jakarta and Semarang suffer from flooding, while inadequate sewerage and waste disposal systems, coupled with the uncontrolled proliferation of unregulated industries has caused air and water pollution in urban areas to become a growing cause for concern. The World Bank has recently estimated that in Jakarta, the cost of boiling drinking water is equal to one per cent of the city's GDP.

Marine resources have also suffered degradation. Many of Indonesia's main fishing grounds have been overfished, and 15 years ago trawlers were banned from operating in western Indonesia, a decree which was later extended to cover most of the country's waters. To control pollution in major rivers, *Prokasih* (*Program Kali Bersih* or the Clean River Programme) was introduced at the end of the 1980s.

Although 'Sustainable' development has become one of the important buzz-words of the 1990s, the concept of *sustainability* is rather complex. The most widely used definition is that contained in the World Commission on Environment and Development's (WCED) report *Our Common Future* in which it is stated that: 'Sustainable development is development that meets the needs of the present without compromising the ability of future generations to meet their own needs.' It is important, however, to note that 'sustainability' almost always means different things to different people.

The complexities of environmental problems in Indonesia are an indication that, apart from certain economic imperatives, there may also be cultural, political and bureaucratic obstacles obstacles to effective environmental management. Lack of empowerment of relevant groups and individuals, insecurity of ownership, bureaucratic inertia and overlap, legal uncertainty, corruption and short-term approaches, are all important reasons why the 'greening' of Indonesia's middle class has yet to make a significant impact on the 'stage' of the environment.

Although Indonesia's environmental problems may at present be growing more acute, the experiences of other Southeast Asian countries show that a valuable first step in finding solutions lies in the acceptance that 'development' does not just mean economic growth, but growth which also respects the fragility and value of the country's environment.

Urban pollution can be serious even in small, regional towns. Rubbish is heaped between these houses in Ternate, Maluku.

A tree nursery in Batu Ampar, East Kalimantan. Replanting programmes aim to protect Indonesia's forest resources.

Conservation and Ecotourism

Conservation is a word people use to express their desire to preserve the wild animals, plants and wilderness areas of the world for themselves and for future generations. It is not just about keeping things as they have been, but rather about maintaining functioning, dynamic ecosystems as repositories of living organisms which live, compete, adapt, evolve, die and decay, responding to environmental changes.

Warning sign at safari park, Cisarua, West Java.

Special protected areas on Komodo island have been set aside to conserve the habitats of the komodo dragon. A dead goat has been provided in a reserve for tourists to watch the dragons during feeding time.

People and Conservation

Conservation sets out to maintain expanses of ecosystems. These must be large enough for natural processes to continue with minimum human intervention. Furthermore they aim to maintain all possible habitats, and thus structural and species diversity. Conservation is also a process by which the preservation of the ecosystem, management of biological diversity and environment, education, and conflict resolution are all integrated within a given area. Thus, in order to protect natural areas it is essential to consider people living around them and to ensure that their food and income supplies are sustainable, that their environment does not degrade, and that there is a desire among the concerned parties to cooperate and resolve conflicts.

Allowance has to be made for traditional needs of people, particularly in tribal areas, so that human suffering does not result from the protection policies.

At the same time steps must be taken against those who violate the regulations concerning protected areas and protected species. This requires the enforcement of existing laws, and the understanding and support of the judiciary. Much of this infrastructure is already in place in Indonesia under the authority of the Directorate General of Forest Protection and Nature Conservation in the Ministry of Forestry, but insufficient manpower and budgets frustrate their best efforts.

Costing Conservation

There are many reasons for conserving areas of natural ecosystems, but they fall into two categories–social or moral, and economic. The social and moral reasons include maintaining quality of life, accepting a responsibility not to leave future generations less than we received (inherent in notions of sustainable development), not depriving other species of existence, and national pride. The economic arguments for conservation simply consider the monetary benefits of such areas which must be

PROTECTED AREAS AND PARKS

SUMATRA
KALIMANTAN
SULAWESI
JAVA
BALI
NUSA TENG
Gunung Leuser National Park
Dolok Sembelin
Singkil Barat
Taitai Batti Nature Reserve
Siberut National Park
Kembang Lubok Niur
Kerinci Seblat National Park
Bukit Barisan Selatan National Park
Ujung Kulon National Park
Gunung Halimun National Park
Gunung Gede-Pangrango National Park
Segara Anakan
Nusa Kambangan
Bromo-Tengger-Semereu National Park
Meru Betiri National Park
Alas Purwo National Park
Gunung Rinjani National Park
Tamboro Complex
Gunung Wanggameti
Gunung Mutis/Tin
Kerumutan
Tanjung Datuk and Pulau Bakung
Seberida
Tanjung Jabung
Berbak National Park
Banyuasin-Musi/Sembilang River
Way Kambas National Park
Kepulauan Seribu Marine Park
Gunung Palung National Park
Kepulauan Karimunjawa Marine Park
Gunung Kawi-Keludu
Bali Barat National Park
Kayan Mentarang
Gunung Bentuang Karimun
Danau Sentarum
Bukit Baka/Bukit Raya National Park
Tanjung Puting National Park
Maura Sebuku
Ulu Sembakung
Sangkulirang
Bunaken Manado Tu Marine Par
Lore Lindu National Park
Bagani Nani Watabone National Park
Marisa
Kepulauan Togiar
Morowa Nature Res
Rawa Aopa Watumahai National Park
Danau Matano Mahalona
Gunung Olet Sangenges
Komodo National Park
Ruteng
Laut Taka Bonerata M
Kakabia
Danau Kelim National Par
Gunu Kelapat
M
D

Exisiting and proposed protected areas: (scientific reserves; strict nature reserves; national parks; national monuments; natural landmarks; managed nature reserves; nature conservation reserves; and wildlife sanctuaries).

International boundary

balanced against their costs. This approach is fraught with problems, however, because not all the benefits or costs can be counted at the present, and the burdens and advantages are not borne and appreciated by the same people. The overall economic benefits of conservation areas tend to be rather low at the local level, higher at the national and regional level, and potentially significant at the global level. Conversely, the overall economic costs tend to be significant locally and nationally while being insignificant globally.

There are rather limited economic incentives for a country to spend its money protecting conservation areas, and this situation is apparent in Indonesia where many conservation areas are under significant threat because of grossly inadequate budgets. If the economic books are required to balance, then the imbalances need to be dealt with through donor grants, increasing local and regional and national benefits from tourism, and integrated conservation and development projects.

Ecotourism

There are some who point to 'ecotourism' as a source of salvation for the richest wildlife areas, based on the model of East African safari parks. Unfortunately the model is inappropriate for a number of reasons, not least the total discrepancy in the visibility and accessibility of the animal life; it is simply not possible to drive up to a Sumatran rhino and take its photograph. The main exceptions to this are probably Komodo where visitors come to see and photograph the huge, wild Komodo Dragons, and sites in Sumatra and Kalimantan such as the Bohorok Orang-Utan Rehabilitation centre in the Gunung Leuser National Park where orang-utans can be encountered at close quarters. There are a number of specialist ecotourism companies exploiting these few niches but the number of tourists involved is small and probably insignificant in the context of the entire tourism sector. In some respects this is just as well, for example, the endangered Bali starling, for example, has enough problems without being disturbed by tourists. This is not to say that increasing numbers of tourists are not finding their way to some of the exceptionally beautiful and rich natural areas of Indonesia and being rewarded and inspired by wonderful natural sights. It is also true that tourists who visit tribal peoples in Kalimantan and Irian Jaya should also be included under the category 'eco-tourists'. The tribal peoples are, in some senses, just as much a part of the natural environment as the animal and plant life, and the reasons motivating tourists to opt for this type of travel are also similar. Interestingly, the most-visited national parks and nature reserves reflect much more the importance of *geo*-tourism, since they tend to be centred on the attractions of dramatic volcanoes, whitewater rivers, waterfalls and rugged coastlines rather than on biological interests. For example, Bromo-Tengger-Semeru National Park in East Java is widely promoted internationally (nearly one-third of all visitors are from overseas), but virtually all the visitors come only to see the sunrise from the Bromo crater after which they leave. Hardly any tourists venture to see the biological interest the Park has to offer.

Foreign tourists are more inclined to enter forests than domestic tourists, but the volume of the latter is slowly increasing. Part of the reluctance of domestic tourists to explore the forest stems from a traditional battle against the forest. Pioneers in any area had to beat back the forest to build their houses and establish their fields, and the forest in its turn would grow back if allowed. In addition, most of the ancient underlying animist religions of Indonesia view the forest as an eerie, evil and frightening dwelling-place of spirits. One can question whether Indonesia's natural biological diversity has generated any significant or genuine interest, inspiration or concern among the general populace of Indonesia so far. It would seem not, but to dismiss the importance of conservation misses the very noticeable increase in young hikers and campers in Java's wilder areas and the growing understanding of environmental issues among a better-informed public.

Agro-tourism on a coffee plantation in East Java. Enthusiasts can spend their vacation studying plants.

Indonesia has many areas of great natural beauty with potential for geo-tourism. Here tourists are visiting Mount Bromo, Java.

Many of Indonesia's ethnic groups are producing traditional craft items for sale to tourists. In some cases, tourist demand has stimulated the production of crafts that were previously disappearing. The Asmat of Irian Jaya have become well-known for the wood carvings they produce for the tourist trade.

Glossary

A

abangan: a form of Islam which blends Hindu and Buddhist elements.

adat: custom, locally accepted code of behaviour.

agen: brokers who usually buy direct from the producer, often on behalf of a third party. They also scout for produce and arrange delivery to a depot when supplies are scarce.

ani-ani: traditional finger knife used for harvesting rice.

B

bakmi: noodles.

bakso: meat soup.

bakul: general term for different kinds of market trader, most commonly applied to women traders buying and selling in the market, or at the roadside.

bawon: share of rice received by a villager for helping another villager with the harvesting.

Bhinneka Tunggal Ika: Indonesia's national motto; usually translated as 'unity in diversity'.

bubur ayam: chicken porridge.

bupati: regent, government officer in charge of a *kapupaten.*

C

cendol: shredded fruit and syrup 'drink'.

convergent plate boundary: area where the plates making up the surface of the earth move towards each other.

D

Daerah Istemewa*:* special administrative regions (applies to Aceh and Yogyakarta).

Daerah Khusus Ibukota (DKI): the special administrative region of Jakarta.

depot: wharehouse, usually for bulk agricultural produce.

desa: village.

divergent plate boundary: area where the plates making up the earth's surface move away from each other.

E

Extended Metropolitan Region: term used to describe the sprawling urban regions of Asia where urban and rural intermingle.

G

gubenur: governer (of a province).

H

hulu: term referring to upriver direction.

hilir: term referring to downriver direction.

I

Inner Islands: metropolitan islands of Java, Bali and Madura.

J

Jabotabek: a region including districts of Bogor, Tangerang and Bekasi, as well as Jakarta.

jamu: herbal health tonic.

juragen: traders mainly concerned with bulking or wholesale dealing, usually men.

K

kabupaten: regency, area headed by a *bupati.*

kaki lima: food vendor.

kampung: village; the English word 'compound'is sometimes said to be derived from *kampung.*

kebun campuran: mixed gardens.

kebun talun: forest gardens.

kecamatan: sub-district.

kepala desa: village head.

klian subak: elected *subak* leader.

kotadesasi: the urbanisation of the countryside. Literally "city/village", to indicate the extension of the town into rural areas to form an extended metropolitan region.

kotamadya: urban municipality, urban district.

krupuk: prawn cracker.

L

langganan tetep: long-term, fixed credit relationship whereby traders obtain goods from a factory or wharehouse, paying their outstanding debt at the end of the year.

lateral plate boundary: area where the plates making the earth's surface move side by side.

M

martabak: savoury pancake.

N

negara: both capital and state; usually associated with the interior states of Java.

ngalap-nyaur: short-term credit relationship.

O

Outer Islands: those islands excluding Java, Bali and Madura.

P

Pancasila: "the five principles", Indonesia's state philosophy.

penebas: a middleman who buys crops still standing in the field and who employs his own labour to harvest it.

pasar: market place, and more generally any place, street side etc. where buying and selling takes place.

pasisir: term used to refer to the coastal areas, or former coastal trading states of Java.

pedagang pikulan: vegetable hawkers.

pekarangan: diverse, multi-crop home gardens.

pisang goreng: deep fried bananas.

priyayi/priai: elite, sometimes broadened to include officials and the upper middle class in general.

propinsi: province.

putu: steamed coconut cakes.

R

rumah makan: restaurant.

S

santri: form of Islam associated with the coastal *pasisir* states, 'purer' than the *abangan* Islam of the interior.

sate: grilled, skewered beef or chicken.

sawah: wet rice cultivation.

sial: oceanic crust of the earth's outer surface.

sima: continental crust making up the outer shell of the earth.

structural change: change in the relative balance between sectors of an economy.

subak: Balinese irrigation association.

swiddening: shifting cultivation.

T

tebesan: produce bought while still in the field.

tahu: beancurd

tempe: fermented soybean cake.

toko: shop, which may be large and purpose-built or simply the front room of a house; *toko* usually deal in more expensive consumer items and in bulk.

Total Fertility Rate: the number of children on average, women would have if they went through their whole childbearing period conforming to the age specific patterns of fertility of a given year.

W

warteg: from "*warung Tegal*", food stall selling inexpensive food.

Wallace line: theoretical line running between Lombok and Bali, and marking the transition zone between the Asiatic and Australasian zoogeographic regions.

warung: food stall or kiosk, selling any kind of item, including prepared foods, usually dealing in small units.

Bibliography

Abeyasekere, S. 1987. ***Jakarta, a History.*** Singapore: Oxford University Press.

Airriess, C.S. 1991. "Global Economy and Port Morphology in Balawan, Indonesia". ***Geographical Review*** 81(2):183-96.

Alexander, Jennifer. 1987. ***Trade, Traders and Trading in Rural Java***, Singapore: Oxford University Press.

Archibold, Richard 1941: "Unknown New Guinea". ***National Geographic Magazine*** 79:315-344.

Arndt, H.W. 1983. "Transmigration: achievements, problems, prospects". ***Bulletin of Indonesian Economic Studies.*** 19(3):50 73

Australian Centre for International Agricultural Research. 1985. ***Smallholder Rubber Production and Politics***. Canberra.

Babcock, T. 1986. "Transmigration: the regional impact of a miracle cure". in Colin McAndrews (ed). ***Central Government and Local Development in Indonesia.*** Singapore: Oxford University Press.

Barnes, Robert H. and Barnes, Ruth. 1989. "Barter and Money in an Indonesian Village Economy". ***Man*** NS 24(3):399-418.

Bhattacharya, Amar and Mari Pangestu. 1993. ***Indonesia: Development, Transformation and Public Policy.*** Washington D.C.: World Bank.

Booth, Anne. 1988. ***Agricultural Development in Indonesia.*** Sydney: Allen and Unwin.

Booth, Anne (ed). 1992. ***The Oil Boom and After: Indonesian economic policy and performance in the Suharto era.*** Singapore: Oxford University Press.

Brass, L.J.1941. "Stone Age Agriculture in New Guinea". ***Geographical Review***. 31:555-569.

Collier, W.L., Soentoro, Gunawan Wirada and Makali, 1974. "Agricultural Technology and Institutional Change in Java". ***Food Research Institute Studies***. 13(2):169-194.

Dewey, Alice G. 1962. "Trade and Social Control in Java". ***Journal of the Royal Anthropological Institute*** 92:177-90.

Dick, H., Fox, J.J., and J. Mackie (eds).1993. ***Balanced Development: East Java in the New Order***. Singapore: Oxford University Press.

Dove, M.R. 1985. ***Swidden Agriculture in Indonesia: the subsistence strategies of the Kalimantan Kantu.*** Berlin and New York: Mouton.

Dove, M.R. 1993. "Smallholder Rubber and Swidden Agriculture in Borneo: a sustainable adaptation to the ecology and economy of the tropical forest". ***Economic Botany.*** 47(2):136-147.

Eng, Pierre van der. 1992. "The Real Domestic Product of Indonesia, 1880-1989". ***Explorations in Entrepreneurial History*** 29:342-73.

Fell, R.T. 1991. ***Early Maps of South-East Asia.*** Singapore: Oxford University Press.

Forbes, D.K. 1990. "Jakarta Towards 2005: planning mechanisms and issues". ***Bulletin of Indonesian Economic Studies.*** 26(3):111-120.

Fox, James (ed). 1993. ***Inside Austronesian Houses: perspectives on domestic designs for living***. Canberra: Department of Anthropology, Research School of Pacific studies, ANU.

Furnivall, J.S. 1944. ***Netherlands India.*** Cambridge: Cambridge University Press. (reprinted by B. M. Israel, Amsterdam, 1976).

Geertz, Clifford. 1956. "Religious Belief and Economic Behaviour in a Central Javanese Town: some preliminary considerations". ***Economic Development and Cultural Change.*** 4:134-58.

————————. 1963. ***Peddlers and Princes: social change and economic moderniation in two Indonesian towns.*** Chicago: University of Chicago Press

——————————. 1966. ***Agricultural Involution: the process of ecological change in Indonesia.*** Berkeley: University of California Press.

Graaf, J. de. 1986. ***The Economics of Coffee.***

Wageningen: Pudoc.

Guiness, P. 1986. ***Harmony and Hierarchy in a Javanese Kampung.*** Singapore: Oxford University Press.

Haberle, S.G., Hope, S.G. and Y. DeFretes. 1991. "Environmental Change in the Baliem Valley, Montane Irian Jaya, Republic of Indonesia". ***Journal of Biogeography.*** 18:25-40.

Hayami, Y. and A. Hafid. 1979. "Rice Harvesting and Rural Wefare in Rural Java". ***Bulletin of Indonesian Economic Studies.*** 15(2):94-112.

Hanson, A.J. 1981. "Transmigration and Marginal Land Development". in Gary Hansen (ed). ***Agricultural and Rural Development in Indonesia.*** Boulder, Colorado: Westview Press.

Hardjono, Joan. 1977. ***Transmigration in Indonesia***, Kuala Lumpur: Oxford University Press.

——————————. 1986. "Spontaneous Rural Settlement in Indonesia". in ***Spontaneous Settlement Formation in Rural Regions.*** HABITAT, Nairobi.

——————————. 1988. "The Indonesian Transmigration Program in Historical Perspective". ***International Migration.*** 26(4):427-439.

—————————— (ed). 1991. ***Indonesia: Resources, Ecology and Environment.*** Singapore: Oxford University Press.

Hardjono, J. and Maspiyati. 1990. ***Production, Organisation and Employment in the West Java Poultry Industry.*** Institute of Social Studies, West Java Rural Non-Farm Sector Research Project, Working Paper No. B-8, Bandung.

Heider, Karl. 1991. ***Grand Valley Dani: peaceful warriors.*** Case Studies in Cultural Anthropology. Fort Worth: Holt Rinehart and Winston Inc., (2nd edition).

Hitchcock, M., King, V.T. and M.J.G. Parnwell. (eds). 1993. ***Tourism in Southeast Asia.*** London: Routledge.

Hugo, G.J. 1985. "Circulation in West Java, Indonesia", in R. Mansell Prothero and Murray Chapman (eds). ***Circulation in Third World Countries.*** London: Routledge and Kegan Paul.

Hugo, G.J., Hull, T.H., Hull, V.J. and G.W. Jones. (eds). 1987. ***The Demographic Dimension in Indonesian Development.*** Singapore: Oxford University Press.

Indonesian Demographic and Health Survey (IDHS). 1992. ***Indonesian Demographic and Health Survey 1991***. Central Bureau of Statistics, National Family Planning Co ordinating Board and Ministry of Health, Jakarta.

Jellinek, Lea. 1977. "The Life of a Jakarta Street Trader". in J. Abu-Lughod and R. Hay (eds). ***Third World Urbanization***. Chicago: Maaroufa Press.

————————. 1977. ***The Life of a Jakarta Street Trader-Two Years Later***. Working Paper No. 13, Centre of Southeast Asian Studies, Monash University, Melbourne.

———————— 1991. ***The Wheel of Fortune: the history of a poor community in Jakarta.*** Sydney, Allen and Unwin and ASAA.

Kartawinata, K., Soedjito, H., Jessup, H., Vadya, A. and C. Colfer. 1984. "The Impact of Development on Interactions between People and Forests in East Kalimantan: a comparison of two areas of Kenyah Dayak settlement". ***The Environmentalist.*** 4. Supp. 7: 87-95.

Kis-Jovak, J.I.; Nooy-Palm, H; Schefold, R. and U. Schulz-Dornburg. 1988. ***Banua Toraja: changing patterns in architecture and symbolism among the Sa'dan Toraja, Sulawesi, Indonesia.*** Royal Tropical Institute, The Netherlands.

King, V.T. 1985. ***The Maloh of West Kalimantan: an ethnographic study of inequality and social change among an Indonesian Borneo people.*** Verhandelingen van het Koninklijk Instituut voor Taal-, Land- en Volkenkunde No. 108. Dordrecht, Holland: Foris

Laird, J. 1991. "Southeast Asia's Trembling Rainforest". ***Our Planet*** 3(4):4-11

Lansing, Stephen J. 1983. ***The Three Worlds of***

Bibliography

Bali. New York: Praeger.

————————. 1991. ***Priests and Programmers: technologies of power in the engineered landscape of Bali.*** Princeton, New Jersey: Princeton University Press.

Mackie, J.A.C. 1971. "The Indonesian Economy, 1950-63". in Bruce Glassburner (ed). ***Economics of Indonesia: selected readings.*** Ithaca: Cornell University Press.

McGee, T.G. and Yeung, Y.M. 1977. ***Hawkers in Southeast Asian Cities: planning for the bazaar economy.*** Ottawa: International Development Research Centre.

McGee, T.G. 1989. "Urbanisasi or Kotadesasi? Evolving Patterns of Urbanization in Asia". in Frank J. Costa, Asok K. Dutt, Lawrence J. C. Ma and Allen G. Noble (eds). ***Urbanisation in Asia: spatial dimensions and policy issues.*** Honolulu: University of Hawaii Press.

—————. 1991. "The Emergence of Desakota regions in Asia: expanding a hypothesis". in Norton Ginsburg, Bruce Koppel and T. G. McGee (eds). ***The Extended Metropolis: settlement transition in Asia.*** Honolulu, University of Hawaii Press.

Michon, G. and J. Bompard. 1987. "The Damar Gardens (*Shorea javanica)* in Sumatra". ***Proceedings of the Third Round Table Conference on Dipterocarps.*** ed. A.J. Kostermans. UNESCO, Jakarta, 3-17.

Moll, H.A.J. 1987. ***The Economics of the Oil Palm.*** Wageningen: Pudoc.

Murray, Alison J. 1991. ***No Money, No Honey: A Study of Street Traders and Prostitutes in Jakarta.*** Singapore: Oxford University Press.

Nas, P. (ed). 1986. ***The Indonesian City: studies in development and planning.*** Dordrecht: Foris.

Paauw, Douglas. 1963. "From Colonial to Guided Economy", in Ruth McVey (ed). ***Indonesia*** HRAF

Padoch, C. and C. Peters. 1993. "Managed Forest Gardens in West Kalimantan, Indonesia". in ***Perspectives on Biodiversity: case studies in genetic resource conservation and development.*** C.S. Potter, J.I. Cohen and D. Jawczenski (eds). Washington: American Association for the Advancement of Science.

Plattner, S. 1985. "Equilibriating Market Relationships". ***Markets and Marketing,*** (Monograph economic Anthropology 4). Lanham: University Press of America.

Schiller, J. 1991. "Public and Private Participation in Urban Planning: A Political Economy Perspective". ***Prisma: the Indonesian Indicator.*** No. 51: 23-31.

Seavoy, R. 1973. "The Transition to Continuous Rice Cultivation in Kalimantan". ***Annals of the Association of American Geographers.*** 63(2):218-25.

Sherman, D. George. 1990. ***Rice, Rupees and Ritual: economy and society among the Samosir Batak of Sumatra.*** Stanford: Stanford University Press.

Sondakh, L. . 1989. ***The Coconut Industry in Indonesia: an overview***. Manado: Pusat Penelitian Universitas Sam Retulangi.

Spencer, J.E. 1966. ***Shifting Cultivation in Southeastern Asia***. University of California Publications in Geography No.19. Berkeley and Los Angeles: University of California Press.

Stoler, A.I. 1985. ***Capitalism and Confrontation in Sumatra's Plantation Belt*** *1870-1979.* New Haven: Yale University Press.

Sullivan, J. 1993. ***Rukun Kampung and Kampung: state-community relations in urban Yogyakarta.*** Singapore: Oxford University Press.

Syarifuddin Baharsyah and Soetatwo Hadiwigeno. 1982. "The Development of Commercial Crop Farming" in Mubyarto (ed). ***Growth and Equity in Indonesian Agricultural Development.*** Jakarta: Yayasan Agro Ekonomica.

Thee, K.W. 1979. ***Plantation Agriculture and Export Growth: an economic history of east Sumatra, 1863-1942.*** Jakarta: National Institute of Economic and Social Research.

Wallace, Alfred Russel. 1896. ***The Malay***

Archipelago: the land of the orang utan and the bird of paradise; a narrative of travel with studies of man and nature. London: Macmillan.

Warren, M.D., Slikkerveer, L.J. and S.O. Titilola. (ed). 1989. ***Indigenous Knowledge Systems: implications for agriculture and international development.*** Studies in Technology and Social Change No. 11, Iowa State University, Ames.

Warren, M.D. 1991. ***Using Indigenous Knowledge in Agricultural Development.*** World Bank Discussion Paper No. 127. Washington: World Bank.

Waterson, Roxana. 1990. ***The Living House: an anthropology of architecture in South-East Asia.*** Singapore: Oxford University Press.

Weinstock, J. 1983. "Rattan: ecological balance in a Borneo rainforest swidden". ***Economic Botany*** 37(1): 58-68.

————. 1990. ***Study on Shifting Cultivation in Indonesia.*** Phase 1 report on FAO Project UTF/INS/065/INS, Rome, FAO.

World Bank. 1988. ***Indonesia: the transmigration program in perspective,*** Washington D. C.

JOURNALS

Borneo Review

Contemporary Southeast Asia

Crossroads

Ekonomi dan Keuangan Indonesia

Indonesia

Indonesia Circle

Indonesian Journal of Geography

Journal of Geography

Indonesian Quarterly

Irian

Inside Indonesia

Journal of Southeast Asian Studies

Malaysian Journal of Tropical Geography

Singapore Journal of Tropical Geography

Index

Photo Credits

Chapter openers: The Indonesian World [Mahakam River system, Menado/Bunaken and Batang Hari River by Pt Bumi Prasaja], Sense of Place: The Archipelago [Spot image of Java and Sumatra reproduced by kind permission of NASA and Anak Krakatau by Bruno Barbey], The Human Context [All pictures by Rio Helmi], Padi and Sawah: Rice in Indonesia [Rice terraces in Bali by Luca Tettoni, Harvested rice in bundles by John Feltwell (Wildlife Matters), Aerial view of rice fields by Guido Rossi and Harvesting rice with ani–ani by Alain Compost], Field and Forest [Sago tree ceremony and Dayak cleaning damar by Alain Compost, Man applying pesticide on apple trees by Tantyo Bangun and Swiddeners planting seedlings on newly burnt grounds by Mahendra Singh], Littoral Livelihoods [Homecoming fishing boats by Guido Rossi, Fishing boat with a net trolley and traditional boat building by Alain Compost, Floating lift nets by Conner Bailey], City and Town Life [Market in Bali by Paul Koh, Aerial of Jakarta by Guido Rossi, Street scenes in Yogya and Becak driver by Tara Sosrowardoyo], Development and Change [Container Terminal by Koes, Aircraft by Back Tohir and Palindo Jaya 500 by Secneg].

Harvesting knife, p. 60, reproduced by the kind permission of the National Museum of Jakarta (photographed by Tara Sosrowardoyo).
Immunisation of infants in a government clinic or school, p. 128, reproduced by kind permission of UNICEF.
Jonathan Rigg, pp. 29, 47, 78, 111, 126, 132, 133, 134 and 135.
Lea Jellinek, pp. 106 and 107.
Roxana Waterson, pp. 42 and 43.
Darwis Triadi, p. 117.
Martin Kers, p. 122.
Ivan Polunin, pp. 28, 120, 123 and 134.
Mike Parnwell, p. 48.
Dean Forbes, p. 104.
Garth Sheldon, p. 43.
Joan Hardjono, pp. 84 and 94.
Lesley Potter, pp. 72 and 73.
Colin Barlow, p. 82.
Stephen Lansing, p. 58 and 59.
Adrian Horridge, pp. 98 and 99.
John Falconer, pp. 10, 13, 32, 38 and 60.
Mike Hosken, pp. 22 and 76.
Auscape, pp. 72 and 94.
Robin Moyer, p. 91.
Basil Pao, p. 108.
Michael Yamashita, p. 108.
Mahendra Singh, pp. 11, 46, 69, 74 and 90.
Ping Amranand, p. 133.
Femdi Siregar, p. 44.
Luca Tettoni, p. 85.
Georg Gerster, p. 23.
Leong Ka Tai, p. 45.
Guido Rossi, pp. 105, 118 and 120.
Martin Westlake, p. 104-105.
Bernard Hermann, p. 29.
Rio Helmi, pp. 16, 22, 39, 88, 89 and 136.
Bruno Barbey, pp. 8, 55, 64 and 102.
Raghu Rai, p. 22.
Paul Koh, pp. 15, 28, 77 and 125.
IRRI, pp. 55, 61, 62 and 63.
Alain Compost, pp. 14, 26, 34, 39, 44, 51, 69, 72, 75, 76, 77, 80, 81, 82, 83, 90, 94, 95, 105, 119, 122, 123,128, 129 and 137.
Agus Leonardus, p. 131.
Kal Muller, pp. 16, 30, 32, 33, 35, 58, 68, 79 and 88.
Victor Esbensen, pp. 13, 30, 31, 39, 50, 54, 68, 77, 79, 83, 84, 96, 119, 126 and 127.
Tara Sosrowardoyo, pp. 10, 20, 39, 85, 103, 110, 112, 113, 124 and 131.
Tantyo Bangun, pp. 47, 55, 62, 63, 65, 76, 84, 95, 97, 104, 121, 128, 132, 134 and 136.
Jill Gocher, pp. 24, 39, 49, 70, 71, 85, 96, 109, 110, 111, 112, 116, 124 and 130.
Leo Haks, pp. 20, 22, 39, 42, 60, 80, 81, 83, 102, 108, 110, 117, 118 and 129.
TAP, pp. 11, 64, 82, 121 and 132.
Bruce Coleman Wildlife Private Limited, pp. 14 and 135.
Paul Chesley, p. 20.
Luca Tettoni, p. 26.